Introduction to

Social
Networking

Introduction to

Social Networking

Michael Miller

Prentice Hall

Boston   Columbus   Indianapolis   New York   San Francisco   Upper Saddle River
Amsterdam   Cape Town   Dubai   London   Madrid   Milan   Munich   Paris   Montreal   Toronto
Delhi   Mexico City   São Paulo   Sydney   Hong Kong   Seoul   Singapore   Taipei   Tokyo

Editor in Chief: Michael Payne
Acquisitions Editor: Samantha McAfee
Product Development Manager: Eileen Bien Calabro
Editorial Project Manager: Meghan Bisi
Development Editor: Karen Misler
Editorial Assistant: Erin Clark
Director of Digital Development: Zara Wanlass
Editor-Digital Learning & Assessment: Paul Gentile
Product Development Manager-Media: Cathi Profitko
Editorial Media Project Manager: Alana Coles
Production Media Project Manager: John Cassar
Director of Marketing: Kate Valentine
Marketing Manager: Tori Olson Alves
Marketing Coordinator: Susan Osterlitz
Marketing Assistant: Darshika Vyas
Senior Managing Editor: Cynthia Zonneveld
Associate Managing Editor: Camille Trentacoste
Production Project Manager: Ruth Ferrera-Kargov
Manager of Rights & Permissions: Hessa Albader
Operations Specialist: Renata Butera
Production Manager: Renata Butera
Art Director: Anthony Gemmellaro
Interior Design: Anthony Gemmellaro
Cover Design: Anthony Gemmellaro
Cover Illustration/Photo: Shutterstock Images
Manager, Cover Visual Research & Permissions: Karen Sanatar
Full-Service Project Management: Saraswathi Muralidhar
Composition: PreMediaGlobal
Printer/Binder: Banta Menasha
Cover Printer: Banta Menasha
Text Font: 11/12 Garamond3

Credits and acknowledgments borrowed from other sources and reproduced, with permission, in this textbook appear on appropriate page within text.

Library of Congress Cataloging-in-Publication Data

Miller, Michael
    Introduction to social networking / Michael Miller. — 1st ed.
        p. cm.
    Includes index.
    ISBN-13: 978-0-13-706374-1
    ISBN-10: 0-13-706374-1
 1. Social networks.   2. Information technology—Social aspects.   I. Title.
    HM742.M555 2011
    006.7'54—dc22

                                                    2010038679

Prentice Hall
is an imprint of

www.pearsonhighered.com

10 9 8 7 6 5 4 3 2
ISBN 13: 978-0-13-706374-1
ISBN 10: 0-13-706374-1

About the Author

Michael Miller has written more than 100 non-fiction how-to books over the last two decades, including *Absolute Beginner's Guide to Computer Basics*, *Windows 7 Your Way*, *YouTube for Business*, *The Complete Idiot's Guide to Music Theory*, and the *Introduction to Google Apps* textbook. His books have collectively sold more than 1 million copies worldwide. Miller has established a reputation for his conversational writing style and for clearly explaining complex topics to casual readers. More information can be found at the author's website, located at www.molehillgroup.com.

Dedication: To Sherry: Who needs a whole network when I have you?

Contents

Visual Walk-Through

Many of today's introductory computing courses are moving beyond coverage of just the traditional Microsoft® Office applications. Instructors are looking to incorporate newer technologies and software applications into their courses, and on some college campuses new alternative courses based on emerging technologies are being offered.

The NEXT Series was developed to provide innovative instructors with a high-quality, academic teaching solution that focuses on the next great technologies. There is more to computing than Microsoft® Office, and the books in *The NEXT Series* enable students to learn about some of the newer technologies that are available and becoming part of our everyday lives.

The NEXT Series...making it easy to teach what's *NEXT!*

► Whether you are interested in creating a new course or you want to enhance an existing class by incorporating new technology, *The NEXT Series* is your solution.

Included in this series are books on alternative productivity software application products, Google Apps and OpenOffice.org, as well as new technologies encompassed in Web 2.0, and Social Networking.

▶ *Introduction to Social Networking* is a teaching and learning tool that was designed for use in a classroom setting, encouraging students to learn by using these new technologies hands-on.

The text includes in-chapter Hands-On Exercises, end of chapter exercises, and instructor supplements.

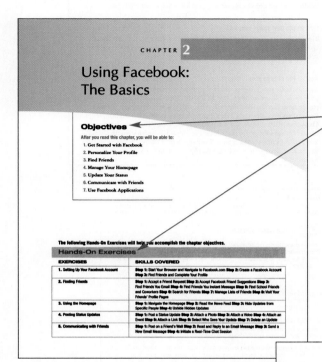

Each chapter opens with a list of numbered **Objectives**, clearly outlining what students will be able to accomplish after completing the chapter. The **Hands-On Exercises** are also outlined at the beginning of the chapter, letting students know what they will be doing in each chapter.

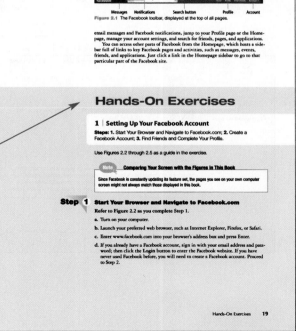

Learn-by-doing approach

Students learn how to use Social Networking technologies and websites by completing a series of **Hands-On Exercises**. These Exercises are clearly distinguished from the explanatory text because the pages are shaded in green.

Question & Answer Format

Each section begins with a question, engaging students in a dialog with the authors and drawing them into the content.

Key terms are defined in the margins.

Objective 2

Personalize Your Profile

What is the Profile page?

Your Profile page is your personal page on Facebook (Figure 2.6). The main part of your Profile page hosts the *Wall*, which displays your latest status updates as well as posts made to you by your friends. Other tabs on your Profile page hold your personal information, photos, videos, events, and so forth. Additional personal information is found in boxes that appear in the sidebar on the left side of the page. Finally, your Profile picture appears at the top left corner of your Profile page.

How do you post status updates?

The *Publisher box*, sometimes called the Share box, is where you post your status updates. Type a message into the Publisher box and click the Share button, and your status update is posted to your Profile page and all your friends' Homepages.

How do you change your Profile picture?

You can change your Profile picture at any time. Navigate to your Profile page and point to your picture, and then click the Change Picture link that appears. When the pop-up menu appears, select from where you want to obtain the picture: Upload a Picture (from your computer), Take a Picture (from your computer's webcam), or Choose from Album (to use a picture previously uploaded to Facebook). If you selected Upload a Picture, click the Browse or Choose File button when the Upload Your Profile Picture window appears. When the Open or Choose File to Upload dialog box appears, navigate to and select the picture to upload. Then click the Open button.

Wall The primary section of a Facebook member's Profile page, which displays the member's status updates as well as messages from other users.

Publisher box The box at the top of your Profile and Homepages; used to post status updates. There is also a Publisher box at the top of friends' Homepages; use this Publisher box to post a message to that friend's Profile page.

Alert boxes call attention to items that might cause students to get hung up.

ferring online friendships to the physical world. Don't put yourself at risk when meeting strangers: remember, until you get to know him or her in person, anyone you correspond with online remains a stranger when it comes to the physical world.

> **Alert** **Don't Meet in Person**
>
> You should never arrange to meet privately with an online friend whom you've never met in person. It's not unheard of for predators to arrange meetings with unsuspecting victims over a social network. If you must meet an online friend in person, take someone else with you and meet in a public place.

Objective 5

Recognize Social Networking Do's and Don'ts

What things should you do when participating in a social network?

In general, you should use caution and discretion when posting to any social network. Here are some specific things you should try to do when social networking:

- **Post frequently but not too frequently.** A social network is a community, and to be a member of that community you have to actively participate. If you wait too long between posts, people will forget that you're there. On the other hand, if you post too frequently, other members might view you as overbearing or

Recognize Social Networking Do's and Don'ts **9**

---

b. To view the *Profile* of a person requesting to be your friend, click his or her name or profile picture.

c. To accept this friend request, click the **Confirm** button. To refuse this request, click the **Ignore** button.

Click to view pending friend requests

Click to accept friend request

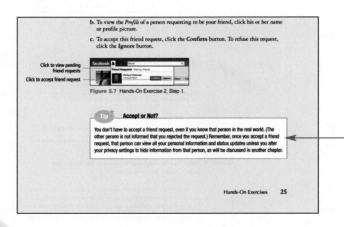

Figure 2.7 Hands-On Exercise 2, Step 1.

> **Tip** **Accept or Not?**
>
> You don't have to accept a friend request, even if you know that person in the real world. (The other person is not informed that you rejected the request.) Remember, once you accept a friend request, that person can view all your personal information and status updates unless you alter your privacy settings to hide information from that person, as will be discussed in another chapter.

Tip boxes provide students with useful tips and tricks.

Hands-On Exercises **25**

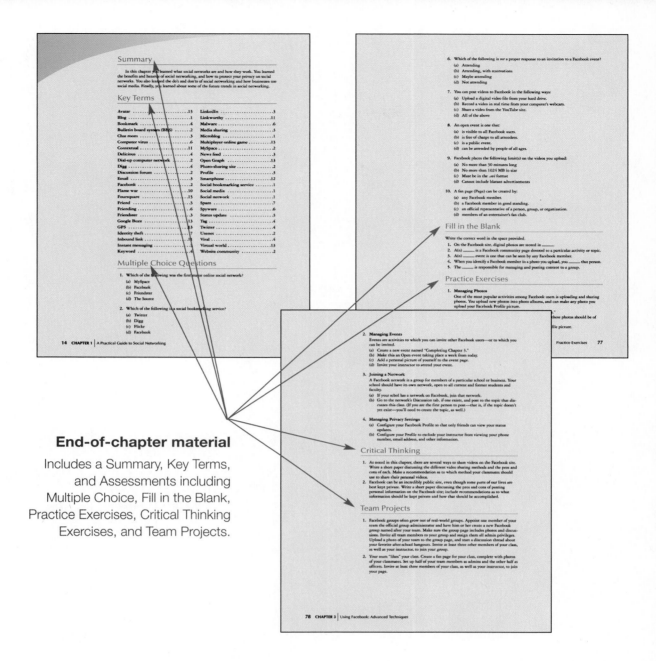

End-of-chapter material

Includes a Summary, Key Terms,
and Assessments including
Multiple Choice, Fill in the Blank,
Practice Exercises, Critical Thinking
Exercises, and Team Projects.

Supplements for Instructors

Instructor Resource CD with:

- PowerPoint Presentations
- Test Bank
- Instructor's Manual
- Solution Files

TestGen Test Bank

www.pearsonhighered.com/nextseries

Supplements for Students

Companion Website with:

- Objectives
- Glossary
- Chapter Summary
- Online Study Guide

www.pearsonhighered.com/nextseries

CHAPTER 1

A Practical Guide to Social Networking

Objectives

After you read this chapter, you will be able to:

1. **Understand Social Networks**

2. **Recognize the Benefits of Social Networking**

3. **Comprehend the Hazards and Limitations of Social Networking**

4. **Protect Your Privacy**

5. **Recognize Social Networking Do's and Don'ts**

6. **Appreciate How Businesses Use Social Networking**

7. **Realize the Future of Social Networking**

Social media Websites, services, and platforms that people use to share experiences and opinions with each other.

Social bookmarking service A web-based service, such as Digg and Delicious, that helps users bookmark and share popular websites, web pages, and articles.

Social network A website, such as Facebook or MySpace, where users can form communities with like-minded people and share details of their lives with friends, family, fellow students, and coworkers.

Blog Short for *web log*, a shared online journal consisting of entries from the site's owner or creator.

Microblog A web-based service, such as Twitter, that enables users to post short text messages to interested followers.

Objective 1

Understand Social Networks

What are social media?

Social media are those websites, services, and platforms that people use to share experiences and opinions with each other. They cover everything from *social bookmarking services* (users share the sites and articles they like) to *social networks* (users share the details of their own lives) and include *blogs*, *microblogs*, and other forms of online communities.

What is social networking?

Social networking is, perhaps, the most popular social medium of communication today. A social network is a large website that hosts a community of users and facilitates public and private communication between those users. Social networks enable users to share experiences and opinions with each other via short posts or status updates.

Some social networks, such as school or alumni networks, are devoted to a specific topic or community. Other social networks, such as *Facebook*, are more broad-based, which allows for communities within the overall network devoted to specific topics.

Facebook The largest social networking site on the web, with more than 500 million users.

MySpace A social networking site that is popular among musicians and other entertainers.

Dial-up computer network A commercial online service that connects multiple computers via a dial-up telephone connection. Examples include CompuServe, Prodigy, and America Online.

Bulletin board system (BBS) A private online discussion forum, typically hosted on a single computer and accessed by other computers via a dial-up telephone connection.

Discussion forum An online space where users can read and post messages on a given topic.

Usenet A subset of the Internet, created in 1980, that hosts and distributes topic-based discussion forums, called *newsgroups*.

Website community A website designed to promote a community around a specific topic.

Photo-sharing site A website where users can upload, store, and share digital photos with other users.

Friendster One of the earliest social networking websites, today Friendster is one of the largest social networking sites in Asia.

LinkedIn A social network for business professionals, with more than 60 million users.

Why are social networks so popular?

Over the past several years, large social networking sites have become enormously popular. According to the research firm Alexa, Facebook is currently the number two most popular site on the web (after Google), with *MySpace* also appearing in the top 20.

These and other social networking sites are popular because they enable easy and immediate interaction with friends, family members, fellow students, and coworkers. Users can interact via public posts, private communication, event calendars, and even community-based games and applications. It's a way to be social with large numbers of people without having to interact personally with each and every individual.

In short, social networks help people keep up-to-date on what others are doing and keep others updated on what they are doing. They also help establish a sense of community based on shared experiences at school, in the workplace, or at play.

How did social networks get started?

The concept of online virtual communities dates to the earliest *dial-up computer networks*, *bulletin board systems* (BBSs), and online *discussion forums*, including The Source, The WELL, CompuServe, Prodigy, America Online, and *Usenet*. These proto-communities, many of which predated the formal Internet, offered topic-based discussion forums and chat rooms, as well as rudimentary forms of private electronic communication.

What were some of the other early components of social networking?

Other components of what is currently considered social networking developed in the 1990s and 2000s. The concept of topic-based *website communities*, as typified by iVillage, Epicurious, and Classmates.com, arose in the mid-1990s. Personal blogs, which let users post short articles of information and opinion, emerged around 2000. And *photo-sharing sites*, such as Flickr and Photobucket, became a part of the Internet landscape in the early 2000s.

In 2003, *Friendster* combined many of these online community features into the first large-scale social networking site and introduced the concepts of *friends* and *friending* to the social web. Friendster enjoyed immediate popularity (more than 3 million users within the first few months of operation), but was soon surpassed by MySpace, which launched later the same year. MySpace became the most popular social networking site in June 2006, and remained the top social network for almost two years.

Another social networking site, *LinkedIn*, was also launched in 2003. Unlike Friendster and MySpace, LinkedIn targeted business professionals, and became known as a site for career networking.

The year 2004 saw the launch of Facebook (initially called *Thefacebook*), which was introduced as a site for college students. Sensing opportunity beyond the college market, however, Facebook opened its site to high school students in 2005, and to users of all ages (actually, users above the age of 13) in 2006. This broadening in Facebook's user base led to a huge increase in both users and pageviews, which led to Facebook surpassing MySpace in April 2008.

Who uses social networks?

While college and high school students used to comprise the bulk of the active audience for social networks, the audience makeup is rapidly changing. In fact, the fastest-growing demographic for social networks today is the 45-and-older age group.

In practice, then, social networks are home to all sorts of users, including

- business colleagues who use the site for networking;
- friends who want to talk online;
- singles who want to meet and match up with other singles;
- classmates who need study partners and homework advice;

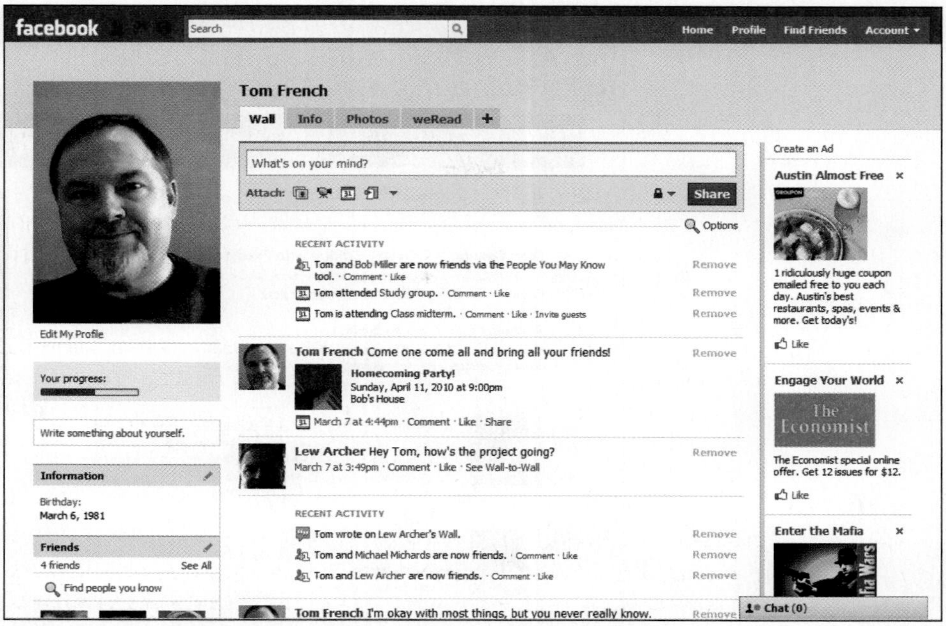

Figure 1.1 A typical user profile page on the Facebook site.

Profile A collection of personal information, including photos, contact information, likes and dislikes, and recent posts for a member of a social networking site.

Status update A short text post from a member of a social networking site, conveying the user's current thoughts, actions, and such.

Friend On a social network, another user with whom you communicate.

News feed On a social network, a collection of posts or status updates from a person's friends.

Chat room A web page that hosts real-time text communication between multiple users.

Email Short for *electronic mail*, a means of sending messages over the Internet or a closed computer network.

Instant messaging A means of conducting a one-to-one text communication in real time over the Internet or a closed computer network.

Media sharing The act of uploading, storing, and sharing various types of media files (photos, videos, and music) with other users over the web.

Digg A social bookmarking service that enables users to submit web pages and other content and then rate that content.

Delicious Formerly known as del.icio.us, a popular social bookmarking service that enables users to tag bookmarked pages with their own index terms.

- hobbyists looking for others who share their interests;
- people looking for long-lost friends;
- musicians, actors, and celebrities connecting with their fans.

In addition to, of course, college and high school students.

How do social networks work?

Most social networks revolve around users' personal *profiles* and ongoing *status updates*.

A profile is a collection of personal information posted by an individual user (Figure 1.1). Each user of the social networks posts his or her own personal profile, which appears on a profile page. There is enough personal information in each profile to enable other users with similar interests to connect as *friends*; one's growing collection of friends helps to build a succession of personal communities.

Users keep their friends informed of current activities via short text posts or status updates. Users read updates from their friends via some sort of *news feed*, thus keeping up to date on their friends' activities.

What are the key components of a social network?

For most social networks, the user's profile page serves as the "home base" for most activities. Most profile pages include some form of blog, discussion forum, or *chat room* so that friends can communicate with the person profiled. In many instances, individual users also post a running list of their current activities so that their friends always know what they're up to.

Many social networks include various means of user-to-user communication, including private *email* and one-to-one *instant messaging*. Most social networks also include various forms of *media sharing*, including digital photos, videos, and the like.

How does a social bookmarking service differ from a social network?

Social bookmarking services, such as *Digg* and *Delicious*, represent a subset of the features found on a social network. A social bookmarking service lets users share their favorite websites with friends and colleagues online (Figure 1.2). A user visits a

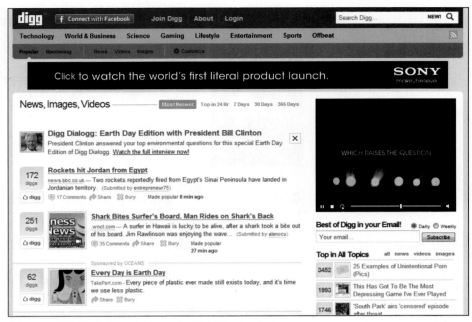

Figure 1.2 Social bookmarks on the Digg website.

Bookmark A means of identifying a web page for future viewing or sharing with other users.

Tag A label used to describe a specific item.

Keyword A word or phrase used to construct a search.

Viral Achieving immense popularity via word of mouth on the Internet.

Bookmark A means of identifying a web page for future viewing or sharing with other users.

Tag A label used to describe a specific item.

Keyword A word or phrase used to construct a search.

Viral Achieving immense popularity via word of mouth on the Internet.

Twitter A popular microblogging service where users post short text messages (tweets) which other users can then follow.

website, web page, news article, or blog post that he or she likes, and clicks a button or link to *bookmark* that site. This bookmark then appears in his or her master list of bookmarks on the social bookmarking service site; the user can share all or some of these bookmarks with anyone he or she designates.

Most social bookmarking services use *tags* to help users find bookmarked sites. When a user bookmarks a site, he or she adds a few tags or keywords to describe the site. Other users can then search by *keywords* to find the most popular matching bookmarked sites, just as they search Google and other traditional search engines.

Social bookmarking services are great ways to spread timely and interesting content. The most notable bookmarks on these sites quickly turn *viral*, as one user after another shares his or her links with other users.

How does a microblogging service differ from a social network?

When you separate the short text messages or status updates from a social network into a separate feed, you have a microblogging service (Figure 1.3). Microblogs, typified by *Twitter*, exist solely to distribute short text posts from individual users to groups of "followers." These posts are similar to traditional blog posts but are much shorter, typically in the 140-character range.

Microblogs do not offer many of the community features found on larger social networking sites. A microblog does not offer topic-based groups, one-to-one private messaging, photo sharing, and the like. The only service a microblog offers is public message distribution.

With a typical microblogging service, registered users post short text messages. Other users sign up to follow the posts of individual members; they are then notified when someone they follow makes a new post. Microblog posts are used to convey personal information and opinions; businesses also use them to make commercial announcements.

Many of the most-followed microbloggers are celebrities; fans follow their posts to learn more about the celebrities' activities. Major news organizations also use microblogs to post breaking stories, while individuals post details of their personal lives to interested friends and family followers.

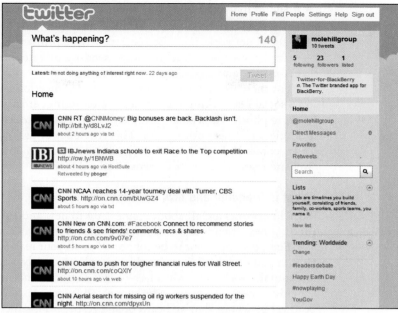

Figure 1.3 Following tweets on the Twitter microblogging site.

Objective 2

Recognize the Benefits of Social Networking

What do people do on social networking sites?

Social networks are all about hanging out, virtually. Typical users spend much of their time online cruising through the profiles, looking for people they know or who share similar interests. They play music and watch videos posted on other profile pages. They see who's online and they communicate via public posts, private emails, and instant messages.

In addition, users spend time updating their own profile pages: their face to the online world. Depending on the site, they redecorate their pages by changing templates, changing color schemes, adding new backgrounds and images, even adding pictures of themselves and their friends. And they post updates about their own activities, which is how their friends know what they've been doing.

Why do people use social networks?

More than a half-million people frequent social networking sites on a regular basis. They do so to communicate with people they know, as well as with those who share common interests or backgrounds with them.

For many users, social networking is a time saver. Most people today simply don't have time to meet face to face with all their friends, family members, and colleagues. It's easier to catch up with one another on a social network, where a single status update is broadcast to an entire community of online friends.

As such, social networks enable you to reach out to old friends and classmates with whom you might otherwise lose touch. The social network becomes a way to maintain these relationships, even if on a somewhat superficial basis.

In addition, social networks make it easy to extend one's network of friends. Most social networks facilitate meeting others with similar interests, as well as the sharing of experiences with these people. These virtual communities bring together like-minded people for discussions and the exchange of information and materials.

Finally, one's social network profile serves as a somewhat prominent contact point, especially for young people whose lives have yet to settle down. As home addresses, email addresses, and phone numbers change throughout life, you can always be contacted via your profile on Facebook or another social network.

Are social networks replacing other forms of online activity?

Many people consolidate some or all of their online activities through a social network. The social network, then, becomes the user's primary means of communication, and is used for posting public messages, sending private messages, sharing photos and other media, and engaging in group discussions.

For these users, separate forms of communication are superseded by those features on a social networking site. Instead of blogging, emailing, instant messaging, and sharing photos via separate sites and applications, users perform all these activities on a single social networking site. This efficiency of usage helps explain the popularity of Facebook and other social networks; it's easier to do all these things on a single website than on several different sites and services.

What is friending and how does it work?

Friending The act of adding someone to a social network friends list.

Social networks are all about connecting to new and existing friends. The process of finding new friends is called *friending*, and involves some specific rules.

First, it's important to be connected to all your real-world friends and acquaintances. Just as you communicate with these people physically, you use the social network to communicate virtually when face-to-face contact is inconvenient or impossible.

Most users also want to be connected to people whom they might not personally know, but whom they've heard of and respect. This includes friends of friends, as well as famous and semi-famous people open to these virtual connections.

In fact, many social network users try to establish as many friend connections as possible. In some circles, the number of friends you have is important; the more friends you have, the more connected you are. (In other circles, of course, quality is more important than quantity.)

Know, however, that when you add someone as a friend, that doesn't imply that the person is a friend in the traditional use of the word. It doesn't even mean that you know that person, or want to know that person; it only means that you've added him or her to your friends list.

Objective 3

Comprehend the Hazards and Limitations of Social Networking

Is social networking safe?

There are potential hazards involved in virtually every online activity, from reading emails to web browsing. Such hazards also exist with the use of social networks.

That said, social networking is only as hazardous—or as safe—as the individual user makes it. Users who post a plethora of personal information are less safe than those who are more discreet. Those who avoid posting personal details about their lives are safer from potential attackers or identity thieves than those who post liberally about their activities.

The only way to avoid all possible dangers is to cease using all social media. Short of that, however, you can network in relative safety by being smart about what you post and what you respond to online.

What are the potential hazards faced by social networkers?

Computer virus A malicious software program capable of reproducing itself across multiple computers and causing damage to an infected computer.

Spyware A malicious software program that obtains information from a user's computer without the user's knowledge or consent.

Malware Short for malicious software. Any computer program designed to infiltrate or damage an infected computer. Computer viruses and spyware are the two most common types of malware.

The hazards posed by social networking are both minor and major. These potential dangers include the following:

- **Computer viruses and other malware.** Like any website, a social networking site can contain links to *computer viruses*, *spyware*, and other forms of *malware*. Clicking on a bad link, often disguised as a link to an interesting website or application, can infect your computer with this type of malicious software.

Spam Unsolicited commercial email, or junk email.

Identity theft A form of fraud in which one person pretends to be someone else, typically by stealing personal information, such as a bank account number, credit card number, or Social Security number. The intent of identity theft is often to steal money or obtain other benefits.

- **Spam.** Users who publicly post their email addresses on social networking sites can find themselves the target of unwanted junk email, or *spam*. Spammers harvest email addresses from social networking sites, and add theses addresses to their email mailing lists for spam messages.

- **Identity theft.** Posting other personal information publicly on a social networking site can result in *identity theft*. Identity thieves can use this public information to assume a user's identity on the social network or on other websites, to apply for credit cards and loans in the user's name, to legitimize undocumented foreign workers, and to gain access to the user's banking and credit card accounts.

- **Online stalking.** Online stalkers like to follow their victims from one website to another. If granted friend status, these online bullies, often pretending to be someone that they're not, will try to become close to their potential prey, whether for their own personal enjoyment or to cause the victim discomfort, embarrassment, or actual harm.

- **Physical stalking or harassment.** Some online predators take their stalking to the physical world. This is facilitated when people post personal information, including phone numbers and home addresses, on social networking sites. This information helps predators physically contact their victims, which can result in harassment or even physical violence.

- **Robbery.** Have you ever posted about going out for dinner on a given evening or getting ready to take a long vacation? When you do so, you're telling potential robbers when your home will be empty and that your belongings are ripe for the taking.

It's surprising how much personal information people make publicly available on social networks. The information posted on Facebook and other social sites is public; unless you change your profile's default settings, virtually anyone can see everything you post. This public availability of private information is what leads to the potential hazards found in social networking.

Is social networking a substitute for face-to-face communication?

Another hazard presented by social networking is one that is more subtle. As people move more and more of their conversations into the virtual space of social networks, physical face-to-face communication decreases. While you may be "talking" to more so-called friends online, you're actually talking to fewer real friends in the real world. Relationships in the real world could suffer if you spend too much time communicating virtually on social networks.

Can you believe who people say they are online?

When you have hundreds of people on your social network friends list, how well do you really know any of them? It's possible that some of the people you call "friends" really aren't the people they present themselves to be. For whatever reason, some people adopt different personas, including fake names and profile pictures, when they're online; it's possible that you're establishing relationships on these social networks that have no basis in reality.

Objective 4

Protect Your Privacy

How private is your personal information on a social network?

Many of the potential hazards of social networking revolve around personal information posted publicly. Since most social networking sites encourage or require you to enter some degree of private information about yourself, it's possible that some or all of this information won't remain private.

Of first concern is the information in your social networking profile. Most sites require certain information, such as your email address, and allow you to enter additional information, such as your postal address or phone number. In some sites, this information is displayed by default on your profile page, which enables anyone on the site to contact you. Fortunately, most sites give you the option of hiding some or all of this information. If you would like to enhance your privacy, you should take advantage of this option.

The other private information that may become public is anything you may post as part of your regular status updates: what you did last night, whom you're seeing, what you think of your teacher or boss. These posts are typically public by default, which means that anyone can read them. As with the information on your profile page, however, most sites include privacy options that allow you to limit who can view these posts; you can avoid full public disclosure of your private information if you so desire.

How can your private information be used?

The personal information you provide to a social network can be used, legitimately, in a number of ways.

For example, a social network can use your profile information, age, gender, education, and so forth, to display targeted third-party advertisements on your profile page. These targeted ads may be marginally more appealing than generic advertisements, but are still, at least to some, a violation of an individual's privacy.

Similarly, your profile information can be used for targeted invitations of various sorts. For example, a social network may determine your interests from your profile data and invite you to play a particular game, use a certain application, join a given group, or add someone as a friend. These may appear to be helpful invitations, but still rely on the use of your private information.

Some social networks not only use your personal data internally but also sell it to interested third parties. Once they sell the data to a particular company, you will typically receive one or more email messages advertising that company's wares. This isn't spam; you no doubt implicitly agreed that the social network could share this data when you accepted the site's terms of service, and these are legitimate marketers. But it's still an annoying use or abuse of your private information.

All these uses of your private information are perfectly legal, and you probably agreed to them, assuming you read the fine print, of course. This points out the necessity of reading the social network's terms of service before you sign up—and not participating if you don't like what you read.

Beyond these legal invasions of your privacy, there are many ways your personal information can be used illegally. These illegal invasions of your privacy can result in everything from spam to identity theft; you can guard against them by limiting the amount of personal information you publicly post on a social networking site.

How much personal information should you disclose online?

Most social networks require you to enter contact information (email address, home address, and such) when you sign up for the site. You do not, however, have to display this information for the rest of the world to see. To keep people from contacting you outside of the social network, you should opt to display as little contact information as possible. After all, do you really want complete strangers calling you or showing up at your door? They might, if you make this information public.

When you update your status or add an everyday post to a site, you need to be discreet about discussing your private life in what is essentially a public forum. The innermost thoughts that you post on Facebook or Twitter can be embarrassing when a parent, partner, teacher, or employer reads them. Too much personal information can derail a job application, grad school request, or even a future personal relationship.

While it's tempting to share intimate details with your online friends, think about who these "friends" really are. How many of your social network friends are close, intimate friends? How many are merely acquaintances or just people you go to school with or work with? How many are people you really don't know at all?

And it's not just friends. Many social networks, by default, make your postings available to *all* members of the network. That means that millions of people could be reading about your behavior at last night's party, or about your current relationship issues, or about how you really feel about your boss and coworkers. It's not hard to imagine how this personal information can come back to haunt you.

Do you really want everyone reading about everything you do? Ultimately, this is the question you need to ask yourself. Just how much personal information do you want other people to know? If you consider this carefully, you might come to the conclusion that you want to keep much of your private information private.

What you have to remember is that, on a social network, you're not invisible. A social network is a public community; everything you post may be read by anyone. Post only information that would be safe enough for your parents (or teacher or boss) to read.

What can you do to protect your privacy on a social network?

Most social networks have a variety of privacy settings you can configure to hide some or all of your personal information from some or all of the site's members. For example, you may be able to configure your settings so that your contact information is not displayed publicly on your profile page. You may also be able to select which users or groups of users can read your personal posts or status updates.

Beyond configuration of a site's privacy settings, you should be circumspect about the information you make public and with whom you personally communicate. Think twice before posting personal information or potentially incriminating photos; resist the urge to share all the intimate details of your life in such a public arena. In addition, you should refrain from broadcasting your every move via the social network. Potential thieves don't need to know when your house will be empty, nor do potential stalkers need to know where you're eating dinner tonight. It's okay to have a private life and keep it private.

Finally, don't view Facebook or the other social networks as online dating services. Yes, you may meet new friends on these social networks, but use caution about transferring online friendships to the physical world. Don't put yourself at risk when meeting strangers: remember, until you get to know him or her in person, anyone you correspond with online remains a stranger when it comes to the physical world.

 Don't Meet in Person

You should never arrange to meet privately with an online friend whom you've never met in person. It's not unheard of for predators to arrange meetings with unsuspecting victims over a social network. If you must meet an online friend in person, take someone else with you and meet in a public place.

Objective 5

Recognize Social Networking Do's and Don'ts

What things should you do when participating in a social network?

In general, you should use caution and discretion when posting to any social network. Here are some specific things you should try to do when social networking:

- **Post frequently but not too frequently.** A social network is a community, and to be a member of that community you have to actively participate. If you wait too long between posts, people will forget that you're there. On the other hand, if you post too frequently, other members might view you as overbearing or annoying. The best frequency is somewhere between once a week and a few times per day.

- **Keep your posts short and sweet.** People don't want or expect to read overly long musings on a social networking site. Instead, they tend to graze, absorbing the gist of what's posted rather than reading entire missives. On a site like Facebook, that means keeping your posts to no more than a few sentences. On a microblog like Twitter, simply adhere to the 140-character limit.

- **Use proper spelling.** While you don't have to use complete and proper grammar and punctuation (see the next tip), blatant misspellings can mark you as less educated than you might actually be. Take the time to spell things correctly; it's literally the least you can do.

- **Take shortcuts.** While you should always use proper spelling, you don't have to use full sentences when posting to a social network. In fact, when working with a limited number of characters (as typical of Twitter and other microblogs), it's okay to use common abbreviations and acronyms, such as BTW (by the way) and LOL (laughing out loud). Avoid unnecessary words and punctuation if you're approaching the character limit.

- **Link to additional information.** You don't always have space to provide a lot of background information in a post. Instead, you can link to web pages or blog posts that offer more details.

- **Be discrete.** Post only information that you'd want your parents (or spouse or teacher or employer) to read.

- **Be cautious.** You don't have to be paranoid about it, but assume that there are some dangerous people out there. Don't do anything that would put you in harm's way.

What things should you *not* do when participating in a social network?

In general, you should avoid posting personal information in any public forum, including those provided by social networks. Here are some specific things you should avoid when social networking:

- **Don't accept every friend request you receive.** You don't have to have a thousand friends. It's better to have a smaller number of true friends than a larger number of people you really don't know.

- **Don't post if you don't have anything interesting to say.** Some of the most annoying people on social networks are those who post their every action and movement. ("I just woke up," "I'm reading my mail," "I'm thinking about having lunch.") Post if there's something interesting happening; avoid posting just to be posting. Think about what you like to read about other people, and post in a similar fashion.

- **Don't assume that everyone online will agree with you.** Some people use social networks as a platform for their opinions. While it may be okay to share your opinions with close (i.e., non–social network) friends, spouting off in a public forum is not only bad form, it's a way to incite a *flame war*.

Flame war A heated or hostile interaction between two or more people in an online forum.

- **Don't post anything that could possibly be used against you.** Want to ensure a poor grade in a class? Post how much you dislike your teacher. You can also put your job in jeopardy by posting negative comments about your workplace or employer. And you may be denied future employment if a potential employer doesn't like what he or she sees in your social network posts. As in most things, with social networking it's better to be safe than sorry; avoid posting overly negative comments that are better kept private.

- **Don't post overly personal information, including contact information.** Don't make it easy for disreputable people to find you offline; avoid posting your phone number, email address, and home address. And think twice before sharing the intimate details of your private life, including potentially embarrassing photos.

- **Don't post your constant whereabouts.** You don't need to broadcast your every movement; thieves don't need to know when your home is empty. It's okay to post where you were after the fact, but keep your current whereabouts private.

Objective 6

Appreciate How Businesses Use Social Networking

Why are social networking and social media important to businesses?

Many businesses are realizing that social media can be an important part of their marketing plans. That's because social media can deliver a large number of highly targeted potential customers at a relatively low cost.

Traditional advertising is expensive; building word of mouth through social media, less so. To that end, for example, if a business can build a large friends or fans list on Facebook, get bookmarked on Digg, or become the subject of a popular tweet on Twitter, that company's website can see a significant spike in traffic, as well as a lasting long-term increase in its customer base. Social networks have a lot of users, and getting in front of them can make or break a company's traffic goals.

Inbound link A link from another website to a given website.

An added benefit of getting mentioned on any of these social sites is that each link or bookmark creates a new link back to the site. These *inbound links* increase the site's ranking in the search results of Google and other major search engines. That's because search ranking is at least partly dependent on the number of inbound links a site receives.

It's important to remember that social media marketing is a form of word-of-mouth marketing. Online or off, a strong word-of-mouth campaign trumps any form of paid advertising or promotion. It's quality attention, which results in quality traffic to the company's website.

How can businesses participate in social media?

The most obvious way for a business to participate in social media is to literally participate to become part of the community. That means establishing a page on a social networking site, creating a Twitter feed, and the like. Businesses can use this type of presence to notify interested customers of upcoming products and promotions, as well as to connect one-on-one with the online customer base.

This participation should be two-way. Not only should someone from the company monitor posts to the company's social pages but also that person should post to other people's pages. It's a matter of being an active participant in the community, not just hosting a passive web page.

Linkworthy Content that is useful or interesting enough to warrant linking to.

In addition, a business should make it easy for various social media to link to its website. A business should start by making its website *linkworthy*, so that there's something of interest for people to link to. The site should also include buttons or links that users can click to automatically bookmark the page with the most important social bookmarking services and to share the page with the largest social networks. Having dedicated Digg and Facebook buttons will make it easier for users of social media to link to the given page.

How important is social network advertising?

Contextual Relating to or determined by the context of the item. Contextual advertising places ads on pages that share similar content.

Many social networking sites enable third-party advertising. This advertising is often *contextual*, meaning that the advertiser can target certain demographic qualifiers, such as age range or gender, and have its ad displayed only to users who match those demographics. While advertising on a social network costs more than "free" social media marketing, its targeted nature can make it more effective than other types of online advertising.

Objective 7

Realize the Future of Social Networking

How will people use social media in the future?

The popularity of social networking is increasing, and is likely to increase more in the future. As larger numbers of people access social media on a regular basis, these media, especially social networks, will become a more important hub for people's online activities.

Instead of using individual applications for email, blogging, photo sharing, and the like, people will centralize these activities on a single social network. Applications that aggregate information from multiple social media, displaying posts from Facebook, Twitter, and a user's favorite blogs, will also become more popular, as will applications that make it possible to post a single message to multiple social media.

In short, people are moving to a single hub for all their online information and communications. It's likely that social networks, and applications that aggregate information from multiple social media, will serve this function in the future, making individual applications practically obsolete.

How will people access social networks in the future?

The use of social networks, as with the use of the Internet in general, is quickly shifting from computers to mobile devices. In the past, most people accessed Facebook and other social networks from their personal computers. Today, however, an increasing number of users are accessing social networks from their Internet-enabled mobile phones, so-called *smartphones*, such as Apple's iPhone.

Smartphone A mobile phone with advanced computer-like capability, typically including Internet access.

This move to the mobile web means that people will increasingly use their mobile phones to access social networks, to read and post microblog messages, and to bookmark interesting sites on social bookmarking services. This will be facilitated by more and better mobile applications for the most popular social networks and media, making it easier to keep up to date when users are on the go.

Will social media replace traditional media?

The increasing popularity of social media has led some to speculate that social media will replace traditional media, at least as a source of information. Taken to its extreme, this argues for the death of television and newspapers, with people finding out about news events over Facebook, Twitter, and other such social media.

While it's true that traditional media are facing a shakeout of sorts, in terms of both readers/viewers and advertising revenue, it's unlikely that social media can fully replace traditional media in terms of news gathering. Opinion, yes: there is no shortage of opinions in the social media space. But while social media can quickly disseminate both news and opinions, they have no built-in facility for reporting on news events. That is, social media can only distribute news reported elsewhere.

This argues for the continuation of traditional media's role in news gathering. Social media such as Twitter can then help to disseminate this news, while social networks and microblogs provide forums for commentary. If traditional media go away, however, it is unlikely that social media can replace them.

A more likely scenario has social media supplementing traditional media offerings. A social network presence, such as a Facebook fan page, can support traditional media programs, as well as offer a forum for community interaction and group discussions. This support can be in real time, as an increasing number of people are accessing the Internet (via either computers or mobile devices) while watching TV. In addition, microblogs such as Twitter can be used to promote traditional media offerings, providing additional information and informing viewers of upcoming developments.

What are the most important trends in social networking?

Social networking, like all Internet-based offerings, is in constant flux. Look for the following changes to happen in the near future:

- **Social networks will offer more protective privacy options.** The days of everyone being able to see everything posted about a person will soon end; users will have an increasing number of privacy options available to hide some or all of their information and posts from unwanted viewers.

- **Teachers and students will use social networks increasingly as a communication tool.** Students have already embraced social networking; teachers will also begin to use social networks to communicate with their students. This will range from tweets about class assignments to Facebook pages with topic discussions, homework assistance, and tests and quizzes. In lower grades, social networks will also be used for parent-teacher communication, without the need to meet face to face or talk over the phone.

- **College students will use social networks increasingly to network with professionals and to seek internship and employment opportunities.** Just as experienced workers are using social networks such as LinkedIn to network with others in their professions, students will be able to take advantage of social networks to find jobs and advance their future careers.

Open Graph Formerly known as Facebook Connect. Facebook's technology platform for connecting other sites and content to the Facebook social network.

Google Buzz A social networking tool that integrates data from a variety of social media, including Twitter, Blogger, and Friend-Feed. Google Buzz (**www.google.com/buzz/**) was launched in 2010, and integrates with Gmail, Google's web-based email service.

GPS A technology that uses satellites to provide positioning and navigation services.

Foursquare A location-based social networking service for mobile phones. Users check into a particular location, and nearby friends are notified of their presence.

Multiplayer online game A computer game that can be played by multiple users over the Internet.

Virtual world An online community that takes the form of a computer-based simulated environment.

Avatar A graphical representation of a computer user, typically in the form of a cartoon character.

- **Social networks will increasingly link to other information and applications.** Facebook is already doing this, via its *Open Graph* platform. Open Graph lets other websites connect their users to Facebook, to share links, likes, and such. Along the same lines, expect your contacts list in both your email program and your mobile phone to be linked to your social network friends list, eliminating any separation between contacts and social friends. In this regard, social media will become part of a single cross-platform experience. You won't have to log in to Facebook or Twitter to create new status updates or tweets; you'll be able to post from any number of websites and devices.

- **Social media will become more interconnected.** Today, many people belong to multiple social networks and services. For example, you might have profiles on Facebook, Twitter, and Digg. New services, such as *Google Buzz*, will make it easier to aggregate information on multiple services, and to use a single interface for accessing all social sites.

- **Social media will become location based.** Social networks will use *GPS*, short for global positioning system, technology embedded in mobile devices to geotag users' posts, as well as to inform nearby friends of a user's presence. Separate services such as *Foursquare*, which enable users to notify others that they're nearby, will be incorporated into more full-featured social networks.

- **Businesses will embrace social media for intercompany communications and collaboration.** In the business world, social media aren't just for promotion; they can also be used to connect employees in different offices and locations and to facilitate collaboration between those employees.

- **Social media will merge with virtual worlds.** Social networking doesn't have to be text based; an immersive, 3D environment can enhance the social networking experience. Look for *multiplayer online games* and *virtual worlds* to acquire more social networking features, and for some social networks to enable *avatar*-based usage. Even those social networks that don't go fully 3D will add more graphical means of communicating and collaborating with other users. The concept of a friends map, for example, will help users see which of their friends are online at a given moment, interested in a given topic, and the like.

Summary

In this chapter you learned what social networks are and how they work. You learned the benefits and hazards of social networking, and how to protect your privacy on social networks. You also learned the do's and don'ts of social networking and how businesses use social media. Finally, you learned about some of the future trends in social networking.

Key Terms

Avatar	13	LinkedIn	2
Blog	1	Linkworthy	11
Bookmark	4	Malware	6
Bulletin board system (BBS)	2	Media sharing	3
Chat room	3	Microblog	1
Computer virus	6	Multiplayer online game	13
Contextual	11	MySpace	2
Delicious	3	News feed	3
Dial-up computer network	2	Open Graph	13
Digg	3	Photo-sharing site	2
Discussion forum	2	Profile	3
Email	3	Smartphone	12
Facebook	2	Social bookmarking service	1
Flame war	10	Social media	1
Foursquare	13	Social network	1
Friend	3	Spam	7
Friending	6	Spyware	6
Friendster	2	Status update	3
Google Buzz	13	Tag	4
GPS	13	Twitter	4
Identity theft	7	Usenet	2
Inbound link	11	Viral	4
Instant messaging	3	Virtual world	13
Keyword	4	Website community	2

Multiple Choice Questions

1. Which of the following was the first major online social network?

   (a) MySpace
   (b) Facebook
   (c) Friendster
   (d) The Source

2. Which of the following is a social bookmarking service?

   (a) Twitter
   (b) Digg
   (c) Flickr
   (d) Facebook

3. Which of the following should you *not* do on a social network?

    (a) Use proper spelling.

    (b) Keep your posts short.

    (c) Accept all friend requests.

    (d) Include links to other sites.

4. What can you do to protect your privacy on a social network?

    (a) Hide your contact information.

    (b) Avoid posting your current whereabouts.

    (c) Avoid posting incriminating information or photographs.

    (d) All of the above

5. Which of the following social networks targets business professionals?

    (a) Facebook

    (b) LinkedIn

    (c) MySpace

    (d) Friendster

6. Which of the following is *not* a component of a typical social network?

    (a) Voice chat

    (b) User profile pages

    (c) Email

    (d) Media sharing

7. Which of the following is *not* a trend in social networking?

    (a) More protective privacy options

    (b) Increased interconnectivity with other information and applications

    (c) Limiting users based on age and education level

    (d) Increased use by businesses for intercompany communications and collaboration

8. Which of the following can businesses do to take advantage of social media?

    (a) Establish their own social networking pages

    (b) Make it easy for social bookmarking services to bookmark their pages

    (c) Advertise on social networking sites

    (d) All of the above

9. Which of the following is *not* a form of social media?

    (a) Social bookmarking services

    (b) Instant messaging

    (c) Social networks

    (d) Microblogs

10. Which is the largest social network today?

    (a) Friendster

    (b) MySpace

    (c) Twitter

    (d) Facebook

Fill in the Blank

Write the correct word in the space provided.

1. Twitter is a form of social media known as a(n) _____.
2. CompuServe, Prodigy, and America Online were examples of _____ computer networks.
3. On a social network, a(n) _____ is someone with whom you communicate and share information.
4. On a social network, you keep others informed of what you're doing by issuing _____.
5. _____ content on a web page is useful or interesting enough to link to.

Critical Thinking

1. Social networks, social bookmarking services, and microblogs are all different types of social media. Write a short paper that discusses the purposes for which each type of social media is best suited.
2. Some information is best kept private, even on a social network. Write a short paper that discusses what types of information can safely be shared and what types should be kept private.

Team Projects

1. Use the resources at your disposal to investigate the early online communities, including CompuServe, Prodigy, and American Online. Each member of your team should take one site or service to research and then write a one-page paper discussing the history and features of that community.
2. Discuss the ramifications of posting personal information on a public social network. Each member of the team should choose a particular piece of information or situation that should not be posted publicly, along with the possible negative results from posting that information, and write a one-page paper about it.

Credits

Figure 1.1, Facebook.com. Reprinted by permission of Facebook Inc.

Figure 1.2, Digg.com. Reprinted by permission of Digg.com.

Figure 1.3, Twitter.com. Twitter, www.twitter.com. Used by permission.

CHAPTER 2

Using Facebook: The Basics

Objectives

After you read this chapter, you will be able to:

1. Get Started with Facebook

2. Personalize Your Profile

3. Find Friends

4. Manage Your Homepage

5. Update Your Status

6. Communicate with Friends

7. Use Facebook Applications

The following Hands-On Exercises will help you accomplish the chapter objectives.

Hands-On Exercises

EXERCISES	SKILLS COVERED
1. Setting Up Your Facebook Account	**Step 1:** Start Your Browser and Navigate to Facebook.com **Step 2:** Create a Facebook Account **Step 3:** Find Friends and Complete Your Profile
2. Finding Friends	**Step 1:** Accept a Friend Request **Step 2:** Accept Facebook Friend Suggestions **Step 3:** Find Friends You Email **Step 4:** Find Friends You Instant Message **Step 5:** Find School Friends and Coworkers **Step 6:** Search for Friends **Step 7:** Manage Lists of Friends **Step 8:** Visit Your Friends' Profile Pages
3. Using the Homepage	**Step 1:** Navigate the Homepage **Step 2:** Read the News Feed **Step 3:** Hide Updates from Specific People **Step 4:** Unhide Hidden Updates
4. Posting Status Updates	**Step 1:** Post a Status Update **Step 2:** Attach a Photo **Step 3:** Attach a Video **Step 4:** Attach an Event **Step 5:** Attach a Link **Step 6:** Select Who Sees Your Update **Step 7:** Delete an Update
5. Communicating with Friends	**Step 1:** Post on a Friend's Wall **Step 2:** Read and Reply to an Email Message **Step 3:** Send a New Email Message **Step 4:** Initiate a Real-Time Chat Session

Get Started with Facebook

What is Facebook?

Facebook is the Internet's largest social network, with more than 500 million users. People use Facebook to keep their friends informed of their latest activities, as well as to keep in touch with what their friends are doing. The average Facebook user has 130 friends on the site and spends close to an hour each day connected to the Facebook site.

Each member of the community posts his or her own personal profile on the site. Users who know each other or who have similar interests connect as friends; an individual's growing collection of friends helps to build a succession of personal communities.

Who can use Facebook?

Facebook is for anyone. Users range from grade schoolers to senior citizens; although it started out as a site with particular appeal for college students, two thirds of the sites users are now post-college age, with a full 10 percent aged 55 or older. As such, Facebook has become a favorite site not just for friend and family connections but also for business networking. In addition, many businesses are using Facebook to connect with their customers; musicians and other entertainers also use Facebook to connect with their fans.

How do I connect to Facebook?

Most users connect to Facebook over the Internet, via Internet Explorer or some other web browser. You can also connect to Facebook from a smartphone or other mobile device; Facebook offers specialized applications for the Apple iPhone and similar phones.

 Tip   **Facebook Mobile**

To find the Facebook application for your phone, search your phone's apps store or go to **www.facebook.com/mobile/**. You can also point your mobile web browser to **m.facebook.com** to access the mobile version of the Facebook site.

How do I get started with Facebook?

Facebook is free to use, although you do have to establish a Facebook account. Establishing an account involves providing Facebook with your email address and other select personal information. Once you are signed up, you create your own Profile page. Then you can begin looking for friends on the site.

How is the Facebook site organized?

The Facebook site consists of several essential sections. The Facebook *Homepage* is where you keep track of what your friends are doing. This page lists recent status updates from your most important friends. Your own *Profile page* is where all your status updates are listed, and where friends can leave you messages on what Facebook calls your Wall. Other parts of the site let you find new friends, send and receive email messages, and sign up for applications and games.

How do I get to various places on Facebook?

You can access most of these pages from the *Facebook toolbar* found at the top of every Facebook page (Figure 2.1). From here you can review friend requests, read

Homepage The main page for Facebook members, located at www.facebook.com. The Facebook Homepage consists of a news feed of status updates from a member's friends.

Profile page The personal page for each Facebook member. All of a member's personal information and status updates are displayed on his or her Profile page.

Facebook toolbar A strip of buttons or commands located at the top of every Facebook page. Use the Facebook toolbar to navigate to key pages on the Facebook site.

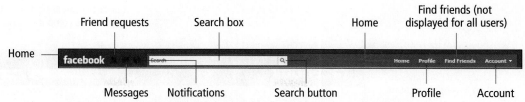

Figure 2.1 The Facebook toolbar, displayed at the top of all pages.

email messages and Facebook notifications, jump to your Profile page or the Homepage, manage your account settings, and search for friends, pages, and applications.

You can access other parts of Facebook from the Homepage, which hosts a sidebar full of links to key Facebook pages and activities, such as messages, events, friends, and applications. Just click a link in the Homepage sidebar to go to that particular part of the Facebook site.

Hands-On Exercises

1 | Setting Up Your Facebook Account

Steps: 1. Start Your Browser and Navigate to Facebook.com; **2.** Create a Facebook Account; **3.** Find Friends and Complete Your Profile.

Use Figures 2.2 through 2.5 as a guide in the exercise.

 Comparing Your Screen with the Figures in This Book

Since Facebook is constantly updating its feature set, the pages you see on your own computer screen might not always match those displayed in this book.

 Start Your Browser and Navigate to Facebook.com

Refer to Figure 2.2 as you complete Step 1.

a. Turn on your computer.

b. Launch your preferred web browser, such as Internet Explorer, Firefox, or Safari.

c. Enter www.facebook.com into your browser's address box and press Enter.

d. If you already have a Facebook account, sign in with your email address and password; then click the **Login** button to enter the Facebook website. If you have never used Facebook before, you will need to create a Facebook account. Proceed to Step 2.

Check to remain signed
in on this computer

Click to sign into an
existing Facebook account

Enter email address and
password if you have an
existing Facebook account

Enter your first
and last names

Enter your email address

Enter your desired password

Select your gender

Click to create a new
Facebook account

Enter your birthdate

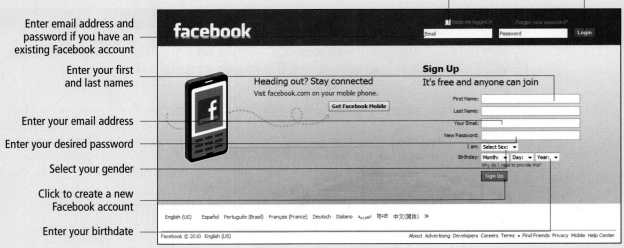

Figure 2.2 Hands-On Exercise 1, Step 1.

Step 2 Create a Facebook Account

Refer to Figure 2.2 as you complete Step 2.

a. From the www.facebook.com page, type your first name into the *First Name* box.

b. Type your last name into the *Last Name* box.

c. Type your email address into the *Your Email* box.

You will use this email address to sign into Facebook each time you enter the site.

d. Enter your desired password into the *New Password* box.

Your password should be at least six characters long.

 More Secure Passwords

To make your password more secure (harder to guess or hack), include a mix of alphabetic, numeric, and special characters (punctuation marks). Longer passwords are also more secure.

e. Select your gender from the *I am (Select Sex)* list.

f. Select your date of birth from the *Birthday (Month/Day/Year)* list.

g. Click the **Sign Up** button.

h. When prompted to complete the Security Check page, enter the "secret words" from the *captcha* into the *Text in the Box* box. Then click the **Sign Up** button.

i. Check your email program or account. When you receive an email message asking you to confirm your new Facebook account, click the link in this email.

Captcha A type of challenge-response test to ensure that the user is a human being, rather than a computer program. Captchas typically consist of warped or otherwise distorted text that cannot be machine read; by requiring input of the captcha text, a web page cuts down on the amount of computer-generated spam.

Step 3 Find Friends and Complete Your Profile

Refer to Figures 2.3 through 2.5 as you complete Step 3.

When you confirm your new Facebook account, you'll be prompted to find friends and family who are already on Facebook.

a. Enter the email address and password for your web-based email account, such as Hotmail or Gmail, into the *Your Email* and *Email Password* boxes. Then click the **Find Friends** button. (If prompted to allow Facebook to access your program or contacts, click **Yes**.)

Enter your web-based email address

Enter the password for your web-based email account

Click to find Facebook members in your email contacts list

Figure 2.3 Hands-On Exercise 1, Step 2a.

Your Facebook page will list people in your email contacts list who are also members of Facebook.

b. To add one or more of these people to your Facebook friends list, check the box next to that person's name and then click the **Add Friend** or **Add as Friends** button. If you do not want to add any of these people, click **Skip**.

> **Note** **Skip This Step**
>
> You don't have to find friends when you first sign up; you can do this at any time on the Facebook site. To skip any part of this process, click the **Skip this step** link or **Skip** button.

Next, Facebook displays a list of your email contacts who are not yet members of Facebook.

c. To invite any of these people to join Facebook, check the box next to that person's name and then click the **Invite to Join** button.

Next, you will be prompted to fill out your *Profile Information*.

d. Type the name of your high school into the *High School* box and select the year of your graduation from the *Class Year* list.

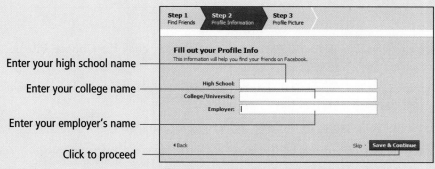

Enter your high school name

Enter your college name

Enter your employer's name

Click to proceed

Figure 2.4 Hands-On Exercise 1, Step 2d.

e. If you graduated from or are attending a college or university, type the name of your college into the *College/University* box and select the year of your graduation from the *Class Year* list.

f. If you are currently employed, type the name of your employer into the *Employer* box.

g. Click the **Save & Continue** button.

If you entered any school or work information, you will be prompted to add as friends people you might know from those schools or businesses.

h. Click the names of any people you know and want as friends; then click the **Save & Continue** button.

Next, you will be prompted to set your *Profile Picture*.

i. To use an existing photo stored on your computer, click the **Upload a Photo** link.

Click to upload your profile picture ———

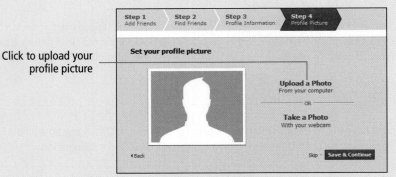

Figure 2.5 Hands-On Exercise 1, Step 2i.

j. When the *Upload Your Profile Picture* window appears, click the **Choose File** or **Browse** button.

k. When the *Open* or *Choose File* dialog box appears, navigate to and select the photo you wish to use. Then click the **Open** button.

You can upload pictures in the *.jpg*, *.gif*, or *.png* formats, up to 4 **MB** in size.

l. When your picture appears on the page, click the **Save & Continue** button.

Objective 2

Personalize Your Profile

What is the Profile page?

Your Profile page is your personal page on Facebook (Figure 2.6). The main part of your Profile page hosts the *Wall*, which displays your latest status updates as well as posts made to you by your friends. Other tabs on your Profile page hold your personal information, photos, videos, events, and so forth. Additional personal information is found in boxes that appear in the sidebar on the left side of the page. Finally, your Profile picture appears at the top left corner of your Profile page.

How do you post status updates?

The *Publisher box*, sometimes called the Share box, is where you post your status updates. Type a message into the Publisher box and click the Share button, and your status update is posted to your Profile page and all your friends' Homepages.

How do you change your Profile picture?

You can change your Profile picture at any time. Navigate to your Profile page and point to your picture, and then click the Change Picture link that appears. When the pop-up menu appears, select from where you want to obtain the picture: Upload a Picture (from your computer), Take a Picture (from your computer's webcam), or Choose from Album (to use a picture previously uploaded to Facebook). If you selected Upload a Picture, click the Browse or Choose File button when the Upload Your Profile Picture window appears. When the Open or Choose File to Upload dialog box appears, navigate to and select the picture to upload. Then click the Open button.

Wall The primary section of a Facebook member's Profile page, which displays the member's status updates as well as messages from other users.

Publisher box The box at the top of your Profile and Homepages; used to post status updates. There is also a Publisher box at the top of friends' Homepages; use this Publisher box to post a message to that friend's Profile page.

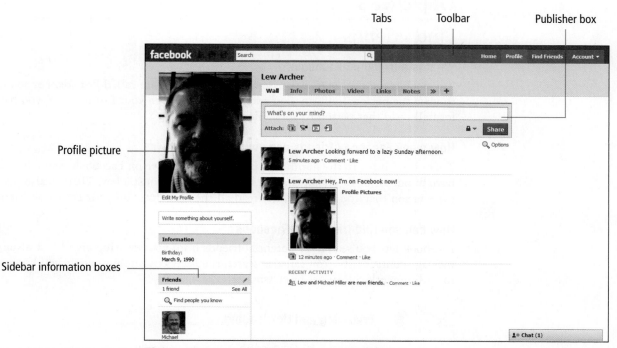

Figure 2.6 A typical Facebook Profile page.

Remove a Picture

To remove the current Profile picture without replacing it with a new picture (resulting in a blank space where your picture should be), point to your Profile picture and select **Change Picture** > **Remove Your Picture**.

How do you select which tabs are displayed on your Profile page?

Different types of information are displayed in separate tabs on your Profile page. To add a new tab, click the + tab and select a new tab from the list. To rearrange the order of your tabs, click a tab and drag that tab to a new position. To delete a tab, select the tab, click the pencil icon, and click Delete Tab.

Pick from the List

Facebook displays up to a half-dozen tabs on your page. If you have more than five tabs, you can view the others by clicking the right arrow tab and selecting the tabs from the list.

Can you change which boxes are displayed on your Profile page's sidebar?

Your Profile page's left sidebar contains various bits of personal information in individual boxes. The Information box and Friends box are displayed by default; you cannot move or delete these boxes. You can, however, reposition any other box by pointing to the title bar of that box until the cursor changes to a four-headed arrow; then drag the box to a new position and double-click to secure. To remove a box, click the Edit Box (pencil) icon and select Remove Box from the pop-up menu.

Objective 3

Find Friends

What is a friend on Facebook?

The people you choose to associate with on Facebook are called Friends. For someone to view the personal information and status updates on your Profile page, you have to formally add that person to your Friends list.

How many Facebook friends can you have?

There is no limit to the number of friends you can have on Facebook. Some people have hundreds of Facebook friends, while others have just a few. There is also no expectation that you will dutifully read all the posts from all your Facebook friends.

How can you find friends on Facebook?

Facebook lets you search for potential friends from your existing email and instant message contact lists. You can also search the Facebook site for people you know, including work colleagues or classmates.

Friending and Unfriending

The process of finding new Facebook friends is called *friending*. When you remove someone from your Friends list, you *unfriend* that person.

How can you organize your Facebook friends?

List A collection of specified Facebook friends; a subset of the member's overall collection of Facebook friends.

If you have large numbers of Facebook friends, handling them all can be difficult. To make that process easier, Facebook lets you create custom *lists* of friends and subsets of friends organized however you wish. You may want to create a list of family members, for example, or a list of people you share a class with. Managing small lists of friends is much easier than dealing with all your friends at once.

Hands-On Exercises

2 | Finding Friends

Steps: 1. Accept a Friend Request; **2.** Accept Facebook Friend Suggestions; **3.** Find Friends You Email; **4.** Find Friends You Instant Message; **5.** Find School Friends and Coworkers; **6.** Search for Friends; **7.** Manage Lists of Friends; **8.** Visit Your Friends' Profile Pages

Use Figures 2.7 through 2.14 as a guide in the exercise.

Step 1 Accept a Friend Request

Refer to Figure 2.7 as you complete Step 1.

Sometimes potential friends find you before you find them. In this instance, they will send you a friend request. You may receive a friend request via email, or you can view friend requests within Facebook.

a. To view pending friend requests, click the **Friend Requests** icon in the Facebook toolbar.

b. To view the *Profile* of a person requesting to be your friend, click his or her name or profile picture.

c. To accept this friend request, click the **Confirm** button. To refuse this request, click the **Ignore** button.

Click to view pending friend requests

Click to accept friend request

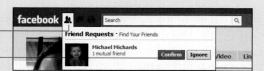

Figure 2.7 Hands-On Exercise 2, Step 1.

 Tip **Accept or Not?**

You don't have to accept a friend request, even if you know that person in the real world. (The other person is not informed that you rejected the request.) Remember, once you accept a friend request, that person can view all your personal information and status updates unless you alter your privacy settings to hide information from that person, as will be discussed in another chapter.

Step 2 · Accept Facebook Friend Suggestions

Refer to Figure 2.8 as you complete Step 2.

Facebook will recommend people to be new friends. These recommendations typically come from mutual associations, that is, they're usually friends of existing friends, or they go to your school or are employed by the same company as you are.

a. To view these friend recommendations, click **Home** on the Facebook toolbar. Then click **Friends** on the sidebar.

b. On the Friends page, scroll to the *People You May Know* section.

c. To send a friend request to a person, click the **Add as friend** link.

d. To ignore a friend suggestion, click the **X** next to that person's name.

Click to ignore this suggestion

Click to send a friend request

Add people you know as friends and become a fan of public profiles you like.

Ricky × Add as friend	Cary × Add as friend	Bigg × Add as friend
Sara × Add as friend	William × Add as friend	Scotty × Add as friend
Mike × Add as friend	Darlene × Add as friend	Psychic × Add as friend

▼ More

Figure 2.8 Hands-On Exercise 2, Step 2.

Step 3 · Find Friends You Email

Refer to Figure 2.9 as you complete Step 3.

If you email someone on a regular basis, you may want to become Facebook friends with him or her.

a. To find people in your email contact list who are also members of Facebook, click **Home** on the Facebook toolbar. Then click **Friends** on the sidebar.

b. On the Friends page, scroll to the *Find People You Email* section.

c. If you use a web-based email service, such as Yahoo! Mail or Gmail, type your email address into the *Your Email* box. Then follow the onscreen instructions. Click the **Find Friends** button to display a list of email contacts who are also Facebook members.

d. If you use a program to manage your email, such as Eudora or Mozilla Thunderbird, click the **Upload Contact File** link. If Microsoft Outlook is your email client, check the **Automatically import my contacts from Outlook** option. If you use another email client, check the **Upload a contact file** option and specify the location of your email contacts file. Click the **Find Friends** button to upload your email contacts list to Facebook and display a list of email contacts who are also Facebook members.

e. Check the box next to each person to whom you'd like to send a friend request; then click the **Add as Friends** button.

Click if you use an email software program

Enter your web-based email address and password

Figure 2.9 Hands-On Exercise 2, Step 3.

Step 4 Find Friends You Instant Message

Refer to Figure 2.10 as you complete Step 4.

If you have someone on your instant messaging service's friends list, you may want to add that person as a friend on Facebook.

a. To find people in your instant messaging friends list who are also members of Facebook, click **Home** on the Facebook toolbar. Then click **Friends** on the sidebar.

> **Note** **IM Services**
>
> At the present time, Facebook can import friends' lists from AOL Instant Messenger (AIM), ICQ, and Windows Live Messenger. It is not yet compatible with Yahoo! Messenger or Google Talk.

b. On the Friends page, scroll to the Find People You IM section.

c. Click the link for the IM service you use: **AOL Instant Messenger**, **ICQ Chat**, or **Windows Live Messenger**.

d. When prompted, enter your IM screen name, number, or ID, along with your password.

e. Click the **Find Friends** button.

Facebook will display a list of your IM friends who are also members of Facebook.

f. Check the box next to each person to whom you'd like to send a friend request; then click the **Add as Friends** button.

Click the link for the
IM service you use

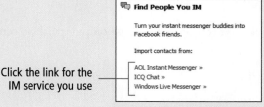

Figure 2.10 Hands-On Exercise 2, Step 4.

Step 5 Find School Friends and Coworkers

Refer to Figure 2.11 as you complete Step 5.

Facebook assumes that classmates or work colleagues might be welcome additions to your friends list.

a. To find your fellow classmates or coworkers, click **Home** on the Facebook toolbar. Then click **Friends** on the sidebar.

b. On the Friends page, scroll to the *Search for People* section.

Facebook should display several links for the schools and businesses you've entered as part of your personal information, in the form of **Find classmates**, **Find coworkers**, and **Find former coworkers**.

c. Click the appropriate link to display a list of classmates or coworkers who are also members of Facebook.

d. Check the box next to each person to whom you'd like to send a friend request. Then click the **Add as Friends** button.

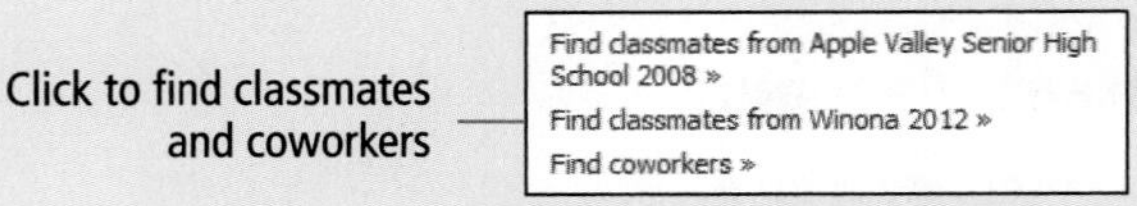

Click to find classmates and coworkers

Find classmates from Apple Valley Senior High School 2008 »

Find classmates from Winona 2012 »

Find coworkers »

Figure 2.11 Hands-On Exercise 2, Step 5.

Step 6 Search for Friends

Refer to Figure 2.12 as you complete Step 6.

Facebook lets you search for friends by either name or email address. You can search from the search box on the Facebook toolbar or the one on the Friends page.

a. To access the Friends page, click **Home** on the Facebook toolbar. Then click **Friends** on the sidebar.

> **Tip** ⭐ **Search by Email Address**
>
> If the friend you're looking for has a relatively common name, such as John Smith, there may be too many people with that name on Facebook for you to find the correct one easily. It may be easier to search for that person by entering his or her email address, if you know it.

b. From the Friends page, scroll to the *Search for People* section.

c. Type a name or email address into the search box. Then click the **Search** button (the magnifying glass) or press Enter on your keyboard.

d. When the search results page appears, make sure that **People** is selected in the sidebar.

e. Click the **Add a Friend** link next to the person to whom you wish to send a friend request.

Click to begin searching

Enter a person's name or email address

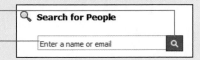

🔍 **Search for People**

Enter a name or email   🔍

Figure 2.12 Hands-On Exercise 2, Step 6.

Step 7 Manage Lists of Friends

Refer to Figure 2.13 as you complete Step 7.

Facebook helps you keep a large number of Facebook friends organized by allowing you to create multiple lists with subsets of friends. For example, you can create lists for family members, coworkers, or even people in a school study group.

a. To create a friends list, click the **Account** link on the Facebook toolbar and select **Edit Friends** from the pull-down menu.

b. Select **All Connections** from the sidebar to display all your friends.

c. Click the **Create New List** button.

d. When the *Create New List* window appears, enter a name for the list into the *Enter a Name* box.

e. Click those friends you want included in this list.

You can select multiple people at once.

f. Click the **Create List** button.

Your new list will appear in the sidebar of the Friends page.

g. Go to the Facebook Homepage and click **Friends** in the sidebar.

When the Friends page appears, all the lists you've created are listed in the *Friends* section of the sidebar.

h. Click a list to display status updates from all of the members of that specific list.

Enter a name for the list ——

Click friends you
want to add to the list ——

Figure 2.13 Hands-On Exercise 2, Step 7.

Step 8 Visit Your Friends' Profile Pages

Refer to Figure 2.14 as you complete Step 8.

Once you've added a person as a Facebook friend and that person has confirmed your request, you can visit that person's Profile page.

a. To display a Profile page, click that person's name anywhere on the Facebook site: in your Friends page, on the Homepage, or in a Friends list.

 Personalized Profiles

Since every Facebook user can personalize the elements displayed on his or her Profile page, some of the items discussed here may not appear on a given individual's page.

b. On your friends' Profile page, select the **Wall** tab to view this person's latest status updates. To comment on a status update, click the **Comment** link, enter your comment, and click the **Comment** button.

c. To post your own public message to this person's Wall, select the **Wall** tab, enter your message into the *Write something...* box, and click the **Share** button.

d. To view personal information about this person, select the **Info** tab.

Basic information is displayed in the *Information* box in the sidebar.

e. To view this person's pictures, select the **Photos** tab.

f. To view this person's friends, scroll to the *Friends* box in the sidebar. To view friends you have in common, scroll to the *Mutual Friends* box.

Click to display personal info

Click to look at pictures

Enter a public message here

Click to comment on a status update

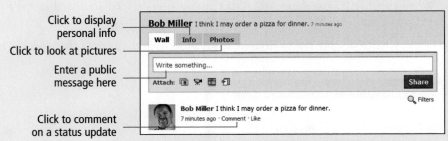

Figure 2.14 Hands-On Exercise 2, Step 8.

Objective 4

Manage Your Homepage

What's on the Facebook Homepage?

The Facebook Homepage (www.facebook.com) is where all the status updates from your friends are displayed in a continuous news feed. It's also a navigational page, with links to other important Facebook features in the left sidebar. You can also use the Homepage to update your own status, via the What's on your mind? box at the top of the page.

What is the news feed?

The news feed is a real-time list of your friends' status updates. By default, Facebook displays the Top News feed, which displays updates only from selected friends—those that Facebook assumes are most important to you. To display updates from *all* your friends, Facebook lets you display the Most Recent feed instead.

How can I comment on friends' status updates?

You don't have to visit a friend's Profile page to comment on his or her status updates. Instead, you can comment on individual updates, or opt to "like" an update, directly from the Facebook Homepage. Just click the Comment **or** Like link beneath the update on your Homepage.

Hands-On Exercises

3 | Using the Homepage

Steps: 1. Navigate the Homepage; **2.** Read the News Feed; **3.** Hide Updates from Specific People; **4.** Unhide Hidden Updates

Use Figures 2.15 through 2.18 as a guide in the exercise.

Step 1 | Navigate the Homepage

Refer to Figure 2.15 as you complete Step 1.

a. To display the Homepage, click either the **Facebook** or the **Home** link on the Facebook toolbar.

A News Feed of friends' status updates is displayed in the center of the Homepage. Links to other Facebook pages are displayed in the left sidebar.

b. Click a link to display the specific page.

Facebook displays a list of suggested activities (possible friends, friends you haven't contacted in a while, and so on) and displays it in the *Suggestions* box at the top of the right sidebar. The right sidebar also includes upcoming events, "pokes" from friends, and advertisements (in the *Sponsored* box).

Right sidebar

News feed

Navigation sidebar

Figure 2.15 Hands-On Exercise 3, Step 1.

Step 2   Read the News Feed

Refer to Figure 2.16 as you complete Step 2.

Your friends' status updates are displayed in the news feed that scrolls down the center of the Homepage.

a. To view older updates, scroll to the bottom of the page and click **Older Posts.**

   By default, Facebook displays what it deems to be the most interesting status updates and other content from your friends.

b. To display a more complete listing of friends' status updates, in real time, click the **Most Recent** link at the top of the Homepage.

c. To comment on a friends' status update, click the **Comment** link under that update and type your comment into the text box. Then click the **Comment** button.

d. To "like" a friends' status update, click the **Like** link under the update.

e. To display a friend's Profile page, click his or her name in the news feed.

Figure 2.16 Hands-On Exercise 3, Step 2.

Step 3   Hide Updates from Specific People

Refer to Figure 2.17 as you complete Step 3.

Over time, you may find that some friends post more often than you like, or post information that you're simply not interested in. Fortunately, Facebook lets you remove updates from specific people from your news feed.

a. Point to a status update from that person to display the **X** button. Click the **X** button.

b. When the prompt box appears, click the **Hide (Friend)** button.

   In some instances, you have the option of only hiding those updates that are automatically posted by selected Facebook games and applications.

c. If this option exists, click the **Hide (Application)** button in the prompt box after you click the initial **X** button.

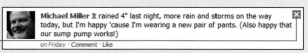

Figure 2.17 Hands-On Exercise 3, Step 3.

Step 4 Unhide Hidden Updates

Refer to Figure 2.18 as you complete Step 4.

If you've hidden posts from a person or application, you can redisplay these posts.

a. Scroll to the bottom of the Homepage and click the **Edit Options** link at the bottom of the *News Feed*.

b. When the *News Feed Settings* window appears, click the **X** button next to the friend or application you wish to see again.

Figure 2.18 Hands-On Exercise 3, Step 4.

Objective 5

Update Your Status

What is your Facebook status?

Status A short text message that indicates what a Facebook user is doing or thinking at the moment. Status updates are displayed in the News Feed of friends' Homepages.

Your Facebook *status* is what you're doing or thinking about at the moment. It's a snapshot into your life, posted as a short text on the Facebook site. You update your status from the top of your Profile page or the Homepage, in the box that asks you "What's on your mind?" When you type something into this box, called the Publisher box, and then click the Share button, your status is automatically updated.

Who sees your status updates?

Your status updates appear in multiple places on the Facebook site. First, your status updates appear on your Profile page, with the most recent at the top, on your Wall tab. (Your most recent status update also appears at the very top of your Profile page, above the Publisher box.) Your status updates also appear on your friends' Homepages, in their news feeds. This way your friends are kept updated as to what you're doing and thinking.

What can you include in your status updates?

A status update starts as a text message. It can be as short as a word or two or several paragraphs long. You can also attach various multimedia elements to your status updates, including digital photographs, videos, events, and links to other web pages. (Various Facebook applications also let you attach application-specific items to your status updates.)

Hands-On Exercises

4 | Posting Status Updates

Steps: 1. Post a Status Update; **2.** Attach a Photo; **3.** Attach a Video; **4.** Attach an Event; **5.** Attach a Link; **6.** Select Who Sees Your Update; **7.** Delete an Update

Use Figures 2.19 through 2.25 as a guide in the exercise.

Step 1 Post a Status Update

Refer to Figure 2.19 as you complete Step 1.

a. Navigate to the Facebook Homepage or your personal Profile page.

b. Type your message into the *Publish* (*What's on your mind?*) box at the top of the page.

c. Click the **Share** button.

Enter update text ——
Click to update status ——

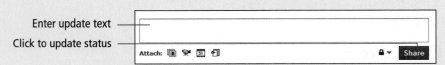

Figure 2.19 Hands-On Exercise 4, Step 1.

Step 2 Attach a Photo

Refer to Figure 2.20 as you complete Step 2.

a. To attach a digital photo to your status update, begin by typing your desired text into the *Publish* box at the top of the Home or Profile page.

b. Click the **Photos** button to display a new Photos panel beneath the *Publish* box.

c. To use a photo stored on your hard drive, click **Upload a Photo**. When the panel changes, click the **Browse** button; when the **Choose File to Upload** dialog box appears, navigate to and select the photo you want. Then click the **Open** button.

d. To use a new photo taken with your computer's webcam, click the **Take a Photo** link. When the panel changes to display your live webcam, click the **Photo** button.

e. Click the **Share** button to post your update.

Click to attach
an uploaded photo

Click to attach a
photo taken via webcam

Figure 2.20 Hands-On Exercise 4, Step 2.

Step 3 Attach a Video

Refer to Figure 2.21 as you complete Step 3.

a. To attach a digital video to your status update, begin by typing your desired text into the Publish box at the top of the page.

b. Click the **Video** button to display a new Video panel beneath the *Publish* box.

c. To attach a video recorded from your webcam, click the **Record a Video** link. When the panel changes to display a live picture from your webcam, click the **Record** button. Click the button again to end your recording.

d. To attach a video already recorded and stored on your computer, click the **Upload a Video** link. When the panel changes, click the **Browse** button; when the **Choose File to Upload** dialog box appears, navigate to and select the video file. Then click the **Open** button.

Videos must be no more than 20 minutes long, and no more than 1024 MB in size. Larger videos can take a long time to upload, especially on slower Internet connections.

e. Click the **Share** button to post your update.

Click to attach
a webcam video

Click to attach a
stored video file

Figure 2.21 Hands-On Exercise 4, Step 3.

Step 4 Attach an Event

Refer to Figure 2.22 as you complete Step 4.

a. To attach a Facebook event to your status update, begin by typing your desired text into the Publish box at the top of the page.

b. Click the **Event** button to display a new *Event* panel beneath the *Publish* box.

c. Type the name of the event into the *Title* box.

d. Type where the event is hosted into the *Location* box.

e. Use the time drop-down boxes to select the start date and time of the event.

f. Click the **Share** button.

Enter the event's name

Enter the event's location

Select the date and time of the event

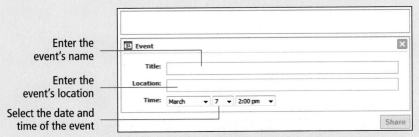

Figure 2.22 Hands-On Exercise 4, Step 4.

Step 5 Attach a Link

Refer to Figure 2.23 as you complete Step 5.

a. To attach a link to another web page to your status update, begin by typing your desired text into the *Publish* box at the top of the page.

b. Click the **Link** button to display a new Link panel beneath the *Publish* box.

c. In the **Link** box, enter the full web address of the page to which you want to link and click **Attach**.

d. If you are prompted to select a thumbnail image from this web page to accompany your link, click the left and right arrow buttons to cycle through the available images, or check the **No Thumbnail** option to include the link without an accompanying image.

e. Click the **Share** button.

Click to select a thumbnail image

Check to attach the link without a thumbnail image

Figure 2.23 Hands-On Exercise 4, Step 5.

Step 6 Select Who Sees Your Update

Refer to Figure 2.24 as you complete Step 6.

By default, Facebook displays your updates to everyone on your Friends list, unless you specify otherwise in your privacy settings. You can, however, restrict the viewing of your status updates on an update-to-update basis. Using this feature will allow you to hide specific updates from specific people.

a. Begin by typing your update into the *Publish* box at the top of the page.

b. Click the **Privacy** button (looks like a padlock) next to the **Share** button.

c. When the pop-up menu appears, select whom you want to see this message: **Everyone**, **Friends of Friends**, or **Only Friends**.

d. If you want to show this message to or hide it from specific people on your friends list, select **Customize** from the pop-up menu to display the *Custom Privacy* window. To display the message only to certain people, pull down the Make this visible to These people list, select **Specific People**, and then enter your friends' names into the *Enter a Name* or *List* box. To hide the message from certain people, enter these names into the *Hide this from These people* box. Click the **Save Setting** button when done.

e. Click the **Share** button to update your status.

Click to display this post to friends and friends of friends only

Click to display this post to all Facebook users

Click to display this post to your friends only

Click to show this message to or hide it from specific people

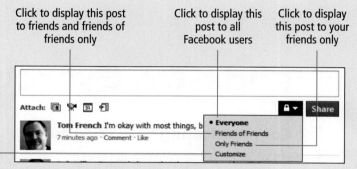

Figure 2.24 Hands-On Exercise 4, Step 6.

Step 7 Delete an Update

Refer to Figure 2.25 as you complete Step 7.

If you change your mind about a status update you made, you can delete that post from Facebook.

a. Navigate to your Profile page.

b. Scroll to the post you want to delete and point to the post until the **Remove** button appears.

c. Click the **Remove** button.

d. When the *Delete Post* confirmation window appears, click the **Delete** button.

Click to delete the post

Figure 2.25 Hands-On Exercise 4, Step 7.

Objective 6

Communicate with Friends

How can you communicate directly with friends on Facebook?

Facebook offers both public and private communications between members. The easiest way to communicate publicly with a friend is to post a comment on that friend's Profile page. The friend can continue the communication by communicating *wall-to-wall*.

Can you also communicate privately with friends?

While Facebook excels in social networking via public status updates, it also facilitates one-to-one communications between members. You can send messages via Facebook's proprietary email system, or you can exchange instant messages in real time via Facebook's *chat* system.

Wall-to-wall Direct communication between two Facebook members, accomplished via consecutive posts on each member's Wall.

Chat Facebook's proprietary instant messaging system, which facilitates one-to-one real-time communication between two friends.

Hands-On Exercises

5 | Communicating with Friends

Steps: 1. Post on a Friend's Wall; **2.** Read and Reply to an Email Message; **3.** Send a New Email Message; **4.** Initiate a Real-Time Chat Session

Use Figures 2.26 through 2.31 as a guide in the exercise.

 Step 1 **Post on a Friend's Wall**

Refer to Figure 2.26 as you complete Step 1.

Any Facebook member can post a message to any of his or her friends' Profile pages. These are posts to a friends' Wall that all of that person's friends can read.

a. To post a message to a friend's Wall, begin by typing your message into the *Publisher* box at the top of that person's Profile page.

 Alert **Public Posts**

All posts you make from the Publisher box on a friend's Profile page are public posts and anyone can read them.

b. If you want to attach an item to the post, click the appropriate button beneath the *Publisher* box.

c. Click the **Share** button.

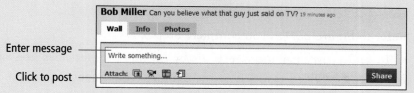

Enter message ⎯⎯

Click to post ⎯⎯

Figure 2.26 Hands-On Exercise 5, Step 1.

Step 2   Read and Reply to an Email Message

Refer to Figures 2.27 and 2.28 as you complete Step 2.

Facebook hosts its own private email system. You can use this system to send private messages to anyone on your friends list. When someone sends you a new message, a number will appear in red over the **Messages** icon in the Facebook toolbar.

a. Click the **Messages** icon on the toolbar to see the messages in your inbox.

New messages are shaded.

b. To read a message in full, click that message.

The message will be displayed on its own page.

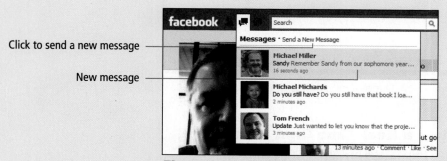

Click to send a new message ⎯⎯

New message ⎯⎯

Figure 2.27 Hands-On Exercise 5, Steps 2a and 2b.

c. To respond to an email message, enter your response into the *Reply* box.

d. If you wish to attach a photo, video, or event to this reply, click the appropriate button under the *Reply* box.

e. Click the **Reply** button.

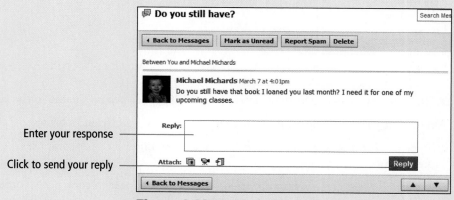

Enter your response ⎯⎯

Click to send your reply ⎯⎯

Figure 2.28 Hands-On Exercise 5, Steps 2c–2e.

Step 3 Send a New Email Message

Refer to Figure 2.29 as you complete Step 3.

a. To send a new email message, begin by clicking the **Messages** icon on the Facebook toolbar.

b. Click **Send a New Message**.

c. When the *New Message* window appears, enter the name of the recipient into the *To* box. The names of friends who match what you're typing are automatically displayed as you type. Select the recipient from the list.

d. Type a subject for this message into the *Subject* box.

e. Type your message into the *Message* box.

f. If you want to attach a photo, video, or link to this message, click the appropriate button underneath the *Message* box.

g. Click the **Send** button.

Enter the recipient's name ————
Enter the message subject ————
Type your message ————

Click to send ————

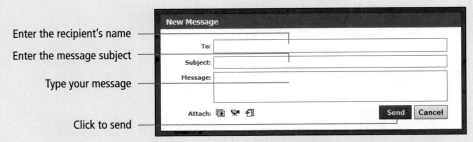

Figure 2.29 Hands-On Exercise 5, Step 3.

Step 4 Initiate a Real-Time Chat Session

Refer to Figures 2.30 and 2.31 as you complete Step 4.

a. Click the **Chat** button at the bottom right of any Facebook page.

A panel now expands to show all your friends who are online. Those friends who are active at the moment have a full green circle by their names; friends who are online but idle have a half-moon by their names.

An active online friend ————
An idle online friend ————

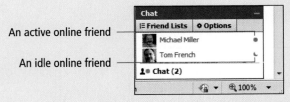

Figure 2.30 Hands-On Exercise 5, Step 4a.

b. To start a chat session with an active friend, click that person's name in the list.

A new chat panel now opens in both your browser and your friend's browser.

c. Type a text message in the bottom box and press Enter on your computer keyboard.

Your messages, along with your friend's responses, appear in consecutive order within the chat panel.

d. Continue typing new messages to progress the chat.

e. To end a chat, click the **X** at the top of the chat panel.

Click to close chat session

Your message

Your friend's reply

Type your message here

Figure 2.31 Hands-On Exercise 5, Steps 4b–4d.

Objective 7

Use Facebook Applications

What are Mafia Wars, Farmville, LivingSocial, and similar items that show up in friends' feeds?

Application On Facebook, a utility or game that runs on the Facebook site.

These items, and others like them, are Facebook *applications*. That is, they are applications and games that run on the Facebook site. You access these applications from their own Facebook pages, and use them while signed into Facebook. Some applications build on the social networking nature of the Facebook site; others are designed for more solitary use.

What kinds of applications are available?

There are many different types of applications available for use on the Facebook site. Facebook organizes applications into the following categories: Business, Education, Entertainment, Friends & Family, Games, Just for Fun, Lifestyle, Sports, and Utilities.

Can I play games on Facebook?

A game is a specific type of Facebook application, developed using the same base technology. You play Facebook games online on the Facebook site. Because they're relatively easy to play and free to use, Facebook games are quite popular; some games have millions of users.

How do I discover new applications?

There are two ways to find new applications and games: by searching or by browsing. To search for an application or a game, enter a description of what you're looking for into the search box in the Facebook toolbar; then click the Search (magnifying glass) button or press Enter on your keyboard. When the search results page appears, click Applications in the sidebar to display only applications in the search results.

To browse for applications by category, navigate to the Facebook application directory, located at www.facebook.com/apps/. From the sidebar, click the category of application you're looking for. (See Figure 2.32.)

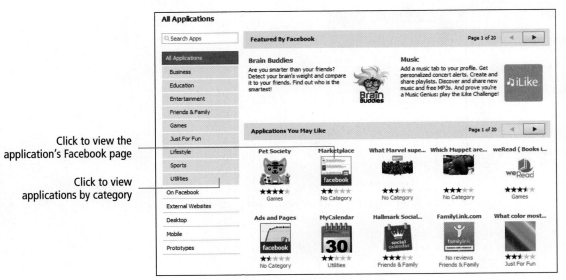

Click to view the
application's Facebook page

Click to view
applications by category

Figure 2.32 The Facebook application directory.

How do I start using an application?

When you find an application you like, click the link for that application to go to that application's Facebook page, which contains important information about that application. To begin using the application or playing the game, click the Go to Application button.

Note **Granting Access**

To use an application or play a game, you have to allow the application access to your Profile information, friends' information, and the like. When prompted, click Allow to allow this access, or Leave Application to halt usage.

Summary

In this chapter you learned how to create a Facebook account, find friends, read friends' profile pages, and post your own status updates. You also learned how to communicate with your Facebook friends, both publicly and privately, via email messages and chat. In addition, you learned how to find and use Facebook applications and games.

Key Terms

Application .41   Profile page 18

Captcha 20   Publisher box 23

Chat 38   Status 33

Facebook toolbar 18   Wall 23

Homepage 18   Wall-to-wall 38

List 25

Multiple Choice Questions

1. You sign into Facebook with your:

    (a) first and last name.

    (b) name and password.

    (c) email address and password.

    (d) last name and ZIP code.

2. Your status updates are displayed in the following places:

    (a) The Wall on your profile page

    (b) Your friends' profile pages

    (c) Your friends' homepages

    (d) Both (a) and (c)

3. Real-time communication between two Facebook users is called:

    (a) wall-to-wall.

    (b) email.

    (c) chat.

    (d) instant messaging.

4. The Facebook toolbar is displayed:

    (a) on every Facebook page.

    (b) on your Homepage only.

    (c) on your Profile page only.

    (d) only when you have a new message waiting.

5. You can add or change your Profile picture via the following method(s):

    (a) Pointing to a photo on the web

    (b) Uploading a photo from your computer

    (c) Taking a still photo from your computer's webcam

    (d) Both (a) and (b)

    (e) Both (b) and (c)

6. By default, Facebook's Homepage displays the following:

   (a) All recent status updates from all your friends
   (b) The most important status updates from selected friends
   (c) Your status updates only
   (d) Status updates from your friends and their friends

7. The following information boxes are displayed by default in the sidebar of your Profile page:

   (a) Information and Friends
   (b) Photos and Videos
   (c) Events and Notification
   (d) Information and Photos

8. Facebook will look for potential friends in your:

   (a) MySpace friends list.
   (b) computer's hard drive.
   (c) instant messaging service friends list.
   (d) business network's user directory.

9. Which of the following *cannot* be included with status updates?

   (a) Digital photos
   (b) MP3 music files
   (c) Video files
   (d) Links to web pages outside of the Facebook site

10. In the Chat panel, a name with a green circle indicates a friend who:

    (a) is online and active.
    (b) wishes to chat with you.
    (c) is online and inactive.
    (d) is not online at the moment.

Fill in the Blank

Write the correct word in the space provided.

1. The box where you enter new status updates is called the _____ box.
2. Facebook's messaging system is a form of proprietary _____.
3. A(n) _____ is someone you communicate with on Facebook.
4. Facebook allows you to attach _____ to other web pages in your status updates.
5. To signify your approval of a status update, click the _____ link.

Practice Exercises

1. **Creating a Facebook Account**

   You must create a Facebook account before you can start using the social network. Once you have created an account, you can add friends and post status updates to inform those friends what you are doing at the moment.

(a) Create a new Facebook account. (If you already have a Facebook account, create a second account using your middle name as your first name; you'll also have to use an alternate email address.)

(b) Add at least three people in your class as friends. You should also add your instructor as a friend.

(c) Make a status update detailing what you are doing in class today.

2. **Posting Messages on Friends' Walls**

You can communicate publicly with your Facebook friends by posting messages on their Walls. You do this via the Publisher box at the top of the friend's Profile page.

(a) Navigate to your instructor's Profile page.

(b) Enter a comment into the Publisher box at the top of the page.

(c) Attach a digital photo of yourself to the message.

(d) Click the **Share** button.

3. **Emailing via Facebook**

Facebook's messages are actually internal emails between Facebook users. You send messages when you want to conduct a private conversation with another user.

(a) Create a new Facebook message.

(b) Address the message to your instructor.

(c) In the text of the message, discuss a new website you've recently visited.

(d) Include a link to this website in your message.

(e) Send the completed message to your instructor.

4. **Using Facebook Applications**

A Facebook application is a utility that performs a specific task. Most applications install on a tab on the user's Profile page.

(a) Search or browse for the weRead application.

(b) Click the **Go to Application** button to run the application. Then allow the application access to your information.

(c) Within the weRead application, add one or more books as favorites or to your bookshelf.

(d) Return to your Profile page and add a new tab for weRead.

(e) Email your instructor with a message inviting him or her to check out your weRead tab on your Facebook Profile page.

Critical Thinking

1. The average Facebook user has more than 130 friends on the site. It's unlikely that a person would know all these people personally, outside of Facebook. Write a paper where you discuss how many Facebook friends you have, how many you would know by sight outside of Facebook, why you allow relative strangers to become your friends on Facebook, and what benefit you gain by having more or fewer Facebook friends.

2. Facebook enables you to communicate with friends both publicly, via status updates, and privately, via email messaging and instant messaging chat. Write a brief paper that discusses which types of communication are best suited for public consumption and which are best suited for private, one-to-one messages.

Team Projects

1. Divide your team into multiple groups of two. The first person in a pair should send a Facebook message to the second person, and include a photo with the message. The second person should reply to the first person, and include another photo with the reply. The final message should then be sent to the instructor for evaluation.

2. Divide your team into multiple groups of two. The first person in a pair should initiate a Facebook chat session with the second person. The two teammates should continue their chat for at least five minutes. At the end of the conversation, each teammate should copy the contents of the chat session and paste them into an email message, which he or she should then send to the instructor.

Credits

Facebook screenshots. Reprinted by permission of Facebook Inc.

CHAPTER 3

Using Facebook: Advanced Techniques

Objectives

After you read this chapter, you will be able to:

1. Share Photos and Videos
2. Manage Events
3. Join Groups, Networks, and Fan Pages
4. Create Groups and Fan Pages
5. Network Professionally
6. Manage Your Privacy Settings

The following Hands-On Exercises will help you accomplish the chapter objectives.

Hands-On Exercises

EXERCISES	SKILLS COVERED
1. Sharing Photos and Videos	**Step 1:** Create a Photo Album **Step 2:** Upload New Photos **Step 3:** Edit Photo Information **Step 4:** Manage Your Photos and Albums **Step 5:** Share a Photo **Step 6:** Display the Video Tab **Step 7:** Upload a Video **Step 8:** Share a Video **Step 9:** Post a Video from YouTube
2. Working with Events	**Step 1:** Display Events **Step 2:** Search for Events **Step 3:** RSVP to an Event **Step 4:** Create an Event
3. Working with Groups, Networks, and Fan Pages	**Step 1:** Join a Group **Step 2:** Join a School or Work Network **Step 3:** Become a Fan **Step 4:** Create a New Group **Step 5:** Create a Fan Page **Step 6:** Invite Others to Become Fans
4. Managing Privacy Settings	**Step 1:** Configure Universal Privacy Settings **Step 2:** Customize Individual Privacy Settings **Step 3:** Limit What Information Applications and Websites Can Access **Step 4:** Block People from Interacting with You on Facebook

Objective 1

Share Photos and Videos

Photo album On Facebook, a collection of digital photos organized by some underlying theme or topic.

You can attach photos and videos to a status update; is there any other way to share photos and videos on Facebook?

Facebook enables any member to upload digital photos into online albums. These *photo albums* can then be shared with friends and other users, who view the photos in their own web browsers. You can also upload videos for sharing by clicking on the Video tab on your Profile page.

Does Facebook have any limits as to the types of photos you can share?

Facebook lets you upload photos in the *.jpg*, *.gif*, and *.png* file formats. The maximum file size you can upload is 15 MB. You're limited to 200 photos per album, but can have an unlimited number of albums, which means you can upload an unlimited number of photos.

Tagging The act of formally identifying a Facebook member in a photo uploaded to the Facebook site.

What is photo tagging?

You identify people in your photos by *tagging* them. That is, you click on a person in the photo and then assign a friend's name to that part of the photo. You can then find photos where a given person appears by searching for that person's tag.

What kinds of videos can you upload?

Most people upload their home videos to Facebook, although you can upload other digital videos as well, as long as you're not uploading any copyrighted material. (That is, you can't upload commercial videos, or videos that contain commercial music in the background.) You can upload videos already stored as digital files, or upload videos recorded in real time from your computer's webcam. Videos must be no more than 20 minutes long, and no more than 1024 MB in size. Facebook accepts videos in the following file formats: *.3g2*, *.3gp*, *.3gpp*, *.asf*, *.avi*, *.dat*, *.flv*, *.m4v*, *.mkv*, *.mod*, *.mov*, *.mp4*, *.mpe*, *.mpeg*, *.mpeg4*, *.mpg*, *.nsv*, *.ogm*, *.ogv*, *.qt*, *.tod*, *.vob*, and *.wmv*.

YouTube The Internet's largest video sharing community, located at **www.youtube.com**, where members upload and view millions of video files each day.

Can you also upload YouTube videos to Facebook?

You can embed any public *YouTube* video in a Facebook status update. These can be videos you've uploaded to the YouTube site, or other people's videos. Since these embedded videos are actually hosted by YouTube, Facebook imposes no length or file size limit on these YouTube videos.

> **Tip** ★ **YouTube Videos**
>
> Since YouTube video files can be much larger (2 GB) than those allowed for direct uploading to Facebook, embedding a YouTube video is the better way to share larger video files, such as those recorded in high definition.

Hands-On Exercises

1 | Sharing Photos and Videos

Steps: 1. Create a Photo Album; **3.** Upload New Photos; **3.** Edit Photo Information; **4.** Manage Your Photos and Albums; **5.** Share a Photo; **6.** Display the Video Tab; **7.** Upload a Video; **8.** Share a Video; **9.** Post a Video from YouTube.

Use Figures 3.1 through 3.13 as a guide in the exercise.

Step 1 Create a Photo Album

Refer to Figures 3.1 and 3.2 as you complete Step 1.

You upload photos to specific photo albums, which are displayed on the
Photos tab on your Facebook Profile page.

a. Navigate to your Profile page and click the **Photos** tab.

The **Photos** tab displays all the photos in which you are tagged, as well as your
existing photo albums.

b. To create a new album, click the **Create a Photo Album** button.

Photos tab
Photos in which you are tagged
Click to create new album

Figure 3.1 Hands-On Exercise 1, Step 1b.

c. When the Create Album page appears, type the name for this album into the
Album Name box.

d. Type the location where these photos were taken into the *Location* box.

You can enter a ZIP code, city name, state name, or even just a country name. (This
step is optional; you can leave this box empty.)

e. Type a short description of this album into the *Description* box.

f. To determine who can view the photos in this album, click the **Privacy** button
and select one of the following: **Everyone, Friends and Networks, Friends of
Friends, Friends Only,** or **Customize.**

g. To finalize the album, click the **Create Album** button.

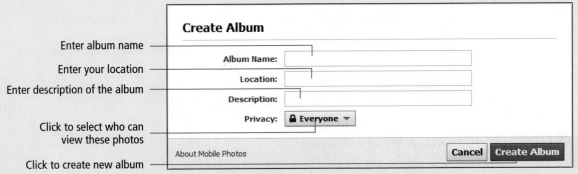

Enter album name ——
Enter your location ——
Enter description of the album ——
Click to select who can view these photos ——
Click to create new album ——

Figure 3.2 Hands-On Exercise 1, Steps 1c–1g.

 Step 2 **Upload New Photos**

Refer to Figure 3.3 as you complete Step 2.

You can add photos to an existing album at any time.

a. Navigate to your Profile page and select the **Photos** tab.

b. Scroll to the bottom of the Photos page and click the album to which you want to upload new photos.

c. When the Album page appears, click the **Add More Photos** link.

> **Note** **Facebook Plug-in**
>
> The first time you upload photos to Facebook you'll be prompted to download and install the Facebook plug-in. Follow the onscreen instructions to install this browser plug-in, which is necessary to upload photos to Facebook.

d. When the Select Photos window appears, use the folder list to navigate to the folder where the photos are located.

e. Click each photo you want to upload.

Note that you can upload multiple photos at one time.

f. Click the **Use Selected Photos** button.

Navigate to photo folder ——
Click photo to select ——
Click to upload selected photos ——

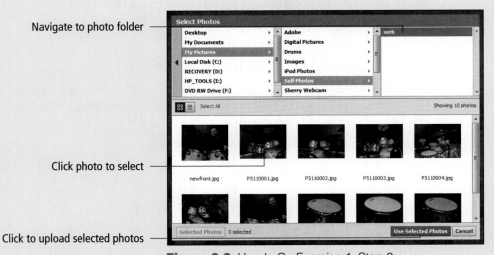

Figure 3.3 Hands-On Exercise 1, Step 2.

Step 3 ▶ Edit Photo Information

Refer to Figures 3.4 and 3.5 as you complete Step 3.

Once a photo is uploaded, you can edit the description of that photo, as well as tag people in the photo, move the photo to another album, or delete the photo.

a. Navigate to your Profile page and select the **Photos** tab.

b. Click the album that contains the photo you wish to edit.

c. Click the photo you wish to edit.

d. To tag a person in the photo, click the **Tag This Photo** link under the photo. Click on the person in the picture whom you want to tag.

You will then see a box around the selected person, along with a list of your friends.

e. Click the correct friend's name in the list, or enter the person's name into the search box. Then click the **Tag** button.

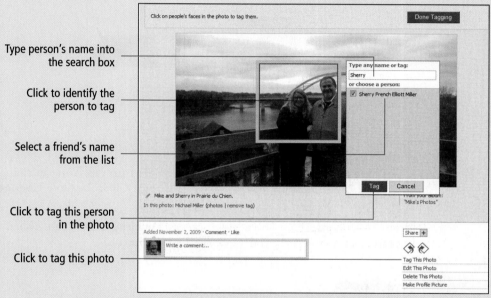

Type person's name into the search box

Click to identify the person to tag

Select a friend's name from the list

Click to tag this person in the photo

Click to tag this photo

Figure 3.4 Figure 3.4 Hands-On Exercise 1, Steps 3d and 3e.

f. To edit the description of this photo, click the **Edit This Photo** link. When the Edit Album page appears, type a caption for this photo into the *Caption* box. Then click the **Save Changes** button.

g. To move this photo to a different album, click the **Edit This Photo** link. When the Edit Album page appears, click the **Move to** list, select the target album, and click the **Save Changes** button.

Enter a caption for the photo

Click to move photo to a different album

Figure 3.5 Hands-On Exercise 1, Steps 3f and 3g.

h. To delete a photo from Facebook, click the **Delete This Photo** link.

Step 4 Manage Your Photos and Albums

Refer to Figure 3.6 as you complete Step 4.

a. To edit the contents of a photo album, begin by navigating to your Profile page and selecting the **Photos** tab.

b. Click the album you wish to edit.

c. Click the **Edit Info** button link above the photos.

d. To change the order of photos in the album, select the **Organize** tab; then click a photo and drag it into a new position. Click the **Save Changes** button when done.

e. To reverse the order of photos in the album, if required, select the **Organize** tab, and click the **Reverse Order** button. Click the **Save Changes** button when done.

Figure 3.6 Hands-On Exercise 1, Steps 4d and 4e.

f. To edit the description of the album, select the **Edit Info** tab. You can change the *Album Name*, *Location*, *Description*, and *Privacy settings*. Click the **Save Changes** button when done.

g. To delete this photo album and all its contents, click the **Delete** tab. When prompted to confirm this action, click the **Delete** button.

Step 5 Share a Photo

Refer to Figures 3.7 and 3.8 as you complete Step 5.

a. To share a photo with others, begin by navigating to your Profile page and selecting the **Photos** tab.

b. Click the album that contains the photo you wish to share.

c. Click the photo you wish to share.

d. Click the **Share** button beneath the photo; this displays the *Post to Profile* window.

e. To share this photo publicly via a status update, type a message to accompany the photo into the main text box. Then click the **Share** button.

Figure 3.7 Hands-On Exercise 1, Step 5e.

f. To share this photo privately via Facebook email, click the **Send as a Message instead** link. When the *Send as a Message* window appears, enter the recipient's name into the *To* box, enter an accompanying message into the *Message* box, and click the **Send Message** button.

Enter recipient's name —

Enter accompanying message —

Click to send —

Figure 3.8 Hands-On Exercise 1, Step 5f.

Step 6 Display the Video Tab

Refer to Figure 3.9 as you complete Step 6.

Sharing videos is similar to sharing photos, but without requiring videos to be organized into albums. Videos are displayed as a group on the *Video* tab. Before you can upload videos to Facebook, you must display the *Video* tab on your Profile page. (This tab is not displayed by default.)

a. Navigate to your Profile page.

b. Click the **+** tab at the end of the row of tabs.

c. Select **Video** from the list of available tabs.

Click to add a new tab —

Click to display the Video tab —

Figure 3.9 .Hands-On Exercise 1, Step 6.

Step 7 Upload a Video

Refer to Figure 3.10 as you complete Step 7.

a. Navigate to your Profile page and select the **Video** tab.

b. Click the **Upload** button.

c. When the Create a New Video page appears, make sure the **File Upload** tab is selected; then click the **Choose File** or **Browse** button.

d. When the **Open** or **Choose File to Upload** dialog box appears, navigate to and select the file to upload; then click the **Open** button.

e. While the video is uploading, enter the title, description, and privacy level for this video; then click the **Save Info** button.

Click to upload video file

Videos in which you are tagged

Click to record webcam video

Videos you've uploaded

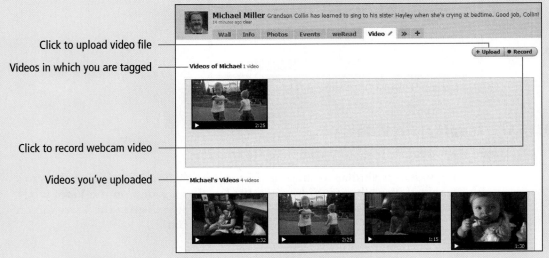

Figure 3.10 Hands-On Exercise 1, Step 7.

Step 8 Share a Video

Refer to Figure 3.11 as you complete Step 8.

Just as with photos, any video you've uploaded can be shared publicly or privately with your friends.

a. Navigate to your Profile page and select the **Video** tab.

b. Click the video you wish to share.

Click to share this video

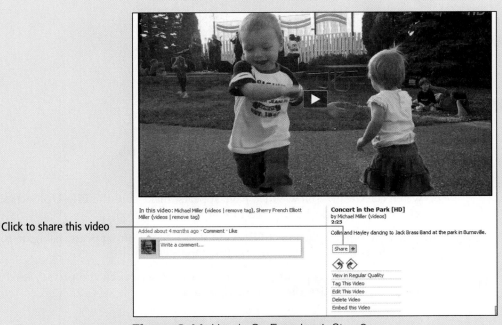

Figure 3.11 Hands-On Exercise 1, Step 8.

c. When the page for the selected video opens, click the **Share** button to display the *Post to Profile* page window.

d. To share this video publicly as a status update, enter an accompanying message in the large text box. Then click the **Share** button.

e. To share this video privately via Facebook email, click the **Send as a Message instead** link to switch to the *Send as a Message* window. Enter the recipient's name into the *To* box, enter an accompanying message into the *Message* box, and click the **Send Message** button.

Step 9 Post a Video from YouTube

Refer to Figures 3.12 and 3.13 as you complete Step 9.

You can embed any public YouTube video as a status update on Facebook.

a. Navigate to **www.youtube.com** and log into your YouTube account.

b. Navigate to the video you want to post to Facebook.

c. Underneath the video player, click the **Share** button to expand the *Share* panel.

d. Click the **Facebook** button.

Click to display Share panel ──

Click to post this video to Facebook ──

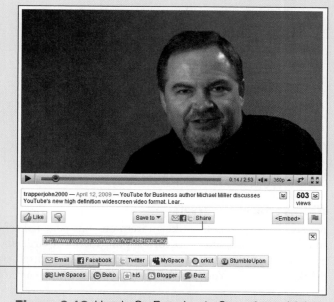

Figure 3.12 Hands-On Exercise 1, Steps 9c and 9d.

> **Note** **Facebook Login**
>
> The first time you share a YouTube video, you'll see the Facebook *Login* window. Enter your email address and Facebook password. Then click the **Login** button.

e. When the *Post to Profile* window appears, enter an accompanying message into the *What's on your mind?* text box.

f. Select a thumbnail to display (if more than one thumbnail image is available), or check the **No Thumbnail** option to post the video without a corresponding thumbnail image.

g. Click the **Share** button.

The video will now be posted as a status update to Facebook.

Enter accompanying message

Click to select a thumbnail

Click to post without a thumbnail

Click to post video to Facebook

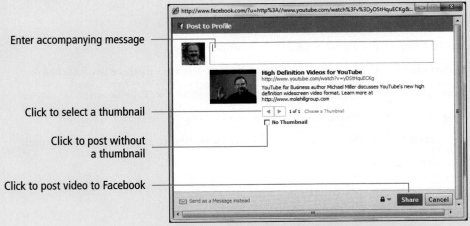

Figure 3.13 Hands-On Exercise 1, Steps 9d–9g.

Objective 2

Manage Events

What is a Facebook event?

Event On the Facebook site, a scheduled activity, much like an item on a personal schedule.

An *event* on Facebook is like an item on your personal schedule. An event can be small and private, like a doctor's appointment, or large and public, like a museum opening. You can use events to invite friends to cocktail parties, soccer games, or just drinks after class. You can also use Facebook events to remember friends' birthdays.

How do you find events on Facebook?

The best way to find new events is by using the search box in the Facebook toolbar. You can also browse events being attended by your Facebook friends.

Can you create your own Facebook events?

RSVP A response to an invitation to a Facebook event; an indication as to whether you are attending an event or not. (The acronym *RSVP* comes from the French phrase *répondez s'il vous plaît*, or "please reply.")

Facebook members can *RSVP* to scheduled events, or schedule events of their own. Creating a new event is as simple as filling in a few forms and inviting those friends you'd like to attend.

Hands-On Exercises

2 | Working with Events

Steps: 1. Display Events; **3.** Search for Events; **3.** RSVP to an Event; **4.** Create an Event.

Use Figures 3.14 through 3.17 as a guide in the exercise.

Step 1 Display Events

Refer to Figure 3.14 as you complete Step 1.

a. To display events to which you've been invited, begin by navigating to the Facebook Homepage.

b. Click the **Events** link in the sidebar.

This displays all events to which you've been invited. Your RSVP status, whether you've accepted or declined the invitation, is displayed beside each event listed.

> **Tip** **Friends' Events**
>
> Many users find that they're interested in events their friends are attending. To display your friends' events, go to the Events page and click the **Friends' Events** link in the sidebar.

c. To display the Facebook page for an event, click the event title in the list.

> **Note** **Birthdays**
>
> To display upcoming birthdays for people on your friends list, go to the Events page and click the **Birthdays** link in the sidebar.

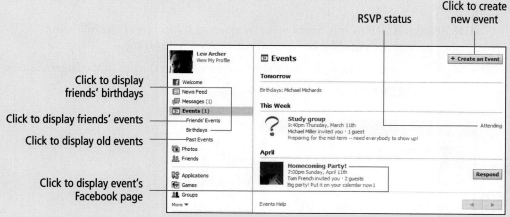

Figure 3.14 Hands-On Exercise 2, Step 1.

Step 2 Search for Events

Refer to Figure 3.15 as you complete Step 2.

a. To find new events to attend, type one or more keywords that describe the event into the search box in the Facebook toolbar. Then click the **Search** (magnifying glass) button or press the Enter key on your keyboard.

b. When the Search Results page appears, click **Events** in the sidebar.

c. To filter the resulting events by date or event type, use the lists at the top of the page.

d. Click an event title to view the Facebook page for that event, or click the **RSVP** link to RSVP to the event.

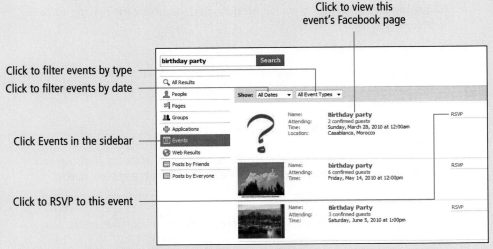

Figure 3.15 Hands-On Exercise 2, Step 2.

Step 3 RSVP to an Event

Refer to Figure 3.16 as you complete Step 3.

a. To RSVP to an event directly from the event listing page, click the **RSVP** link for that event.

b. When the RSVP to this Event window appears, select one of the following options: **Attending, Maybe Attending,** or **Not Attending**.

c. If you're attending the event and want to add a comment, write in the large text box.

d. Click the **RSVP** button to send your response.

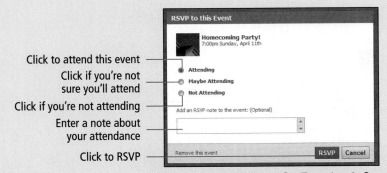

Figure 3.16 Hands-On Exercise 2, Step 3.

Tip ⭐ RSVP from the Event Page

You can also RSVP from an event's Facebook page. Go to the Your RSVP section and select **Attending**, **Maybe Attending**, or **Not Attending**.

Step 4 Create an Event

Refer to Figures 3.17 and 3.18 as you complete Step 4.

a. Go to the Facebook Homepage and select **Events** in the sidebar.

b. From the Events page, click the **Create an Event** button.

c. When the Create an Event page appears, click the controls in the When section to set the start date and time for the event.

d. To set the end time for the event, click the **Add end time** link to display the *End Time* section; then use the controls to set the end date and time.

e. Type the name of the event into the *What are you planning?* box.

f. Type the location of the event into the *Where?* box.

g. Add any additional information about the event into the *More info?* box.

Figure 3.17 Hands-On Exercise 2, Steps 4c–4g and 4i–4k.

h. To invite friends to your event, click the **Select Guests** button. When the Select Guests dialog box appears, click those Facebook friends you want to invite or enter the email addresses of non-Facebook invitees. Then click the **Save and Close** button.

You are now returned to the Create an Event page.

i. To make this a public event that all Facebook members can view, check the **Anyone can view and RSVP (public event)** option.

j. To not display the guest list on the event page, uncheck the **Show the guest list on the event page** option (checked by default).

k. Click the **Create Event** button.

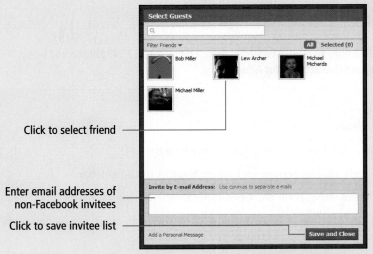

Click to select friend

Enter email addresses of non-Facebook invitees

Click to save invitee list

Figure 3.18 Hands-On Exercise 2, Step 4h.

Objective 3

Join Groups, Networks, and Fan Pages

What is a Facebook group?

Group On Facebook, a topic- or activity-oriented community page.

The Facebook site hosts numerous topic-oriented pages, called *groups*. A group is simply a place for people interested in a given topic to meet online to view information and photos, to exchange messages, and to engage in online discussions about that topic. Each group has its own Facebook page, with different tabs for different activities.

What is a Facebook network?

Network On Facebook, a group devoted to a particular school or company; only students and teachers of a school, and employees of a company, can join that school or company's network.

On the Facebook site, a *network* is a type of group devoted to a particular school or company. That is, you have to be a student, former student, or teacher at the school to join that school's network; likewise, you have to be an employee of the company to join that company's network. Registration to any network is limited to those who have a valid email address for that school or company.

What is a Facebook fan page?

Page Sometimes called a fan page, a group for fans of an entertainer, celebrity, company, or product.

A fan page, technically called a *Page* by Facebook, is a group for fans of a given musician, actor, entertainer, writer, celebrity, or company. Fan pages have similar sections, as do group and network pages, including a message Wall, photos, and discussions. You can join fan pages for your favorite entertainers, or for products or companies you like. For example, there are several fan pages devoted to the Beatles; in the business world, Starbucks has a very popular fan page for its customers.

What's the difference between a group, a network, and a fan page?

While groups, networks, and pages look similar, they serve different purposes. A group is meant to foster group discussion around a particular topic area. A network serves as an online community for a school's students and faculty or a company's employees. Fan pages are designed for public figures and organizations to broadcast information to their fans.

Objective 4

Create Groups and Fan Pages

Can anyone create a Facebook group?

Any Facebook member can create a group. Most groups are organized around a specific interest, activity, or topic. Groups are typically informal communities, as opposed to the official communities that revolve around Facebook fan pages.

> **Note** **200 Groups**
>
> A Facebook member can create up to 200 groups.

Who runs the group?

Admin Short for group administrator, the person responsible for managing and posting content to a group.

A Facebook group is run by the group administrator, called the *admin*. In most cases, the admin is the person who creates the group, although other users can also be granted admin status. The admin is responsible for posting new content to the group, monitoring the Wall and discussion tabs, inviting new members to the group, approving new member applications (if you use that option), and just generally making sure that things run smoothly.

How do admins differ from officers?

Officer An honorary title for a high-level member of a Facebook group. Officers have no privileges beyond that of normal members.

In addition to admins, a group can also have group *officers*. An officer is merely an honorary title; he or she has no privileges beyond that of normal members.

Who can join the group?

When you create a group, you can choose from three different access levels that determine who can join the group, and how. An open group has open membership; any Facebook member can see and join the group without prior approval. A closed group can be seen by all Facebook members, but the group administrator must approve all applications for membership. A secret group cannot be found in any Facebook searches; new members join by invitation (of the admin) only.

What features can a group offer?

Facebook groups can contain many of the same features found on a traditional Facebook Profile page, such as a Wall, photos, videos, events, and the like. In addition, groups can include a discussion tab, where members can engage in thread-oriented discussions, such as those found on web message forums.

How does creating and hosting a fan page differ from creating a group?

While the processes differ slightly, creating a fan page is very similar to creating a group. You have to enter similar information, configure similar settings, and invite other people to join. The day-to-day group/page management is also similar.

Who can create a fan page?

A fan page can be created only by an authorized representative of the entity being honored. That is, you can't create a fan page for an entertainer or product or company just because you like that person or thing; you have to be appointed to the task. If you're an independent fan who wishes to honor a person or organization, you should use Facebook's groups feature instead.

How can you use a fan page to promote your business?

A fan page is a great way to keep in touch with your most loyal customers or fans. You can use your fan page to announce new products and promotions, hold contests, and solicit customer opinions. Obviously, you can also link to your main website from your fan page, so customers can find out more information at the source.

Hands-On Exercises

3 | Working with Groups, Networks, and Fan Pages

Steps: 1. Join a Group; **3.** Join a School or Work Network; **3.** Become a Fan; **4.** Create a New Group; **5.** Create a Fan Page; **6.** Invite Others to Become Fans

Use Figures 3.19 through 3.26 as a guide in the exercise.

Step **Join a Group**

Refer to Figure 3.19 as you complete Step 1.

a. To search for a specific group, enter one or more keywords that describe that group into the search box in the Facebook toolbar. Then click the **Search** (magnifying glass) button or press Enter on your keyboard.

b. When the search results page appears, click the **Groups** link in the sidebar.

c. To view the Facebook page for that group, click the group's name.

d. To join a group, click **Join Group** or **Request to Join**.

> **Note**   **Request to Join**
>
> Most groups are open to all Facebook members to join. Some groups, however, require that the group administrator approve all requests for membership; these groups display a **Request to Join** link or button instead of the normal **Join Group** link. Facebook will notify you when your membership request is approved.

Click to view group page ⟶

Type of group ⟶

Number of current members ⟶

Click to join group ⟶

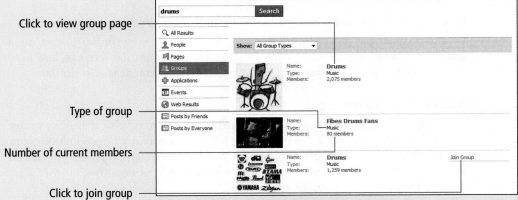

Figure 3.19 Hands-On Exercise 3, Step 1.

Step 2 Join a School or Work Network

Refer to Figure 3.20 as you complete Step 2.

a. Click the **Account** link in the Facebook toolbar and then click **Account Settings**.

b. From the My Account page, click the **Networks** tab.

c. Enter the name of your school or company into the *Network name* box.

   As you type, matching networks appear in a drop-down menu.

d. Select the school or company from the list.

e. If you selected a school, select your school status (*undergrad*, *grad student*, *alumnus/alumni*, *faculty*, or *staff*), the year you graduate(d), and your school email address.

f. If you selected a company, enter your work email address into the *Work Email* box.

g. Click the **Join Network** button.

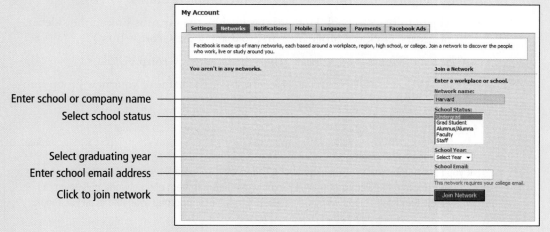

Figure 3.20 Hands-On Exercise 3, Step 2.

Step 3 Become a Fan

Refer to Figure 3.21 as you complete Step 3.

a. To search for a specific fan page, enter one or more keywords that describe the company or entertainer into the search box in the Facebook toolbar. Then click the **Search** (magnifying glass) button or press Enter on your keyboard.

b. When the search results page appears, click the **Pages** link in the sidebar.

c. To view a specific fan page, click the page's name.

d. To join a group, click the **Like** link.

Click to view fan page —

Click to "like" (become a fan) —

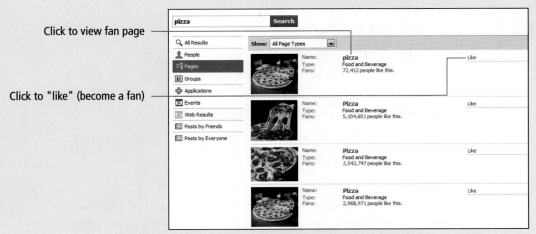

Figure 3.21 Hands-On Exercise 3, Step 3.

Step 4 Create a New Group

Refer to Figures 3.22 through 3.24 as you complete Step 4.

a. Navigate to the Facebook Homepage and click the **Groups** link in the sidebar. (If necessary, click the **More** link first to display the **Groups** link.)

b. When the Groups page appears, click the **Create a Group** button.

c. When the Create a Group page appears, enter the name of your new group into the *Group Name* box.

> **Note** **Networks**
>
> If you're a member of a Facebook network, Facebook displays a Network list on the Create a Group page. To make your group available only to other members of a network, pull down the Network list and select a network. Select **Global** to make your group available to all Facebook members.

d. Enter a short description of the group into the *Description* box.

e. To enter a Group Type, click the **Select Category** arrow, and select a category for your group: *Business, Common Interest, Entertainment & Arts, Geography, Internet & Technology, Just for Fun, Music, Organizations, Sports & Recreation, or Student Groups.*

f. Click the **Select Type** arrow and select the type of group you're creating.

The options here differ depending on the category you selected in the previous step.

g. Enter any important announcements about this group into the *Recent News* box.

h. If the group has an official office, enter the office's name into the *Office* box.

i. If you want to display your email address, enter it into the *Email* box.

j. If you have a website, enter the site's URL into the *Website* box.

k. If you want to display your street address, enter it into the *Street* box.

l. If you want to display your city, enter it into the *City/Town* box.

m. Click the **Create Group** button.

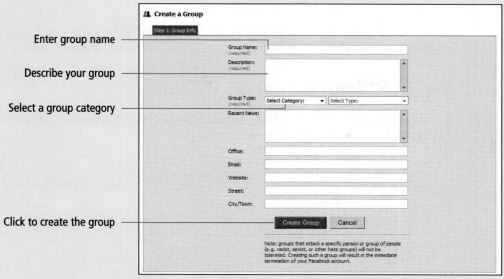

Enter group name

Describe your group

Select a group category

Click to create the group

Figure 3.22 Hands-On Exercise 3, Steps 4c through 4m.

Once you've created the new group, you will see the Customize page, which includes numerous settings you can configure. By default, all group members can write on the Wall; group events are displayed; discussion, photos, and videos tabs are displayed; and links are enabled.

n. To disable any of the features on the Customize page, uncheck their boxes.

o. Select the access level for your group: open, closed, or secret.

p. Click the **Save** button.

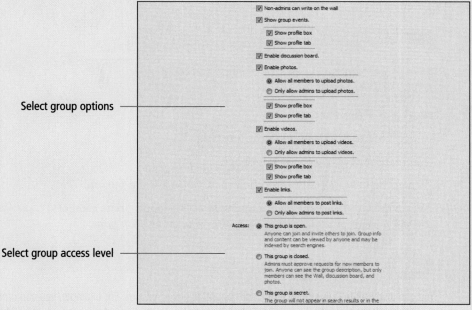

Select group options

Select group access level

Figure 3.23 Hands-On Exercise 3, Steps 4n through 4p.

Next you will be prompted to publish a status update about this group to your Profile page and to your friends' Homepages.

q. Click the **Publish** button to post this update, or click **Skip** to not do so.

Facebook will display the Invite People to Group page.

r. To invite non-Facebook members to join your group, enter their email addresses into the *Invite People via Email* box; use commas to separate multiple addresses.

> **Note** **Inviting New Members**
>
> You can also invite new members from the group's Facebook page. To invite friends to join this group, click each friend's name in the list.

s. Enter a message to accompany this invitation into the *Add a Personal Message* box.

t. Click the **Send Invitations** button.

Click friends to invite

Enter email addresses to invite non-Facebook members

Click to send invitations

Figure 3.24 Hands-On Exercise 3, Steps 4r through 4t.

Step 5 Create a Fan Page

Refer to Figure 3.25 as you complete Step 5.

a. Navigate to www.facebook.com/pages/.

b. When the next page appears, click the **Create a Page** button.

c. When the Create a Page page appears, select the appropriate category: *Local business*; *Brand, product, or organization*; or *Artist, band, or public figure*.

> **Note** **Community Pages**
>
> You can also create Community Pages for general topics or causes. For example, you can create a Community Page to support a candidate for elected office or to support a grassroots charitable movement. You don't have to be an official representative to create a Community Page.

d. After you select the category, click the associated arrow to select the type of page within that category.

For example, if you're creating a page for a local business, you'd select the Local category and make a further selection from the list: *Automotive, Banking and Financial Service, Bar, Café, Club,* and so on.

e. Enter the name of your page into the *Page name* box.

f. Check the box stating you are the official representative of this person, business, band, or product and have permission to create this Page.

g. Click the **Create Official Page** button.

Choose page category

Click arrow to select type of page

Enter page name

Click to create page

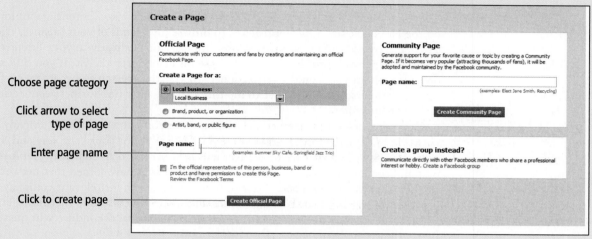

Figure 3.25 Hands-On Exercise 3, Step 5.

Step 6 Invite Others to Become Fans

Refer to **Figure 3.26** as you complete Step 6.

a. Navigate to your fan page and click the **Suggest to Friends** link in the sidebar.

b. When the *Suggest to Friends* window appears, click the names of friends you'd like to invite to be fans.

c. Click the **Send Invitations** button.

Click friends to invite

Click to send invitations

Figure 3.26 Hands-On Exercise 3, Step 6.

Objective 5

Network Professionally

How useful is Facebook for professional networking?

While Facebook has its roots in personal social networking, it has also become a useful site for establishing professional connections. Workers at all levels use Facebook to connect with other professionals in their industries and other business people in their cities, and to seek out new employment. In fact, Facebook is second only to LinkedIn for job hunters and for employers seeking to fill new positions.

How can you find other business professionals on Facebook?

There are many ways to find other business professionals (and potential employers) on the Facebook site. One approach is to browse for friends of your business friends.

Begin by identifying a business professional who is already in your Friends list. Go to that person's profile page and browse his or her Friends list. If you find someone with whom you would like to connect, invite that person to become your friend. Peruse that person's Friends list to identify further potential business connections and so on and so on.

If you're looking for connections within your company, join your company's network, as explained in Hands-On Exercise 3. Search for your company and, if a network exists, join that network. You will have access to all company employees, past and present, who are Facebook members and who have joined that network.

You can also use Facebook's search function to search for relevant company names, industry buzzwords, and the like. Filter the search results by people, and you'll see a list of people who work for the company or in the industry in question. Invite these people to be your Facebook friends.

How do I manage my professional contacts on Facebook?

Once you've added a number of professional contacts to your Facebook friends list, it's good practice to create a list of just these professional friends. Once you've created a separate list of professional contacts, you can send email messages to this entire list. Create a single message; then enter the list name into the message's *To* box. The message will be sent to all members of this list.

You can also filter the status updates and other information sent to the members of this professional contacts list. Doing so allows you to display personal information to your personal friends and hide that personal information from your professional friends.

How important are Facebook groups for professional networking?

Facebook hosts a large number of groups focused on professional topics. These are groups devoted to a particular company, industry, or profession, and tend to be where you'll find like-minded professionals on the Facebook site.

Use Facebook's search function to search for keywords related to your company, profession, or industry. When the search results page appears, filter the results by group. You can then join those groups that are most closely related to what you're looking for professionally.

Once you join a professional group, become an active participant. Participate in group discussions, respond to questions asked by other group members, and start your own conversations with others in the group. When you post, be sure to provide useful and relevant information and advice to the group. Over time you will become familiar with other group members, and you can invite them to join your Friends list.

You should also consider creating your own professional group, related to your profession or industry, and see which professionals it attracts. When you create such a group, make sure that it offers unique value not found in other similar groups. Invite your professional Facebook friends to this group; you should also invite non-Facebook members to join, via the email join feature. Encourage all group members to invite their professional friends to join the group, as well. The more successful your group, the more professional connections you will make.

Can you mix your personal and professional lives on Facebook?

When you're using Facebook for professional purposes, you have to be careful about mixing your personal and professional lives. For example, you probably don't want to broadcast gossip (or even photos!) about your drunken behavior at a weekend party to your boss, or to potential employers. It makes sense to practice discretion about what you post in your status updates, and to utilize Facebook's numerous privacy settings to limit what you display to whom online.

Objective 6

Manage Your Privacy Settings

How private is your information on Facebook?

Facebook is a social network. Being social means sharing information about yourself—who you are and what you're doing. As such, much of the personal information you provide to Facebook is available for anyone to see, as are the photos you post and the status updates you make. When you participate in the Facebook community, your private life becomes public.

Is there a way to hide some information and posts from some people?

While most of what you provide to Facebook is public by default, there are several mechanisms available to hide that information from some or all Facebook members. Facebook provides a full page of privacy settings you can configure; you can also select, on a post-by-post basis, who can see your status updates. If you properly manage your privacy settings, you can forge a balance between private information and public participation in the Facebook social network.

What is the harm in making all your information public?

We might like to think that people other than our friends aren't that interested in our private lives, but that isn't true. Online stalkers do exist, tracking every online move of their potential victims; sometimes this stalking moves to the physical world, with real physical danger. In addition, criminals can peruse your Profile page to find out when you're away from home, thus targeting your empty house or apartment for burglary.

Less spectacular but equally devastating is what happens when people you don't want observing your private activities find out just a little bit too much about what you're doing, via your Facebook posts. Do you really want your parents or teachers to know what you did at that wild party last weekend? Does a future boyfriend or girlfriend need to know all about your past liaisons? What might a potential employer think about your private musings on your Profile page, including those bad things you have to say about your current boss? It's simple common sense; you don't want to make your private life totally public.

In addition, making all your information public makes it easier for advertisers, spammers, and scammers to target you with all manner of unwanted solicitations. There is value in not sharing all your personal information with everyone.

How do Facebook applications treat your private information?

When it comes to sharing your personal information, it's not just your Profile page and status updates you have to worry about. Many Facebook applications work by accessing your private information and the private information of your friends. Playing a Facebook quiz might seem like innocent fun, but you've just provided that application, and the application's developers, private information about you and possibly your friends. That information can be used to send more unsolicited advertising and spam your way, or just to annoy you while you're using Facebook.

What information you should you keep private?

What information you do or don't share depends on how private you want to be. Some users are comfortable sharing all their information, including phone number and street address with the entire Facebook population. Others carefully guard all their personal info, including real name and facial photo. At the very least, you probably want to keep your contact information private; you may also want to filter specific information or status updates to particular people or groups of people. That might mean sharing your most personal posts only with a select few friends, or keeping strangers from viewing personal photos.

Can you rely on Facebook's privacy settings?

Facebook's privacy settings work well, when you use them. For most people, however, these settings should be supplemented with a combination of good sense and discretion. While it might seem fun at the time to brag about your recent off-hours exploits, know that anything you post publicly, on Facebook or another site, can and will come back to haunt you. Even a seemingly innocuous remark, such as wanting to "kill" someone who annoys you, can be taken out of context and made to seem more serious than you intended.

You have to remember that Facebook is a very public site; just how public do you really want your private life to be? It's often better to be discreet and leave some things unsaid.

Hands-On Exercises

4 | Managing Privacy Settings

Steps: 1. Configure Universal Privacy Settings; **2.** Customize Individual Privacy Settings; **3.** Limit What Information Applications and Websites Can Access; **4.** Block People from Interacting with You on Facebook.

Use Figures 3.27 through 3.35 as a guide in the exercise.

Step Configure Universal Privacy Settings

Refer to Figures 3.27 and 3.28 as you complete Step 1.

Facebook displays most of its privacy options on the Choose Your Privacy Settings page. You can choose from Facebook's recommended settings or opt to display items to Everyone (all Facebook members), Friends Only, or Friends of Friends (your friends and their friends).

a. From the Facebook toolbar, click **Account**; then click **Privacy Settings**.

b. When the Privacy Settings page appears, go to the *Sharing on Facebook* section.

All the individual privacy options are displayed in a table on the right side of this section. For each option, a bullet indicates whether that item can be viewed by Everyone, Friends of Friends, or Friends Only. These selections change based on the universal setting you select from the left side of this section.

c. To accept Facebook's recommended settings, make sure that **Recommended** is selected.

 Friends of Friends and Networks

If you're a member of a Facebook network, you also see an option for Friends and Friends and Networks. This option includes people on your Friends list, people on *their* Friends lists, and people in your network(s).

d. To make most items visible to all Facebook members, select **Friends of Friends.**

e. To make most items visible to only those on your friends list, select **Friends Only.**

f. To make most items visible to your friends and their friends, select **Friends of Friends.**

g. Click **Apply These Settings** when done.

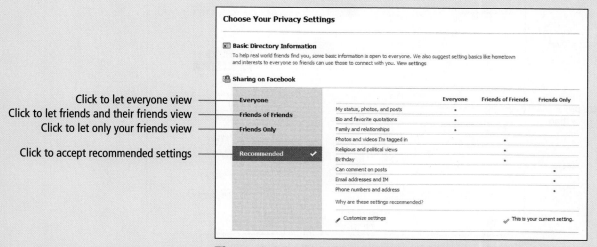

Figure 3.27 Hands-On Exercise 4, Step 1.

Step 2 Customize Individual Privacy Settings

Refer to Figures 3.28 through 3.30 as you complete Step 2.

The universal settings on the Choose Your Privacy Settings page work well for many users. You can also, however, configure dozens of individual privacy settings on the Facebook site.

a. From the Facebook toolbar, click **Account**; then click **Privacy Settings**.

b. When the Privacy Settings page appears, click **Customize settings** in the *Sharing on Facebook* section.

Click to customize individual settings

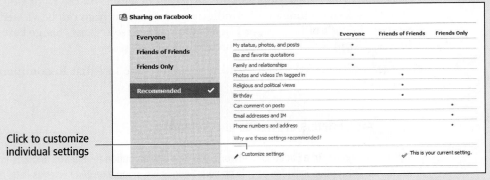

Figure 3.28 Hands-On Exercise 4, Step 2b.

c. When the Customize settings page appears, scroll to the item you want to configure.

d. Click the Privacy Setting button to the right of that item and select **Everyone, Friends of Friends,** or **Friends Only**.

e. To further customize who can view a specific item, click that item's Privacy Setting button and select **Customize**.

Click to select privacy level

Click to customize privacy setting

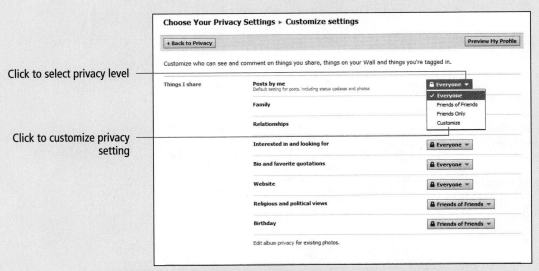

Figure 3.29 Hands-On Exercise 4, Steps 2c through 2e.

Facebook displays the *Custom Privacy* window.

f. To make your posts visible only to selected people, click the **Make this visible to These people** arrow and select **Specific People**. Then enter the names of those friends you want to see your posts.

g. To hide your posts from selected friends, enter their names into the *Hide this from These People* box.

h. Click the **Save Setting** button when done.

Click to make visible to
specific people

Enter names of people you
want to see this item

Enter names of people you
don't want to see this item

Click to save settings

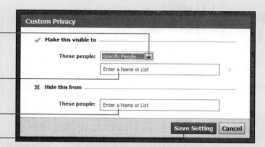

Figure 3.30 Hands-On Exercise 4, Steps 2f through 2h.

 Privacy Lists

It may be easier to create a list of friends you want to see your posts, or whom you wish not to see your posts. You can then enter this list name into the *Custom Privacy* window, rather than entering each friend's name individually.

 Avoid Being Tagged

To keep from being tagged in embarrassing photos posted by your friends, navigate to the Customize Settings page, go to the *Photos and videos I'm tagged in* item, click the **Privacy Settings** button, and select **Customize**. When the *Custom Privacy* window appears, click the **Make this visible to These people** arrow and select **Only Me**.

Step ❸ Limit What Information Applications and Websites Can Access

Refer to Figures 3.31 through 3.33 as you complete Step 3.

You not only have to worry about people viewing things you don't want them to view; you also have to be concerned about Facebook applications and third-party websites accessing your personal information. Fortunately, you can control what information these applications and sites can share.

a. From the Facebook toolbar, click **Account**, and then click **Privacy Settings**.

b. When the Privacy Settings page appears, go to the *Applications and Websites* section and click **Edit your settings**.

Click to edit application
settings

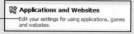

Figure 3.31 Hands-On Exercise 4, Step 3b

You now see the Applications, Games and Websites page.

c. Click the **Edit Settings** button in the *Info accessible through your friends* section.

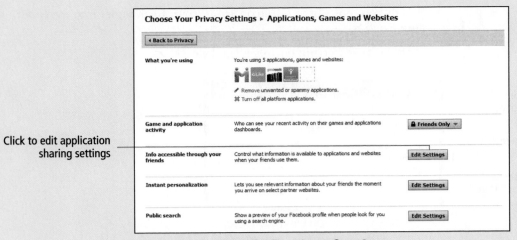

Click to edit application
sharing settings

Figure 3.32 Hands-On Exercise 4, Step 3c.

d. When the next page appears, check those items you're okay to share, and uncheck those items you don't want shared.

e. Click the **Save Changes** button when done.

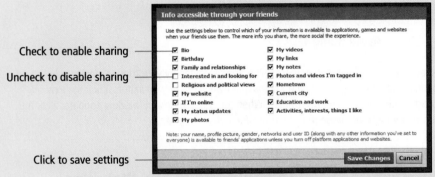

Check to enable sharing

Uncheck to disable sharing

Click to save settings

Figure 3.33 Hands-On Exercise 4, Steps 3d and 3e.

Step 4 Block People from Interacting with You on Facebook

Refer to Figures 3.34 and 3.35 as you complete Step 4.

If you think someone may be stalking you via Facebook, or you just want to avoid dealing with a specific individual, you can block all Facebook interactions with that person, including ending your friend relationship by "defriending" that person.

a. From the Facebook toolbar, click **Account**, and click **Privacy Settings**.

b. When the Choose Your Privacy Settings page appears, go to the Block Lists section and click **Edit your lists**.

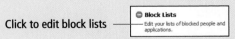

Click to edit block lists

Figure 3.34 Hands-On Exercise 4, Step 4b.

c. When the Block List page appears, enter the Facebook name of that person into the *Name* box, or enter his or her email address into the *Email* box.

d. Click the **Block This User** button.

Enter name of user to block —

Enter email address of user to block —

Click to block user —

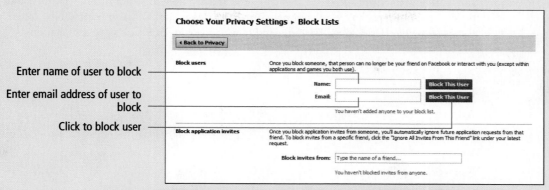

Figure 3.35 Hands-On Exercise 4, Steps 4c and 4d.

Summary

In this chapter you learned how to upload and share photos and videos on the Facebook site, and how to create and manage events. You learned how to join groups, networks, and pages, as well as how to create your own group and fan pages. You also learned how to use Facebook for professional networking, and how to manage Facebook's privacy settings.

Key Terms

Multiple Choice Questions

1. Which of the following can be a Facebook event?

    (a) Your birthday

    (b) A class reunion

    (c) A public concert

    (d) All of the above

2. A Facebook community dedicated to a particular school or company is called a:

    (a) group.

    (b) network.

    (c) forum.

    (d) fan page.

3. You can share photos and videos in the following way(s):

    (a) As an attachment to a Facebook email message

    (b) As an attachment to a status update

    (c) As an attachment to a chat (instant message)

    (d) Both (a) and (b)

    (e) Both (a) and (c)

4. Facebook's privacy settings let you control the following:

    (a) Who can see your status updates

    (b) Who can see your tags in friends' photos

    (c) Who can see your personal contact information

    (d) All of the above

5. When using Facebook for professional networking, you should do the following:

    (a) Create a separate Facebook membership for your professional activities.

    (b) Delete all your private posts.

    (c) Search for and join relevant professional groups.

    (d) Remove all your real-world friends and family from your friends list.

6. Which of the following is *not* a proper response to an invitation to a Facebook event?

    (a) Attending

    (b) Attending, with reservations

    (c) Maybe attending

    (d) Not attending

7. You can post videos to Facebook in the following ways:

    (a) Upload a digital video file from your hard drive.

    (b) Record a video in real time from your computer's webcam.

    (c) Share a video from the YouTube site.

    (d) All of the above

8. An open event is one that:

    (a) is visible to all Facebook users.

    (b) is free of charge to all attendees.

    (c) is a public event.

    (d) can be attended by people of all ages.

9. Facebook places the following limit(s) on the videos you upload:

    (a) No more than 30 minutes long

    (b) No more than 1024 MB in size

    (c) Must be in the *.avi* format

    (d) Cannot include blatant advertisements

10. A fan page (Page) can be created by:

    (a) any Facebook member.

    (b) a Facebook member in good standing.

    (c) an official representative of a person, group, or organization.

    (d) members of an entertainer's fan club.

Fill in the Blank

Write the correct word in the space provided.

1. On the Facebook site, digital photos are stored in _____.

2. A(n) _____ is a Facebook community page devoted to a particular activity or topic.

3. A(n) _____ event is one that can be seen by any Facebook member.

4. When you identify a Facebook member in a photo you upload, you _____ that person.

5. The _____ is responsible for managing and posting content to a group.

Practice Exercises

1. **Managing Photos**

    One of the most popular activities among Facebook users is uploading and sharing photos. You upload new photos into photo albums, and can make any photo you upload your Facebook Profile picture.

    (a) Create a new photo album labeled "Personal Photos."

    (b) Upload at least three photos to this album. One of these photos should be of yourself.

    (c) Make one of the photos you just uploaded your Profile picture.

2. **Managing Events**

Events are activities to which you can invite other Facebook users—or to which you can be invited.

(a) Create a new event named "Completing Chapter 3."
(b) Make this an Open event taking place a week from today.
(c) Add a personal picture of yourself to the event page.
(d) Invite your instructor to attend your event.

3. **Joining a Network**

A Facebook network is a group for members of a particular school or business. Your school should have its own network, open to all current and former students and faculty.

(a) If your school has a network on Facebook, join that network.
(b) Go to the network's Discussion tab, if one exists, and post to the topic that discusses this class. (If you are the first person to post—that is, if the topic doesn't yet exist—you'll need to create the topic, as well.)

4. **Managing Privacy Settings**

(a) Configure your Facebook Profile so that only friends can view your status updates.
(b) Configure your Profile to exclude your instructor from viewing your phone number, email address, and other information.

Critical Thinking

1. As noted in this chapter, there are several ways to share videos on the Facebook site. Write a short paper discussing the different video sharing methods and the pros and cons of each. Make a recommendation as to which method your classmates should use to share their personal videos.
2. Facebook can be an incredibly public site, even though some parts of our lives are best kept private. Write a short paper discussing the pros and cons of posting personal information on the Facebook site; include recommendations as to what information should be kept private and how that should be accomplished.

Team Projects

1. Facebook groups often grow out of real-world groups. Appoint one member of your team the official group administrator and have him or her create a new Facebook group named after your team. Make sure the group page includes photos and discussions. Invite all team members to your group and assign them all admin privileges. Upload a photo of your team to the group page, and start a discussion thread about your favorite after-school hangouts. Invite at least three other members of your class, as well as your instructor, to join your group.

2. Your team "likes" your class. Create a fan page for your class, complete with photos of your classmates. Set up half of your team members as admins and the other half as officers. Invite at least three members of your class, as well as your instructor, to join your page.

Credits

Facebook screenshots. Reprinted by permission of Facebook Inc.

CHAPTER 4

Using MySpace

Objectives

After you read this chapter, you will be able to:

1. Sign Up for and Navigate MySpace

2. Update Your Status

3. Personalize Your Profile Page

4. Find and Communicate with Friends

5. Manage Your Blog

6. Share Photos and Videos

7. Join and Create Groups

8. Promote Yourself or Your Band

The following Hands-On Exercises will help you accomplish the chapter objectives:

Hands-On Exercises

EXERCISES	SKILLS COVERED
1. Set Up a MySpace Account and Update Your Status	**Step 1:** Start Your Browser and Navigate to MySpace.com **Step 2:** Create a MySpace Account **Step 3:** Enter a Status Update
2. Personalize Your Profile Page	**Step 1:** Change Themes **Step 2:** Change Page Layout **Step 3:** Select Content to Display **Step 4:** Edit Advanced Options **Step 5:** Add a Music Player and Playlists
3. Find and Communicate with Friends	**Step 1:** Search for New Friends **Step 2:** Browse for New Friends **Step 3:** Leave a Comment on a Profile Page **Step 4:** Send a Private Message
4. Share Photos and Videos	**Step 1:** Upload a Photo **Step 2:** Upload a Video
5. Join and Create Groups	**Step 1:** Search for and Join a Group **Step 2:** Browse for and Join a Group **Step 3:** Create a New Group

Objective 1

Sign Up for and Navigate MySpace

What is MySpace?

MySpace is one of the original social networking sites on the web. Although MySpace is still popular, its user growth has stagnated in recent years, with many users moving to the competing Facebook site. MySpace remains the number two full-service social networking site, however, with more than 125 million users, and is still one of the top 20 sites on the web in terms of its usage.

 Note   MySpace History

MySpace was founded in 2003 by Tom Anderson and a team of programmers from eUniverse, an Internet marketing company. eUniverse sold MySpace to Rupert Murdoch's News Corporation in 2005.

Who uses MySpace—and why?

Originally, MySpace had a similar user base as Facebook, focusing primarily on college students. Over the years, older users gravitated away from MySpace to Facebook, leaving MySpace with a slightly younger demographic—junior high and high school students, primarily. In recent years, however, MySpace has become known as a site for musicians, actors, comedians, and other entertainers, as well as their fans. It also remains popular in many circles for traditional social networking activities, such as communicating with friends and family, and sharing digital photos, videos, and music.

How is the MySpace site organized?

Stream On MySpace, a constantly updated feed of status updates and other posts from friends.

The MySpace site consists of several essential sections. Once you're logged into your MySpace account, the site's Homepage is where you keep track of what your friends are doing, via a **Stream** of status updates, photos, music, and the like. Beyond the Homepage, your Profile page is your personal page on the MySpace site, where you display information about yourself and post your own status updates, blog entries, photos, music, and such. Other parts of the site let you find new friends, send and receive email messages, find and download digital music, watch videos, play games, and more.

How do I navigate the MySpace site?

Menu bar A horizontal strip that contains clickable or pull-down menus to access specific items or actions.

You can access various parts of the MySpace site using the **menu bar** that appears at the top of every MySpace page (Figure 4.1). You can access some parts of the site (Home, Music, Video, Games, and Events) by clicking that item on the menu bar. You can access other parts of the site via pull-down menus. For example, to access your personal blog, click the Profile menu item and select My Blog from the pull-down menu.

Figure 4.1 The MySpace menu bar, displayed at the top of all MySpace pages.

What is on the MySpace Homepage?

Once you've created a MySpace account and signed onto the site, you access the Homepage by clicking Home on the MySpace menu bar (Figures 4.2 and 4.3). This page contains much useful information, organized into individual content modules. At the top of the Homepage is a box where you enter your status updates for others on the site to read. Beneath that is the Stream module, which displays various pieces of information from people you've added to your Friends list. You can filter the information displayed by clicking the links at the top of this module: All, Status (status updates only), Photos, Music, Videos, Bulletins (official notices from the MySpace site), and More (Links, Apps, Blogs, and Events).

Figure 4.2 The MySpace Homepage (top).

Other content modules on the Homepage include your photo and profile information, Alerts, My Apps, Virtual Gifts, Recommended Events, People You May Know, Games You Should Play, and MySpace Music. At the very bottom of the Homepage is the Friend Space module, where all your MySpace Friends are listed.

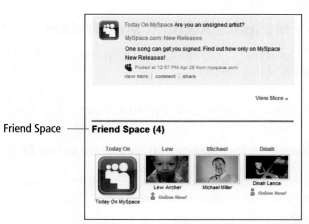

Figure 4.3 The MySpace Homepage (bottom).

How do I manage my account settings?

You can change your MySpace account information at any time. Click My Account in the MySpace menu bar to display the Account Settings page. From here you can select the settings you'd like to change by clicking the appropriate link along the top of the page: Contact Info, Account, Password, Privacy, Spam, Notifications, Applications,

IM, Mobile, Calendar, Miscellaneous, Ad Categories, No More CAPTCHAs, and Sync. Make the appropriate changes on the resulting page; then click the Save Changes button.

Objective 2

Update Your Status

What is your MySpace status?

Your MySpace status is a short text message about what you're doing or thinking about at the moment. It's a snapshot into your life, posted as a short text message on the MySpace site.

You update your status from the top of your Homepage, in the box that asks you "What do you want to share?" When you type something into this box and then press the Share button, your status is automatically updated.

Who sees your status updates?

Mood On the MySpace site, a graphic indication of the user's emotional condition, as represented by the appropriate emoticon.

Your status updates appear in multiple places on the MySpace site. Your most recent status updates appear near the top of both your Profile and Homepages. Your status updates also appear on your friends' Homepages, in their Stream module. This way your friends are kept updated as to what you're doing and thinking.

What can you include in your status updates?

Emoticon Also known as a *smiley*, a graphic representation of the user's mood. For example, a happy mood might be indicated by an emoticon of a smiling face.

A MySpace status update starts as a text message. It can be as short as a word or two or several paragraphs long. You can also attach photos, videos, and links to other web pages to your status updates. In addition, you can indicate a *mood* for your update, in the form of an *emoticon* that appears alongside your update.

Hands-On Exercises

1 | Set Up a MySpace Account and Update Your Status

Steps: 1. Start Your Browser and Navigate to myspace.com; **2.** Create a MySpace Account; **3.** Enter a Status Update

Use Figures 4.4 through 4.6 as a guide in the exercise.

 Comparing Your Screen with the Figures in This Book

Since MySpace is constantly updating its feature set, the pages you see on your own computer might not always match those displayed in this book.

Step 1 Start Your Browser and Navigate to myspace.com

Refer to Figure 4.4 as you complete Step 1.

a. Turn on your computer.

b. Launch your preferred web browser, such as Internet Explorer, Firefox, or Safari.

c. Enter **www.myspace.com** into your browser's address box and press Enter.

d. If you already have a MySpace account, sign in with your email address and password; then click the **Log In** button to enter the MySpace website. If you have never used MySpace before, you will need to create a MySpace account. Proceed to step 2.

Click to create a new account

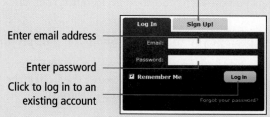

Enter email address

Enter password

Click to log in to an existing account

Figure 4.4 Hands-On Exercise 1, Step 1.

Step ② Create a MySpace Account

Refer to Figure 4.5 as you complete Step 2.

a. From the www.myspace.com page, click the *Sign Up!* tab.

b. When the Sign Up for MySpace page appears, enter your email address into the *Email Address* box.

c. Enter your desired password into the *Password* box.

Your password should be at least six characters long.

 More-Secure Passwords

To make your password more secure (harder to guess or hack), include a mix of alphabetic, numeric, and special characters (punctuation marks). Also, longer passwords are more secure.

d. Enter your first and last name into the *Full Name* box.

e. Use the *Date Of Birth* controls to select the month, day, and year you were born.

f. In the *Gender* section, check either *Male* or *Female*.

g. Click the **Signup Free** button.

Enter email address   Select your gender

Enter desired password

Enter your name

Select the month, day, and year you were born

Click to create your account

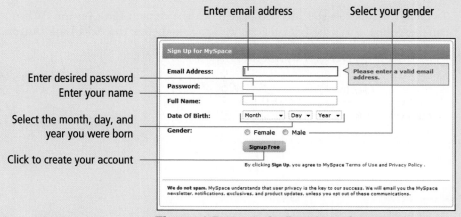

Figure 4.5 Hands-On Exercise 1, Steps 2b–2g.

h. When the next page appears, enter the captcha text into the *Verification* box and click the **Continue** button.

You will receive an email from MySpace; click the link in the email to confirm your registration. MySpace will now suggest people, bands, applications, and video channels you may like.

i. Select those people or things you'd like to add to your account; then click the **Continue** button.

At this point, MySpace will prompt you to upload a photo for your profile.

j. Click the **Browse** or **Choose File** button to display the **Open** or Choose File to Upload dialog box. Browse to and select the file you want; then click the **Open** button. When you return to the previous page, click the **Upload** button.

k. When the next page appears, enter the requested information to connect with classmates of a particular school, for example; then click the **Save** button.

l. When the final page appears, select your country and state, enter your city and postal code, and click the **Save** button.

Step 3   Enter a Status Update

Refer to Figure 4.6 as you complete Step 3.

Once you've created your MySpace account, you can begin entering status updates. Most users change their status on a regular basis, to let their friends know what they're currently doing or thinking.

a. Click the **Home** icon in the MySpace menu bar to go to the MySpace Homepage.

b. Type your message into the *What do you want to share?* box.

c. To indicate your mood, click the **Attach Mood** button. When the panel expands, either click the left down arrow and select a mood from the list or click the right down arrow and select the desired emoticon.

d. To attach a photo to your status, click the **Attach Photo** button. When the panel expands, click **Upload a Photo**. When the *Open* or *Choose File to Upload* dialog box appears, navigate to and select the file you want to attach; then click the **Open** button.

e. To attach a video to your status, click the **Attach Video** button. When the panel expands, click **Upload a Video**. When the *Open* or *Choose File to Upload* dialog box appears, navigate to and select the file you want to attach; then click the **Open** button.

f. To include a link to a specific web page, click the **Attach Link** button. When the panel expands, enter the URL for the web page and click the **Add Link** button.

g. Click the **Share** button to post your status update.

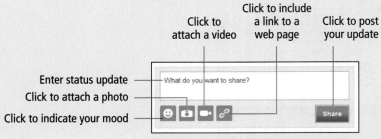

Figure 4.6 Hands-On Exercise 1, Step 3.

Objective 3

Personalize Your Profile Page

What is on your MySpace Profile page?

Your MySpace Profile page is the page all your friends see when they click your name anywhere on the MySpace site (Figure 4.7). Your Profile page contains different types of personal information, including your name, age, location, status updates, list of MySpace friends, and a Stream of your friends' updates.

How can you personalize your Profile page?

Theme On the MySpace site, a preset combination of layout, colors, and graphical elements applied to a Profile page.

You can customize both the content and the look and feel of your Profile page (Figure 4.8). You can add and delete a variety of content modules, so that your Profile page contains precisely the information you want to display. You can also change the page's overall *theme*, column and width layout, and background color or image.

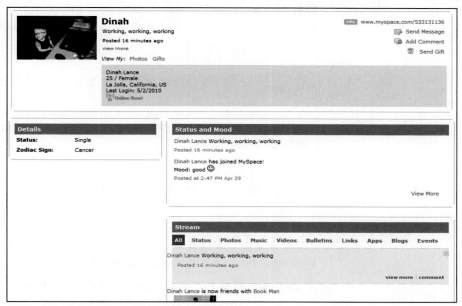

Figure 4.7 The default Profile page layout.

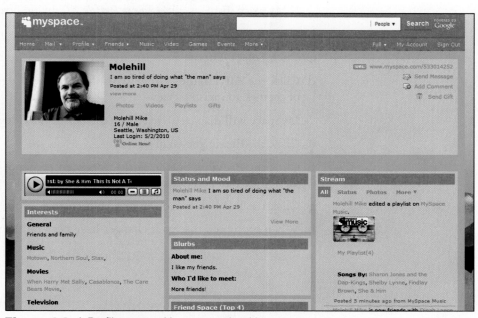

Figure 4.8 A Profile page with a customized layout.

HTML Short for hypertext markup language; the markup language used to create web pages.

CSS Short for cascading style sheets; a technology used within HTML to define and format specific elements on a web page.

Are there any other themes available?
MySpace offers more than 100 built-in themes for your Profile page. In addition, many other websites offer their own MySpace themes that you can apply to your Profile. You can also edit the page's underlying *HTML* and *CSS* codes for further customization.

Hands-On Exercises

2 | Personalize Your Profile Page

Steps: 1. Change Themes; **2.** Change Page Layout; **3.** Select Content to Display; **4.** Edit Advanced Options; **5.** Add a Music Player and Playlists

 Hands-On Exercise 2 covers version 2.0 of MySpace's Profile pages

As this book is being written, MySpace is testing a new version of its Profile pages that changes the customization process somewhat. Use the customization features available to you when you complete this exercise.

Use Figures 4.9 through 4.17 as a guide in the exercise.

 Step 1 **Change Themes**

Refer to Figure 4.9 as you complete Step 1.

a. From any MySpace page, select **Profile > Customize Profile** from the menu bar.

MySpace will then display the *Customize Profile* pane.

If MySpace displays a *Welcome to Profile 2.0* dialog box, click the **Continue** button.

b. Click **Appearance** on the left side of the *Customize Profile* pane.

c. Click **Select Theme** from the middle list of the *Customize Profile* pane.

d. Click the **All Themes** arrow to display a list of categories; then click the category of themes you wish to view.

MySpace will display all available themes in the category you selected.

e. Click the theme you want to use.

f. Click the **Preview** button in the upper left corner of the *Customize Profile* pane to view your changes; click the **Customize** button to return to the editing screen.

g. Click the **Publish** button to save your changes.

h. When prompted that your changes have been published, click **OK**.

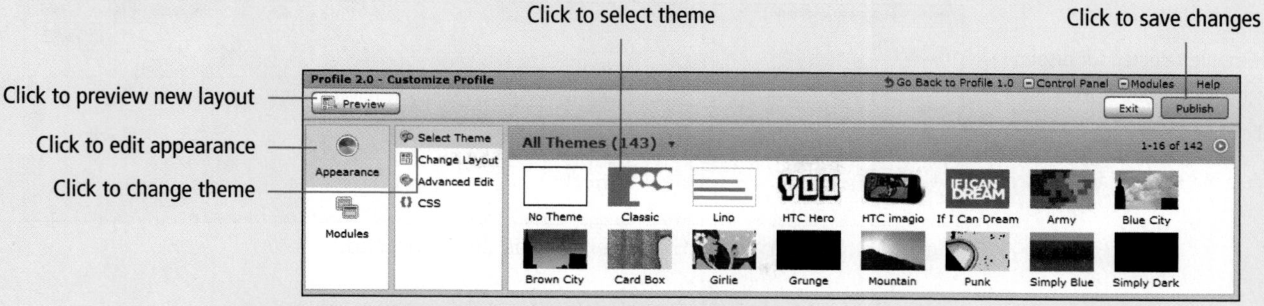

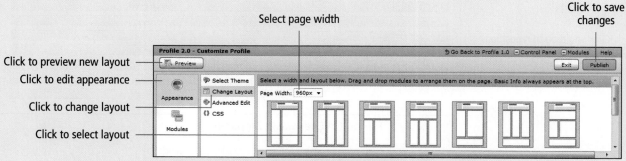

Click to select theme

Click to save changes

Click to preview new layout

Click to edit appearance

Click to change theme

Figure 4.9 Hands-On Exercise 2, Step 1.

Step 2 Change Page Layout

Refer to Figure 4.10 as you complete Step 2.

a. From any MySpace page, select **Profile > Customize Profile** from the menu bar.

b. Click **Appearance** on the left side of the *Customize Profile* pane.

c. Click **Change Layout** from the middle list of the *Customize Profile* pane.

d. Click the **Page Width** arrow to select a page width.

The following page widths are available: 750 pixels, 960 pixels, or 100%. Choose a page width that can best hold the content you select.

e. Click the column layout you want to use.

MySpace offers several different column layouts, including one-, two-, and three-column layouts. Some layouts have areas that span multiple columns.

f. Click the **Preview** button to view your changes; click the **Customize** button to return to the editing screen.

g. Click the **Publish** button to save your changes.

h. When prompted that your changes have been published, click **OK**.

Select page width

Click to save changes

Click to preview new layout

Click to edit appearance

Click to change layout

Click to select layout

Figure 4.10 Hands-On Exercise 2, Step 2.

Step 3 Select Content to Display

Refer to Figures 4.11 and 4.12 as you complete Step 3.

a. From any MySpace page, select **Profile > Customize Profile** from the menu bar.

b. Click **Modules** on the left side of the *Customize Profile* pane.

c. Click each content module you want to display on your page.

When selected, a content module displays a "happy face" above its graphic.

d. To remove a content module from your page, click it again to display the plus sign (+) above the graphic.

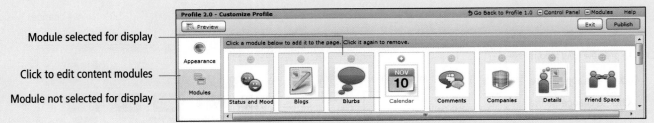

Module selected for display

Click to edit content modules

Module not selected for display

Figure 4.11 Hands-On Exercise 2, Steps 3a through 3d.

e. Click the **Modules** button at the top right corner of the *Customize Profile* pane.

This enables you to reposition the content modules on your page. Each content module appears as its own small box.

f. To reposition a module, use your mouse to click and drag it into a new position.

g. Click the **Preview** button to view your changes; click the **Customize** button to return to the editing screen.

h. Click the **Publish** button to save your changes.

i. When prompted that your changes have been published, click **OK.**

Click to save changes

Click to preview new layout

Click to display available content modules

Click to reposition content modules

Click and drag to reposition module

Figure 4.12 Hands-On Exercise 2, Steps 3e through 3i.

Step Edit Advanced Options

Refer to Figure 4.13 as you complete Step 4.

MySpace lets you configure the following page elements separately: background, content, modules, module headers, and module bodies.

 Third-Party Themes via CSS

Many third-party sites offer MySpace Profile themes. You install these third-party themes by cutting and pasting the CSS code into the CSS section of the Customize Profile pane.

a. From any MySpace page, select **Profile > Customize Profile** from the menu bar.

b. Select **Appearance** on the left side of the *Customize Profile* pane.

c. Click **Advanced Edit** from the middle list of the *Customize Profile* pane.

d. Select the element you wish to edit from the list in the third column.

Each element has its own unique configuration options. For example, you can edit the page background to display a particular color or to display a background image you upload. If you choose to display a background image, you can have the image scroll (or not) when the page scrolls, select a position for the image, or repeat the image on the page.

e. Configure the selected element as desired.

f. Click the **Preview** button to view your changes.

g. Click the **Publish** button to save your changes.

h. When prompted that your changes have been published, click **OK**.

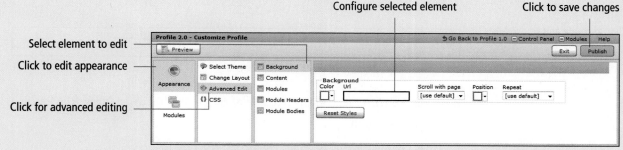

Figure 4.13 Hands-On Exercise 2, Step 4.

Step 5 Add a Music Player and Playlists

Refer to Figures 4.14 through 4.17 as you complete Step 5.

One of the most popular custom elements is the MySpace Music Player. When the Music Player is added to a Profile page, visitors to that page can listen to music selected by the page's owner. The owner creates one or more *playlists* to be played on his or her Profile page, selecting commercial music available to MySpace users.

Playlist A collection of songs.

Figure 4.14 The MySpace Music Player.

a. From any MySpace page, select **Profile > Customize Profile** from the menu bar.

b. Click **Modules** on the left side of the **Customize Profile** pane.

c. Click the Music Player content module.

d. Click the **Publish** button to save your changes.

Click to save changes

Figure 4.15 Hands-On Exercise 2, Steps 5a through 5d.

Click to select Music Player

Click to edit content modules

e. When prompted that your changes have been published, click **OK**.

You then have to create one or more playlists to play back in your Music Player.

f. Click **Music** on the MySpace menu bar.

g. When the MySpace Music page appears, click the **My Music** link at the top of the page.

Click to create and edit playlists

Figure 4.16 Hands-On Exercise 2, Step 5g.

h. In the *Playlists* pane on the left side of the page, click **Add New Playlist**.

A blank box will appear.

i. Type a name for this playlist; then click the **OK** button.

The playlist will appear, ready for editing, in the middle of the page. You can now search for songs to add to the playlist, either by song title or artist.

j. Enter the name of a song or artist into the *Search and add songs to your playlist* box. Then click the **Search** button (magnifying glass) or press Enter.

A list of matching songs will appear in the middle of the page.

k. Click and drag the desired song onto the playlist name on the left side of the page.

Repeat Steps j and k to add more songs to the playlist. To view all the songs in your playlist, click the name of the playlist on the left side of the screen.

Once your playlist is assembled, you can select which playlist plays automatically in your Music Player when visitors view your Homepage.

l. Under *My Profile Playlist*, click the **Please select a playlist** arrow and select the playlist for your Music Player.

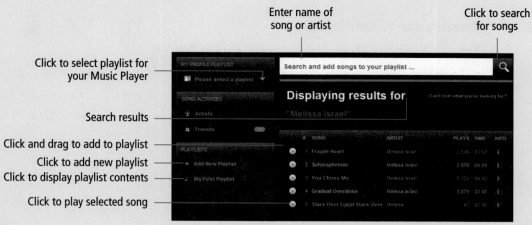

Enter name of song or artist

Click to search for songs

Click to select playlist for your Music Player

Search results

Click and drag to add to playlist

Click to add new playlist

Click to display playlist contents

Click to play selected song

Figure 4.17 Hands-On Exercise 2, Steps 5h through 5l.

Objective 4

Find and Communicate with Friends

What is a friend on MySpace?

Just as they are on Facebook, the people you choose to associate with on MySpace are called *friends*. For someone to view your Profile page, you have to formally add that person to your friends list.

When you add a person to your MySpace friends list, however, that doesn't imply that the person is a friend in the traditional use of the word. You may not even know that person; MySpace friends can be total strangers in real life, or just fans of your work.

How can you find friends on MySpace?

MySpace lets you search for potential friends using their real name, display name, or email address. You can also browse MySpace users by age, location, or other characteristics to find new friends.

How can you communicate with your MySpace friends?

Comment A short message left on a MySpace user's Profile page.

You can communicate publicly with any friend by leaving a *comment* on his or her Profile page. You can also communicate privately by sending email-like messages to that friend within the MySpace system.

Hands-On Exercises

3 | Find and Communicate with Friends

Steps: 1. Search for New Friends; **2.** Browse for New Friends; **3.** Leave a Comment on a Profile Page; **4.** Send a Private Message.

Use Figures 4.18 through 4.23 as a guide in the exercise.

Step 1 Search for New Friends

Refer to Figures 4.18 and 4.19 as you complete Step 1.

a. From any MySpace page, select **Friends > Find Friends** from the menu bar.

b. Enter a person's name, MySpace display name, or email address into the search box.

c. Make sure that *All Name Fields* is selected from the *Search By* list.

d. Click the **Search** button.

Select All Name Fields — Enter person's name or email address —

Click to begin search

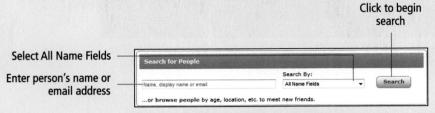

Figure 4.18 Hands-On Exercise 3, Steps 1a through 1d.

e. When the *Search Results* pane appears, find a person you'd like to add as your friend; then click the **Add to friends** link next to that person's name.

MySpace will send an invitation to that person to be your friend. If this person accepts your invitation, he or she will be added to your friends list.

Click to send friend invitation

Click to view person's Profile page

Figure 4.19 Hands-On Exercise 3, Step 1e.

Step 2 Browse for New Friends

Refer to Figure 4.20 as you complete Step 2.

a. From any MySpace page, select **Friends > Browse** from the menu bar.

b. When the Browse Users page appears, click the **Advanced** tab in the *Browse For* pane.

c. To display only users with photos, check the **Show only users who have photos** option.

d. Click the **Gender** arrow and select **Women**, **Men**, or **Both**.

e. Click the **between ages** arrow and select an age range.

f. To further filter the results, click the down arrow next to any filter (who are, and are here for, Ethnicity, and so forth); then check the options that apply.

g. Scroll to the bottom of the *Browse For* pane, pull down the located within list, and select which country to search within.

h. To search in a specific location, click the **Any** arrow and select the desired number of miles. Enter a city, state, or zip code into the *miles from* text box.

i. Click the **Update** button.

The *Search Results* pane will list all MySpace members who match your criteria.

j. To invite a person to be your friend, point to that person's name or photo to display the pop-up; then click **Add to Friends**.

MySpace will send an invitation to that person to be your friend. If this person accepts your invitation, he or she will be added to your friends list.

Click the Advanced tab

Check to display only users
with photos

Click arrow to select gender

Select age range

Click to display and select
additional options

Point to photo to display
pop-up

Click to send friend invitation

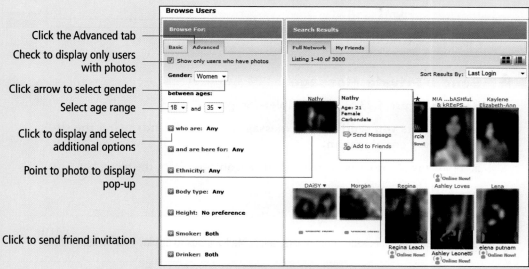

Figure 4.20 Hands-On Exercise 3, Step 2.

Step ❸ Leave a Comment on a Profile Page

Refer to Figures 4.21 and 4.22 as you complete Step 3.

MySpace lets you post public comments to your friends' Profile pages. These comments appear in a Comments module on the Profile page.

a. Navigate to your friend's Profile page.

b. Click the **Add Comment** link.

Click to add a public comment

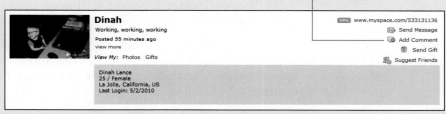

Figure 4.21 Hands-On Exercise 3, Steps 3a and 3b.

c. When the *Add Comment* window appears, type your comment into the text box.

 Attachments

Use the buttons beneath the text box to attach photos, videos, or web links to your comment.

d. Click the **Submit** button.

Enter text

Click to add attachments

Click to submit the comment

Figure 4.22 Hands-On Exercise 3, Steps 3c and 3d.

Step 4 Send a Private Message

Refer to Figure 4.23 as you complete Step 4.

MySpace lets you send private messages to your friends using the site's proprietary email system.

a. From any MySpace page, select **Mail > Compose** from the menu bar.

> **Tip** ⭐ **View Messages**
>
> To view and read messages from others, select **Mail > Inbox** to display your MySpace inbox.

b. Type your friend's name or email address into the *To* box.

c. Type the subject of the message into the *Subject* box.

d. Type your message into the large text box.

e. Use the controls on the formatting toolbar to change font family and point size, add bold or italic, change text justification, and so forth.

f. To attach a file to this message, click the **Add a File** link below the message box; then click the **Browse** button that appears. When the *Open* or *Select File to Upload* dialog box appears, navigate and select the file to upload; then click the **Open** button.

g. To attach a photo to this message, click the **Add a Photo** link. When the photo upload window appears, select the **My Photos** tab to attach a photo already uploaded to MySpace, or click the **Upload Photos** tab to upload a new photo from your computer.

h. To attach a video to this message, click the **Add a Video** link. When the video upload window appears, select the **My Videos** tab; then click the video you want to attach.

i. To attach a link to another web page to this message, click the **Add a Link** link. When the *Add a Link* dialog box appears, enter the page's address into the URL box; then enter any accompanying text into the text box. Click the **Done** button to add the link.

j. Click the **Send** button to send this message to the recipient.

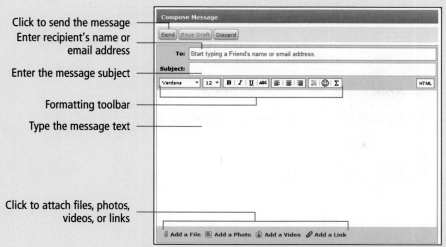

Click to send the message

Enter recipient's name or email address

Enter the message subject

Formatting toolbar

Type the message text

Click to attach files, photos, videos, or links

Figure 4.23 Hands-On Exercise 3, Step 4.

Objective 5

Manage Your Blog

What is a blog?

A blog is an online personal journal. You can post your thoughts and opinions on any topic to your blog, as a series of short text posts.

Why do you need a blog on your MySpace page?

A blog lets you post longer messages to your Profile page than is possible with regular status updates. If you want to let your friends know more about what you're thinking or doing than you can with a short status update, post your thoughts to your MySpace blog.

How do you add a blog to your Profile page?

To display a blog module on your Profile page, like the one in Figure 4.24, select **Profile > Customize Profile** from the MySpace menu bar. When the *Customize Profile* pane appears, select *Modules* from the left-hand list; then click the **Blogs** module to select it. Click the **Publish** button to save your changes.

Click to view full blog

Click to read full post

Figure 4.24 A blog module on a Profile page.

How do you post to your blog?

To make a post to your blog, select **Profile > My Blog** from the MySpace menu bar. When the Blog page appears, click the **Post New Blog** link on the left side of the page. Type the subject of this post into the *Subject* box, select a topic from the *Category* pull-down list, and type your post into the large text box. Click the **Preview & Post** button to preview your post; then click the **Post** button on the following page (Figure 4.25).

Type subject line

Select a category

Enter the text of the post

Figure 4.25 Creating a new blog post.

The subject lines of your most recent posts are displayed in the *Blog* module on your Profile page. To view the full post, your friends can click the subject line for that post. They can then read the post and add their own comments.

Objective 6

Share Photos and Videos

How can you share photos and videos on MySpace?

Like Facebook and other social networks, MySpace lets users share their favorite digital photos and videos with friends (Figure 4.26). You can attach photos and videos to your status updates and email messages, or simply upload photo and video files that your friends can view from your Profile page. Friends can view your photos and videos by clicking the **Photos** or **Videos** link in the *View My* section at the top of your Profile page. (If you haven't yet uploaded any photos or videos, these links won't appear.)

Click to view photos
Click to view videos

Figure 4.26 Viewing photos and videos from a Profile page.

How are photos stored?

Photos are stored in photo albums. MySpace's default photo album is labeled My Photos, but you can create any number of additional photo albums with their own unique names.

What kinds of photos can you share?

MySpace lets you upload photos up to 5 MB in size, in the *.jpg*, *.gif*, *.tiff*, *.png*, and *.bmp* file formats. Photos may not contain copyrighted images or any nudity, or violent or offensive images.

What kinds of videos can you share?

MySpace lets you upload videos up to 500 MB in size and 20 minutes in length. MySpace supports the following video file formats: *.avi, .mov, .wmp, .mpg, .mpeg, .mp4, .qt, .asf, .dv, .gsm, .m4v, .mp4v, .cmp, .divx, .xvid, .rm, .rmvs, .flv, .mkv, .ogm, .3g2, .3gp, .3gp2, .3gpp,* and *.h.264.*

Hands-On Exercises

4 | Share Photos and Videos

Steps: 1. Upload a Photo **2.** Upload a Video

Use Figures 4.27 through 4.34 as a guide in the exercise.

Step 1   Upload a Photo

Refer to Figures 4.27 through 4.30 as you complete Step 1.

a. From any MySpace page, select **Profile > My Photos** from the menu bar.

   MySpace will display any photo albums you've created.

b. Click the **Upload Photos** link.

   If you're prompted to install the ActiveX control, do so; it is necessary in order to launch MySpace's photo uploader.

Click to upload new photos —

Click to return to Profile page —

Photo albums you have already uploaded —

Figure 27 Hands-On Exercise 4, Steps 1a and 1b.

c. On the Upload Photos page, use the folder list on the left to navigate to the location of the photo(s) you want to upload.

d. Click to check the photos you want to upload or click **Select All**.

e. To upload these photos to an existing album, click the **Uploaded to** arrow and select the album. To upload these photos to a new album, enter the album's name into the *create a new album* box.

f. Click the **Upload** button.

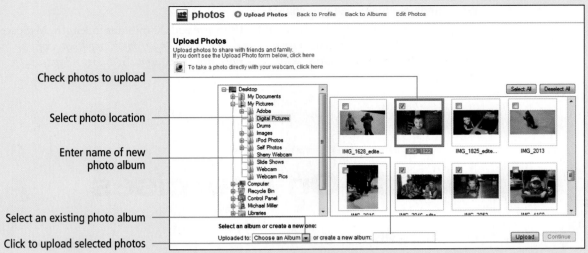

Check photos to upload

Select photo location

Enter name of new photo album

Select an existing photo album

Click to upload selected photos

Figure 4.28 Hands-On Exercise 4, Steps 1c through 1f.

Once you have uploaded the photos, MySpace displays the Edit Captions - My Photos page. You can use this page to provide optional captions for each photo, as well as to tag photos with names of your friends.

g. When the Edit Captions - My Photos page appears, type a description of the photo into the *Add a caption to this photo* box.

Click when done

Enter photo caption

Click to add tags to photo

Figure 4.29 Hands-On Exercise 4, Steps 1g and 1i.

h. To identify friends in a photo, click the **Tag Photo** link. When the *Tag Photo* window appears, click and drag the selection box to highlight the person in the photo you want to tag; then click the name of the person in the accompanying list. When the notification window appears, click **Add Another Tag** to tag another person in this photo, or click the **Finished** button to complete the process.

i. When you're done adding captions and tags, click the **Done Editing** button on the Edit Captions - My Photos page.

Click name of person in photo

Click and drag to highlight person in photo

Click to save tag(s)

Figure 4.30 Hands-On Exercise 4, Step 1h.

Step 2 Upload a Video

Refer to Figures 4.31 through 4.34 as you complete Step 2.

a. From any MySpace page, select **Profile > My Videos** from the menu bar.

MySpace will display your My Videos page, which will include any videos you've previously uploaded. You can also use this page to view your favorite videos from other MySpace users.

b. Click the **Upload** link.

Click to upload a new video

Click to view your uploaded videos

Click to view your favorite MySpace videos

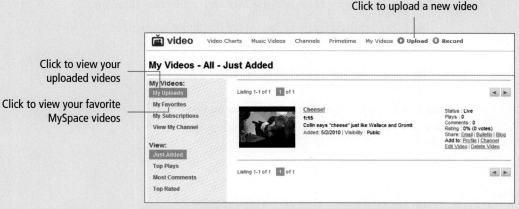

Figure 4.31 Hands-On Exercise 4, Steps 2a and 2b.

c. When the Select Video page appears, click the **Browse** button.

This displays the *Select file to upload* dialog box.

Click to browse for a video file

Click to upload the selected video

Figure 4.32 Hands-On Exercise 4, Steps 2c and 2f.

d. Navigate to and select the video to upload.

e. Click the **Open** button.

You will return to the Select Video page.

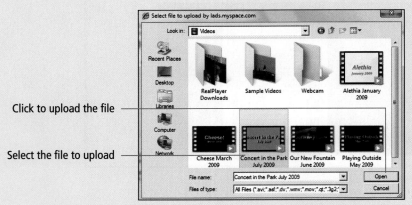

Click to upload the file

Select the file to upload

Figure 4.33 Hands-On Exercise 4, Steps 2d and 2e.

f. Click the **Upload Video** button.

MySpace will display the Video Upload and Basic Information page. The progress of the file upload will be noted at the top of this page.

g. Type a title for the video into the *Title* box.

h. Type a description of the video into the *Description* box.

i. Click the **Category** arrow and select a category for this video.

j. Type any keywords that describe this video into the **Tags** box.

k. Click the **Language** arrow and select the language used in the video.

l. Check the *Terms & Conditions* box.

m. Click the **Save Information** button.

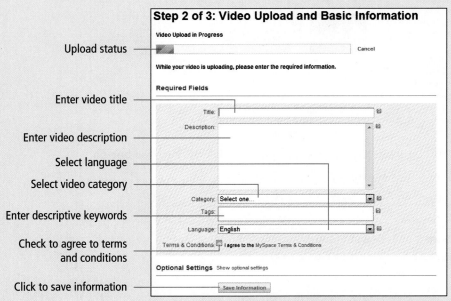

Upload status

Enter video title

Enter video description

Select language

Select video category

Enter descriptive keywords

Check to agree to terms and conditions

Click to save information

Figure 4.34 Hands-On Exercise 4, Steps 2g through 2m.

Objective 7

Join and Create Groups

What is a MySpace group?

A MySpace group is a virtual community for a particular topic or entertainer. Groups host community discussions, in the form of an online forum; they also post photos and bulletins about the topic at hand. A group is a great place to communicate with others who share your interests.

How does one find a group?

You can search for groups by name or keyword, or browse groups by category. Once you find a group you like, you can join the group with a click of a button.

Can anyone start a group?

Any MySpace member can form a new group. All you have to do is give the group a name, assign it to a given category, and choose the desired features for the group. Once you create the group, you can invite your MySpace friends to join it.

Hands-On Exercises

5 | Join and Create Groups

Steps: 1. Search for and Join a Group; **2.** Browse for and Join a Group; **3.** Create a New Group.

Use Figures 4.35 through 4.43 as a guide in the exercise.

Step 1 Search for and Join a Group

Refer to Figures 4.35 through 4.38 as you complete Step 1.

a. From any MySpace page, select **More > Groups** from the menu bar.

   MySpace will display the Groups Homepage. You can use this page to access any groups of which you're a member, to search or browse for new groups, or to create new groups.

b. Click the **Search Groups** link in the navigation box on the left side of the page.

   The Search Groups page will be displayed.

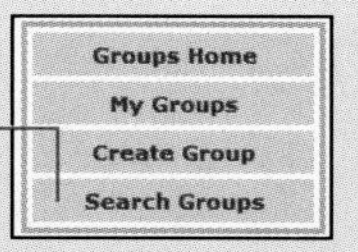

Click to display Search Groups page

Figure 4.35 Hands-On Exercise 5, Steps 1a and 1b.

c. Type one or more words that describe the group you're searching for into the *Keyword* box.

d. In the *Search By* section, click the **Name** option to search group names.

You can also search by keyword, but this typically returns fewer results, as many group creators don't enter keywords for their groups.

e. To confine your search to a particular category of groups, pull down the *Category* list and make a selection.

You can also narrow your search by country, region, or distance from your location.

f. Go to the *Sort by* section and choose how you want your results sorted—newest, most popular, or group name.

g. Click the **Search** button.

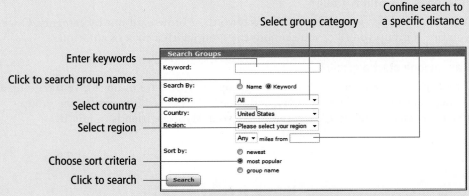

Figure 4.36 Hands-On Exercise 5, Steps 1c through 1g.

h. When the search results page appears, click the **Join Group** link for the group you want to join.

 Tip **Preview Group**

To preview a group before you join, click the group's name on the search results page. You can then join the group from its page by clicking the **Join Group** button there.

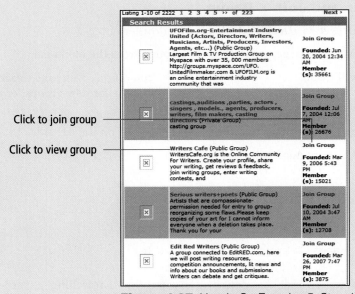

Figure 4.37 Hands-On Exercise 5, Step 1h.

i. When the Confirm Join Group page appears, click the **Join** button.

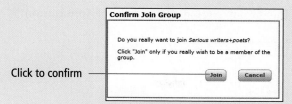

Click to confirm

Figure 4.38 Hands-On Exercise 5, Step 1i.

Step 2 Browse for and Join a Group

Refer to Figures 4.39 through 4.41 as you complete Step 2.

a. From any MySpace page, select **More** > **Groups** from the menu bar.

b. Click the category you're interested in.

Click a category

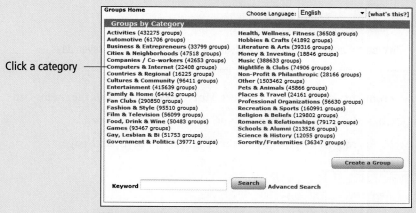

Figure 4.39 Hands-On Exercise 5, Steps 2a and 2b.

MySpace will display a list of all groups within that category. You can sort this list by most popular (default), newest, or group name (alphabetical).

c. Click the **Join Group** link for the group you want to join.

Click to sort by group name   Click to join group

Click to sort by newest first

Click to view group

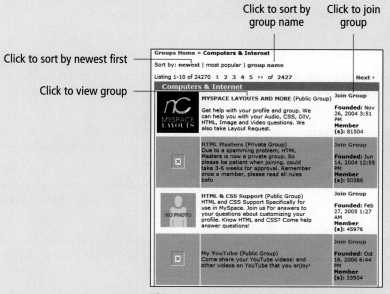

Figure 4.40 Hands-On Exercise 5, Step 2c.

d. When the Confirm Join Group page appears, click the **Join** button.

Click to confirm ——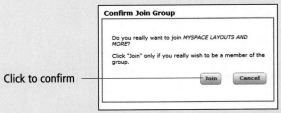

Figure 4.41 Hands-On Exercise 5, Step 2d.

Step 7 Create a New Group

Refer to Figures 4.42 through 4.43 as you complete Step 3.

Note Seven Days

To create a group, you must be a MySpace member for at least seven days.

a. From any MySpace page, select **More > Groups** from the menu bar.

b. Click the **Create Group** link on the left side of the page.

MySpace will display the Create a Group on MySpace! page.

Click to create a new group ——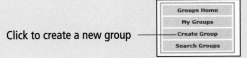

Figure 4.42 Hands-On Exercise 5, Steps 3a and 3b.

c. Type the name for your group into the *Group Name* box.

d. Click the **Category** arrow and select the appropriate category for your group.

e. In the *Open Join* section, check **Yes** to let any MySpace member join your group. Check **No** if you want to manually approve or reject requests to join.

f. In the *Hidden Group* section, check **Yes** to hide your group from public viewing. Check **No** if you want your group to be open to public viewing.

g. In the *Members can Invite* section, check **Yes** to enable group members to invite new members. Check **No** if you want to be the only one capable of inviting new members to join the group.

h. In the *Public Forum* section, check **Yes** if you want group members to be able to post new topics to the group forum. Check **No** if you want to be the only one who can post new topics.

i. In the *Members can Post Bulletins* section, check **Yes** if you want group members to be able to post bulletins to the group. Check **No** if you want to be the only one who can post group bulletins.

j. In the *Members can Post Images* section, check **Yes** if you want group members to be able to upload photos to the group. Check **No** if you want to be the only one who can upload group photos.

k. In the *Mature Content* section, check **Yes** if your group contains adult content; check **No** if the group features content for all ages.

l. Click the **Country** arrow and select the country where the group is based.

m. Click the **Region** arrow and select the state where the group is based.

n. Enter the city where the group is based into the *City* box.

o. Enter your zip code into the *Zip Code* box. (Optional)

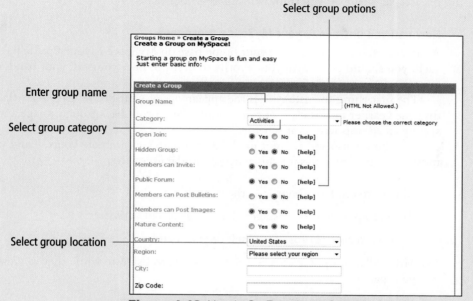

Figure 4.43 Hands-On Exercise 5, Steps 3c through 3o.

p. Enter a brief description of the group into the *Short Description* box.

q. Enter a longer description of the group into the *Description* box. (Optional)

r. Enter the desired web address for the group into the *URL* box.

s. Enter the displayed captcha into the *Verification* box.

t. Click the **Create Group** button.

Once you have created your group, you can upload group photos and invite others to join.

Objective 8

Promote Yourself or Your Band

Why do musicians and entertainers like MySpace?

MySpace is one of the premier web communities for musicians, actors, comedians, entertainers, and celebrities of all stripes. Fans know that they can find their favorite bands and entertainers on MySpace, and musicians especially appreciate the tools that MySpace provides to promote themselves and their music. The result is that MySpace is the number one community site that musicians and other entertainers use to build their fan bases. Many musicians use MySpace as their home base, rather than establishing dedicated websites.

How much work does it take to promote yourself or your music on MySpace?

To succeed on MySpace you have to actively participate in the community. You can't expect your fans to follow you on MySpace (or on any social network) unless you post with some regularity. If you go too long without posting something new, people will quit following you. In reality, that means going online and writing *something* at least once a week. You can talk about upcoming concert dates, recording sessions, album releases, or whatever you think will interest your fans.

How can you customize your MySpace presence?

As an entertainer or musician, your home base on MySpace is your Profile page. As such, you should customize your Profile to best promote yourself, your band, or your music.

The first thing to customize is the appearance of your Profile page. Use the tools discussed earlier in this chapter to use your own custom background image, and to specify an appropriate color scheme.

You should also add content modules that help you promote yourself and your music. The best modules for this purpose are the following:

- Blurbs, to tell fans about you, the artist.

- Blogs, to post longer messages about your recent activities.

- Images, to post photos of yourself or your band.

- Music Player, to play your music for visitors to listen to while they're viewing your page.

- Videos, if you have any music videos for users to view.

- Calendar, to post your upcoming performance schedule.

- Comments, to display comments from your fans.

Summary

In this chapter you learned how to open a MySpace account, navigate the MySpace site, and post status updates. You learned how to personalize your Profile page and add a Music Player, complete with playlists you created. You learned how to find friends and communicate with them. You also learned how to create and post to a MySpace blog, how to upload and share photos and videos, and how to join or create topic-related groups. Finally, you learned how to use MySpace to promote bands and music.

Key Terms

Multiple Choice Questions

1. MySpace is a social networking site especially popular among:
   (a) grade school students.
   (b) senior citizens.
   (c) musicians.
   (d) truckers.

2. You use the following to navigate to specific sections of the MySpace site:
   (a) Toolbar
   (b) Menu bar
   (c) Search box
   (d) Context-sensitive pop-ups

3. You can attach the following item(s) to a MySpace status update:
   (a) Photos
   (b) Videos
   (c) Links
   (d) All of the above

4. You can customize all the following on your MySpace Profile page *except*:
   (a) menu bar contents.
   (b) content modules.
   (c) column layout.
   (d) background image.

5. You use the following content module to play music on your Profile page:

    (a) Media Player

    (b) Music Player

    (c) Playlist

    (d) Jukebox

6. To personalize your MySpace Profile page, you select the following from the Profile menu:

    (a) My Profile

    (b) Edit Profile

    (c) Personalize Profile

    (d) Customize Profile

7. Which of the following is a *private* communication on MySpace?

    (a) Comment

    (b) Status update

    (c) Blog post

    (d) Mail

8. Which of the following is *not* a content module available for a MySpace Profile page?

    (a) Calendar

    (b) Friend Space

    (c) Wall

    (d) Video Player

9. What types of videos can you upload to MySpace?

    (a) Video files

    (b) DVDs

    (c) Webcam videos

    (d) Both (a) and (c)

    (e) All of the above

10. Musicians can do all the following on their MySpace Profile pages *except*:

    (a) Chat live with fans

    (b) Stream free music playlists

    (c) Display music videos

    (d) Post concert schedules

Fill in the Blank

Write the correct word in the space provided.

1. On MySpace, friends' status updates are displayed in the _____.

2. A(n) _____ contains a preset combination of page layout, colors, and graphical elements.

3. Content on a MySpace Profile page is organized into _____, which can be arranged in any order.

4. To play back music on your Profile page, create a(n) _____ of your favorite songs.

5. A(n) _____ is a topic-oriented community on the MySpace site.

Practice Exercises

1. **Personalize Your Profile**

   MySpace differs from Facebook in that you can almost totally customize your Profile page. This is one of the reasons some people prefer MySpace to other social networking sites.

   (a) Select a layout with one small column and a second, wider column.

   (b) Edit the appearance of your page so that it has no theme, a green background, blue content, white modules, and red module headers.

   (c) Display the following content modules on your page: Status and Mood, Calendar, Comments, Details, Friends, Interests, Schools, Stream, and Video Slider.

2. **Add a Music Player**

   The Music Player is one of MySpace's most popular content modules. It's nice to be able to share your favorite music with friends who visit your Profile page.

   (a) Add the Music Player module to your Profile page.

   (b) Create three different playlists, titled Country, Rock, and Hip Hop.

   (c) Select at least six tracks for each playlist.

   (d) Configure Rock as the default playlist for your Profile page.

3. **Create a Group**

   When you want to communicate with others who share your interest in a given topic, you join the appropriate MySpace group. If no group exists for a given topic, you can create a new group. (Remember that you need to be a member of MySpace for seven days before you can create a group.)

   (a) Create a group based around your favorite hobby.

   (b) Configure the group so that it is Open Join, not hidden, and members can invite new members, post new topics to the forum, and post images. Members should not be able to post group bulletins.

   (c) Invite at least three classmates and your instructor to join your group.

4. **Create a Blog**

   Status updates are for posting brief comments and thoughts. For more in-depth musings, you can create a MySpace blog.

   (a) Add a blog module to your Profile page.

   (b) Make at least three posts to your blog.

   (c) Attach a photo to one of your blog posts.

Critical Thinking

1. MySpace offers many of the same features as Facebook, yet is losing members to the competing site. Write a short paper giving the reasons why you think users are leaving MySpace for Facebook, explaining why you like one site over the other and proposing what MySpace can do to retain users going forward.

2. MySpace is extremely popular among musicians. MySpace enables musicians to communicate directly with their fans, and to offer free music (via playlists in the music player). Write a short paper discussing why musicians might want to establish a MySpace page in addition to or in place of a freestanding website.

Team Projects

1. Once you have been a MySpace member for seven days, create a MySpace group for your group. Make it a private group but make sure all group members and your —instructor are invited to join. Each group member should upload at least one photo to the group, as well as make at least two posts to the group's discussion forum.

2. For the purposes of this project, assume that you and your group are members of a band. Create a MySpace page for your band, customize the look and feel of the page to reflect your band's name and music, and add the appropriate content modules to display the band's club schedule, play your music online, play your music videos, and offer news and other updates via a blog.

Credits

MySpace screenshots. © MySpace, www.myspace.com. Used by Permission.

CHAPTER 5

Using LinkedIn

Objectives

After you read this chapter, you will be able to:

1. Sign Up for and Navigate the LinkedIn Site
2. Personalize Your Profile
3. Find New Connections
4. Send and Receive Messages
5. Join and Create Groups
6. Research Companies
7. Look for Employment

The following Hands-On Exercises will help you accomplish the chapter objectives:

Hands-On Exercises

EXERCISES	SKILLS COVERED
1. Editing Your LinkedIn Profile	**Step 1:** Edit Your Snapshot **Step 2:** Add a Profile Picture **Step 3:** Edit Your Current Position **Step 4:** Add a New Position **Step 5:** Edit Your Summary **Step 6:** Add Education Information **Step 7:** Edit Additional Information **Step 8:** Edit Your Personal Information **Step 9:** Add Applications
2. Finding New Connections	**Step 1:** Search Web Mail Contacts **Step 2:** Import Other Address Books **Step 3:** Find Present and Former Colleagues **Step 4:** Find Present and Former Classmates **Step 5:** Invite New Connections
3. Sending and Receiving Messages	**Step 1:** Read and Reply to Messages **Step 2:** Compose a New Message
4. Joining and Creating Groups	**Step 1:** Search for and Join a Group **Step 2:** Visit a Group **Step 3:** Create a New Group
5. Researching Companies	**Step 1:** Finding a Company **Step 2:** Viewing Company Data

Objective 1

Sign Up for and Navigate the LinkedIn Site

What is LinkedIn?

LinkedIn is a business-oriented social networking site, used primarily for professional networking and job hunting. The site was launched in May 2003, and currently has more than 65 million registered users, with an additional 1 million people joining each month.

Who uses LinkedIn?

LinkedIn is used primarily by business professionals. The average age of a LinkedIn user is 41; the average annual income is $109,000. Sixty-four percent of LinkedIn users are male, and 80 percent are college graduates. Most are successful in their chosen professions, with 46 percent describing themselves as "decision makers" in their companies.

How can you use LinkedIn?

People use LinkedIn to expand their list of business contacts, to keep in touch with colleagues, and to keep abreast of developments in their profession. Contacts made on LinkedIn can be used for a number of different purposes, such as finding employment, making a sale, or exploring business opportunities. You can also use LinkedIn to gain an introduction to a specific individual you'd like to know, via connections with mutual contacts.

How do you start using LinkedIn?

LinkedIn membership is free. To join the LinkedIn network, go to **www.linkedin.com** and enter your first and last name, email address, and desired password. Click the Join Now button and you will be prompted to enter information to complete your personal profile, employment status, company, title, and so forth. You will also be prompted to search your email contacts for people who are already on LinkedIn.

LinkedIn will then send a confirmation message to your email address. Click the link in the email to confirm your membership and you're ready to continue building your network and start using the site.

How do you navigate the LinkedIn site?

Use the menu bar at the top of each page to find your way around LinkedIn (Figure 5.1). The menu bar contains links to the LinkedIn Homepage, your personal profile, your LinkedIn contacts, groups you belong to, LinkedIn's job search features, and your message inbox.

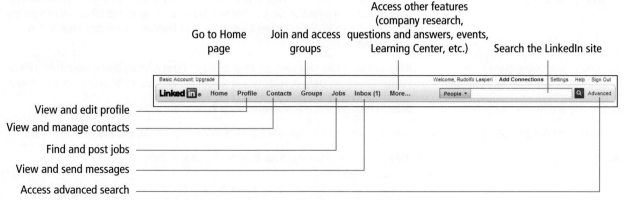

Figure 5.1 The LinkedIn menu bar.

Objective 2

Personalize Your Profile

What is a LinkedIn profile?

Each LinkedIn member has his or her own personal profile page. This profile page is what other LinkedIn users see when they search for you on the site; it's where you make your initial impression to potential employers and people with whom you want to make contact.

What does a LinkedIn profile contain?

A LinkedIn profile is fully customizable; you can select the content that others see. This content can include any or all of the following:

- **Snapshot.** This is an overview of your personal information, including your name, location, current title, past positions, education, recommendations, and links to your Twitter account and website (Figure 5.2). It functions as an online business card, a quick summary of your experience and qualifications. The snapshot section also includes your most recent status update, your personal photo, and a link to your *public* profile, the information that non–LinkedIn members can see when searching the site.

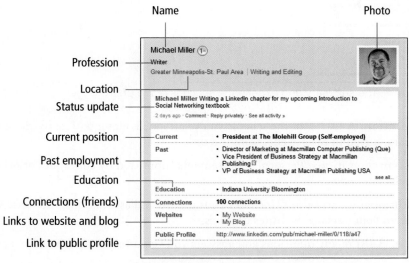

Figure 5.2 A typical LinkedIn snapshot.

- **Links.** This section contains links that let other users send you a message, add you to their professional networks, forward your profile to other users, search through your present and past organizations for potential references, print your profile page, or download your profile as a PDF or *vCard* (Figure 5.3).

vCard A specific file format for electronic or virtual business cards.

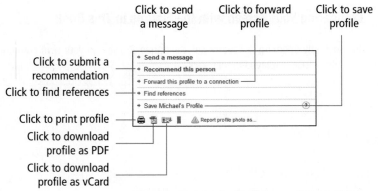

Click to send a message   Click to forward profile   Click to save profile

Click to submit a recommendation

Click to find references

Click to print profile

Click to download profile as PDF

Click to download profile as vCard

Figure 5.3 LinkedIn links on the profile page.

- **Contact information.** Includes your current email address, phone number, and other contact information you choose to share.

- **Summary.** A paragraph or two summarizing your professional experience, specialties, and goals.

- **Experience.** A listing of your current and previous employment positions, sorted in reverse chronological order (Figure 5.4).

Summary

Specialties

Experience

Figure 5.4 The summary and experience sections of the profile page.

- **Education.** A listing of the schools you've attended, along with activities and honors, sorted in reverse chronological order.

- **Recommendations.** Personal endorsements submitted by colleagues or other people you know.

- **Additional information.** Includes your groups and associations, interests, and links to your personal websites or blogs.

- **Q&A.** A list of any questions and answers you've posted to the LinkedIn site.

- **Personal information.** Phone number, address, IM name, birthday, and marital status.

- **Contact settings.** Types of offers or opportunities you're interested in; enables other users to contact you via a LinkedIn message or general email.

- **Activity.** Your most recent activity on the LinkedIn site (Figure 5.5).

Figure 5.5 The activity section of a LinkedIn profile page.

- **Connections.** Displays your top connections on the LinkedIn site.

- **Groups.** Lists those LinkedIn groups to which you belong.

- **Applications.** Displays any LinkedIn applications you've added to your profile page.

Why would you want to personalize your profile?

Since your profile page serves as your de facto résumé on the LinkedIn site, you want to control the information you display to others. Displaying only selected information can help you present yourself in the best possible light.

Can you add any other functionality to your profile?

LinkedIn lets you embed additional features in your profile page by adding individual applications to the page. A LinkedIn application is a *widget*-like utility that adds specific functionality to your profile.

The most popular of these applications include the following:

- **Blog Link**, which lets you display posts from your external blog.

- **Box.net Files**, which lets you manage all your important files online.

- **Company Buzz**, which displays Twitter activity about your company.

- **Events**, which helps you find and display conferences and other professional events.

- **Google Presentation**, which lets you embed a Google or PowerPoint presentation in your profile.

- **Huddle Workspaces**, which provides a private, secure workspace for online collaboration.

- **My Travel**, which displays your current and upcoming travel schedule.

- **Polls**, which allows you to conduct market research and collect data from visitors to your profile page.

- **Reading List by Amazon**, which lets you share the books you're reading with other LinkedIn users.

- **SAP Community Bio**, which displays your *SAP* credentials and contributions.

- **SlideShare Presentations**, which lets you upload and share your presentations.

- **Tweets**, a Twitter client you can use from your LinkedIn profile page.

- **WordPress**, which syncs your WordPress blog posts with your LinkedIn profile.

Widget A small single-purpose application installed on a web page.

SAP The self-named enterprise planning software distributed by the German SAP software company.

Hands-On Exercises

1 | Editing Your LinkedIn Profile

Steps: 1. Edit Your Snapshot; **2.** Add a Profile Picture; **3.** Edit Your Current Position; **4.** Add a New Position; **5.** Edit Your Summary; **6.** Add Education Information; **7.** Edit Additional Information; **8.** Edit Your Personal Information; **9.** Add Applications.

Use Figures 5.6 through 5.27 as a guide in the exercise.

Step 1 Edit Your Snapshot

Refer to Figures 5.6 through 5.7 as you complete Step 1.

a. From the LinkedIn menu bar, select **Profile > Edit Profile**.

   LinkedIn will display the Edit My Profile page.

b. In the snapshot section, click the **Edit** link next to your name.

Click to edit snapshot —

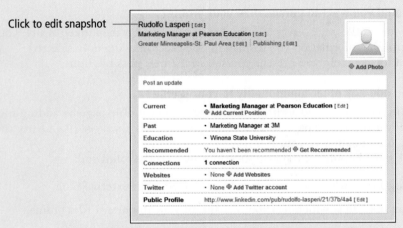

Figure 5.6 Hands-On Exercise 1, Step 1b.

c. When the Basic Information page appears, edit your first and last names as appropriate. You can also edit your profession (*Professional "Headline"*), country, zip code, and industry. Click the **Save Changes** button when you're done.

Edit first name —
Edit last name —
Enter former or maiden name —
Check how you want your name displayed —
Enter a professional headline —
Select country —
Edit zip code —
Select industry —
Click to save changes —

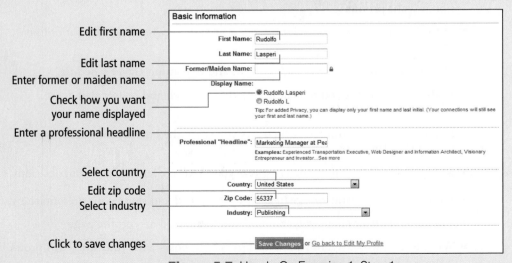

Figure 5.7 Hands-On Exercise 1, Step 1c.

Step 2 Add a Profile Picture

Refer to Figures 5.8 through 5.11 as you complete Step 2.

a. From the LinkedIn menu bar, select **Profile > Edit Profile**.

b. In the snapshot section of the Edit My Profile page, click the **Add Photo** link underneath your picture.

If you've already added a photo, you can change the photo by clicking the **Edit** link instead.

Click to add photo

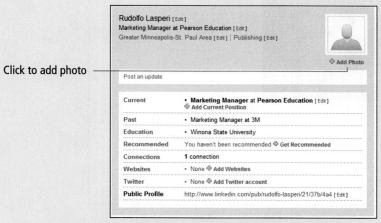

Figure 5.8 Hands-On Exercise 1, Step 2b.

c. When the next page appears, click the **Choose File** or **Browse** button.

Click to choose photo

Click to upload photo

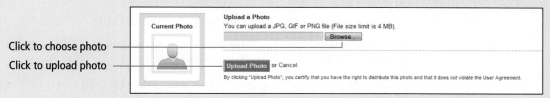

Figure 5.9 Hands-On Exercise 1, Steps 2c and 2e.

d. When the *Open* or *Choose File to Upload* window appears, navigate to and select the photo you want to use; then click the **Open** button.

Click to select photo

Click to upload photo

Figure 5.10 Hands-On Exercise 1, Step 2d.

e. When you're returned to the previous page, click the **Upload Photo** button.

f. When you're presented with a preview of your photo, drag the yellow border to crop the photo as necessary.

g. Click the **Save Photo** button.

Click to save photo —

Click and drag to crop photo —

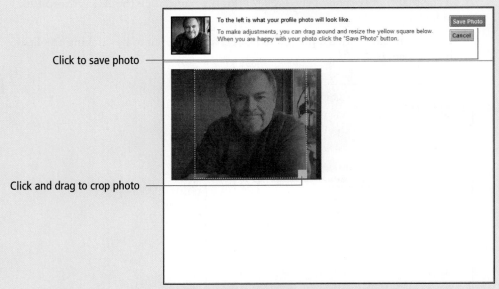

Figure 5.11 Hands-On Exercise 1, Steps 2f and 2g.

Step ③ Edit Your Current Position

Refer to Figures 5.12 through 5.14 as you complete Step 3.

a. From the LinkedIn menu bar, select **Profile > Edit Profile**.

b. In the snapshot section of the Edit My Profile page, click the **Edit** link to the right of your current employment information.

If you haven't yet added your current position, click the **Add Current Position** link instead.

Click to edit current position —

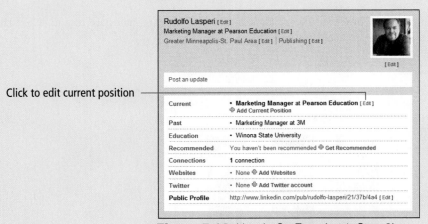

Figure 5.12 Hands-On Exercise 1, Step 3b.

c. When the Edit Position page appears, click the **Change Company** link.

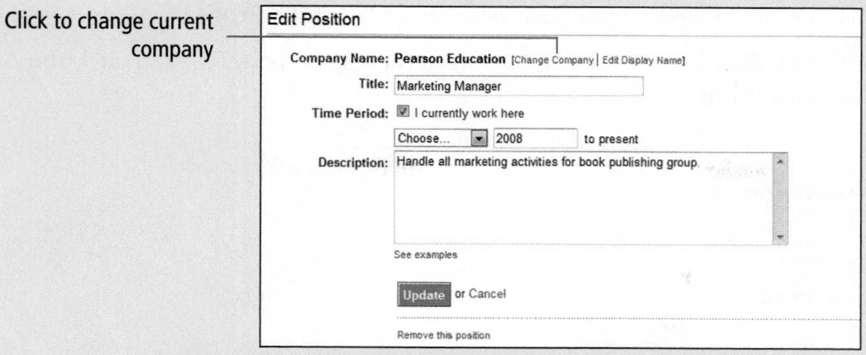

Click to change current company

Edit Position

Company Name: **Pearson Education** [Change Company | Edit Display Name]

Title: Marketing Manager

Time Period: ☑ I currently work here

Choose... ▾ 2008 to present

Description: Handle all marketing activities for book publishing group.

See examples

[Update] or Cancel

Remove this position

Figure 5.13 Hands-On Exercise 1, Step 3c.

d. Next, type the name of the company where you work into the *Company Name* box.

> **Note**   **New Companies**
>
> If you're entering a new company that LinkedIn does not have on file, you'll see a More information about this company box after you enter the company name. Enter the URL for the company's website into the Website box; then pull down the Industry list and select the appropriate industry in which the company operates.

e. Type your current position into the *Title* box.

f. Check the *I currently work here* option.

g. Use the month and year controls to select your starting date with this company.

h. Enter a description of your position into the *Description* box.

i. Click the **Save Changes** or **Update** button.

Select starting month and year

Enter company name

Enter job title

Check to indicate current employment

Enter job description

Click to update current employment

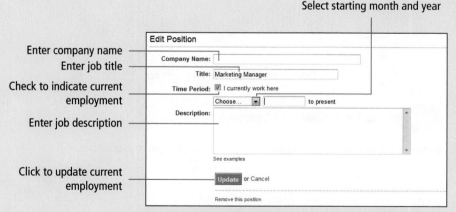

Edit Position

Company Name:

Title: Marketing Manager

Time Period: ☑ I currently work here

Choose... ▾ to present

Description:

See examples

[Update] or Cancel

Remove this position

Figure 5.14 Hands-On Exercise 1, Steps 3d through 3i.

Step 4   Add a New Position

Refer to Figures 5.15 through 5.16 as you complete Step 4.

You can, at any time, add other employment experience to your LinkedIn profile. It's a good idea to list your complete employment history, especially when using LinkedIn to seek a new job.

a. From the LinkedIn menu bar, select **Profile > Edit Profile**.

b. On the Edit My Profile page, scroll to the *Experience* section and click the **Add Position** link.

Click to add new position

Figure 5.15 Hands-On Exercise 1, Step 4b.

c. When the Add Position page appears, type the name of the company you worked for into the *Company Name* box.

d. Type your job title at this company into the *Title* box.

e. Use the month and year controls to select your starting and ending dates with this company.

f. Enter a description of your position into the *Description* box.

g. Click the **Save Changes** button.

Select ending date and year

Enter company name
Enter job title

Select starting month and year

Enter job description

Click to save changes

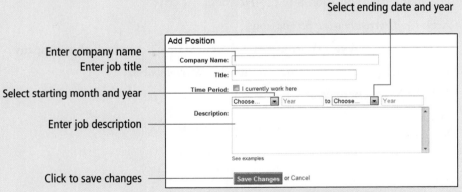

Figure 5.16 Hands-On Exercise 1, Steps 4c through 4g.

 Tip **Enter Additional Employment**

Repeat Step 4 as many times as necessary to enter all your previous positions.

 Step 5 **Edit Your Summary**

Refer to Figures 5.17 through 5.18 as you complete Step 5.

The summary section of your profile page is the place to summarize your job skills and employment history. You can edit your summary at any time.

a. From the LinkedIn menu bar, select **Profile > Edit Profile**.

b. Scroll to the *Summary* section of the Edit My Profile page and click the **Edit** link.

If you haven't yet created your summary, click the **Add Summary** link instead.

Click to edit summary

Figure 5.17 Hands-On Exercise 1, Step 5b.

c. When the Summary page appears, enter a summary of your job skills and experience into the *Professional Experience & Goals* box.

 Write Well

Appearances matter to future employers. For the Professional Experience & Goals section, write in complete sentences, using proper grammar and punctuation. For the Specialties section, enter short, direct items rather than full sentences, which are easier for employers to scan at a glance.

d. Enter your unique skills or areas in which you specialize, for example, marketing or accounting, into the *Specialties* box.

e. Click the **Save Changes** button.

Enter professional summary

Enter areas of expertise

Click to save changes

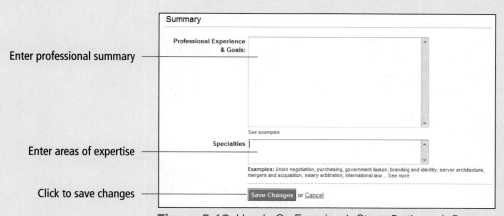

Figure 5.18 Hands-On Exercise 1, Steps 5c through 5e.

Step 6 **Add Education Information**

Refer to Figures 5.19 through 5.20 as you complete Step 6.

a. From the LinkedIn menu bar, select **Profile > Edit Profile**.

b. Scroll to the *Education* section of the Edit My Profile page and click the **Add Education** link.

Click to add school

Figure 5.19 Hands-On Exercise 1, Step 6b.

c. When the Add Education page appears, type the name of the school into the *School Name* box.

If you don't see the *School Name* box, select a country and state first. (The *School Name* box should then appear.)

d. Enter the degree you received into the *Degree* box.

e. Enter the field(s) you studied, such as economics or history, into the *Field(s) of Study* box.

Separate multiple fields with commas.

f. Use the *Dates Attended* controls to enter the years you attended this school.

If you are a current student, enter your expected graduation year as the end year.

g. If you participated in any extracurricular activities, enter them into the *Activities and Societies* box.

Separate multiple activities with commas.

h. Enter any additional notes about your experience at this institution into the *Additional Notes* box.

i. Click the **Save Changes** button.

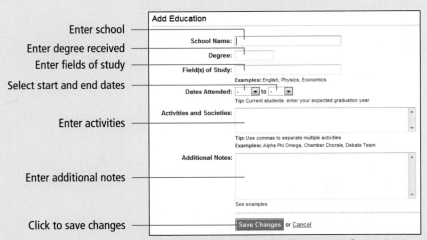

Figure 5.20 Hands-On Exercise 1, Steps 6c through 6i.

Step 7 Edit Additional Information

Refer to Figures 5.21 through 5.22 as you complete Step 7.

a. From the LinkedIn menu bar, select **Profile > Edit Profile**.

b. Scroll to the *Additional Information* section of the Edit My Profile page and click the **Edit** link.

If you haven't yet added any additional information, click the **Add Information** link instead.

> ✛ Additional Information [Edit]
>
> | Websites: | Add up to 3 websites to your profile. |
> | Twitter: | Add your Twitter account to your profile. |
> | Interests: | New technology |
> | Groups and Associations: | Add groups or associations you are involved in to your profile. |
> | Honors and Awards: | Add honors and awards you have received to your profile. |

Figure 5.21 Hands-On Exercise 1, Step 7b.

The Additional Information page will appear.

c. If you have a personal web page, click the first *Websites* arrow, select **My Website**, and enter the site's URL in the accompanying box.

d. If you have a personal blog, click the next *Websites* arrow, select **My Blog**, and enter the blog's URL into the accompanying box.

e. Enter any relevant personal interests into the *Interests* box.

Separate multiple interests with commas.

f. If you belong to any relevant groups or associations, enter them into the *Groups and Associations* box.

Separate multiple entries with commas.

g. If you've received any relevant honors or awards, enter them into the *Honors and Awards* box.

Separate multiple entries with commas.

h. Click the **Save Changes** box.

Tip ⭐ **Twitter Feed**

If you have a Twitter feed you'd like to share with others on LinkedIn, click the Twitter Settings page link at the bottom of the Additional Information page, or the Add Twitter Account link in the snapshot section of the Edit My Profile page. When the next page appears, click the Add your Twitter account link. When the Twitter window opens, enter your Twitter username or email and password; then click the Allow button.

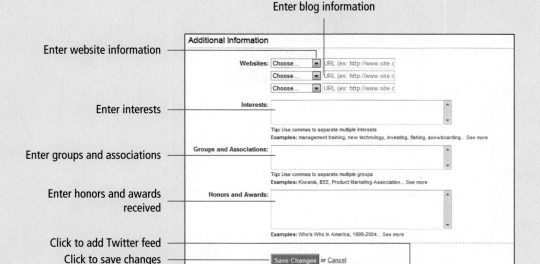

Enter blog information

Enter website information

Enter interests

Enter groups and associations

Enter honors and awards received

Click to add Twitter feed
Click to save changes

Figure 5.22 Hands-On Exercise 1, Steps 7c through 7h.

Step 8 Edit Your Personal Information

Refer to Figures 5.23 through 5.24 as you complete Step 8.

If you wish, you can display a wealth of personal contact information on your LinkedIn profile page. If you value your privacy, you may opt **not** to display all or some of this information; enter only that information you want to be publicly visible.

a. From the LinkedIn menu bar, select **Profile > Edit Profile**.

b. Scroll to the *Personal Information* section of the Edit My Profile page and click the **Edit** link.

Click to edit personal information

✛ Personal Information [Edit]	
Phone:	Add a phone number to your profile.
Address:	Add your address to your profile.
IM:	Add an IM to your profile.
Birthday:	Add your birthday to your profile.
Marital status:	Add your marital status to your profile.

Figure 5.23 Hands-On Exercise 1, Step 8b.

c. To display your phone number on your profile, enter your number into the *Phone Number* box; then click the accompanying arrow and select whether this is your *Home, Work,* or *Mobile* number.

d. If you want to display your instant messaging information on your profile, enter your IM name into the *IM* box; then click the accompanying arrow and select which instant messaging service you use: AIM, Skype, Windows Live Messenger, Yahoo! Messenger, ICQ, or GTalk (Google Talk).

e. If you want to display your postal address on your profile, enter that address into the *Address* box.

f. If you want to display your birthday on your profile, use the *Birthday* controls to select the month and date you were born; then use the *Birth year* control to select your year of birth.

g. If you want to display your marital status (married or single), make a selection from the *Marital status* list.

h. Click the **Save Changes** button.

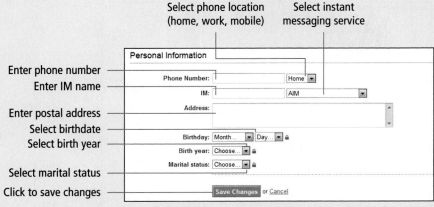

Select phone location (home, work, mobile)
Select instant messaging service

Enter phone number
Enter IM name
Enter postal address
Select birthdate
Select birth year
Select marital status
Click to save changes

Figure 5.24 Hands-On Exercise 1, Step 8c through 8h.

Step 9 Add Applications

Refer to Figures 5.25 through 5.27 as you complete Step 9.

a. From the LinkedIn menu bar, select **Profile > Edit Profile**.

b. Scroll to the *Applications* section of the Edit My Profile page and click the **Add Application** link.

Click to add applications ────

Figure 5.25 Hands-On Exercise 1, Step 9b.

LinkedIn will display the Applications page.

c. Click the title of the application you want to add.

Click to add application ────

Figure 5.26 Hands-On Exercise 1, Step 9c.

LinkedIn will display the page for that application.

d. Under *Application Info*, make sure the *Display on my profile* check box is checked. If you also want to display the application on your home page, leave checked the *Display on LinkedIn homepage* check box; uncheck this box to not display the application on your home page.

e. Click the **Add Application** button.

f. Follow the specific instructions for adding the selected application.

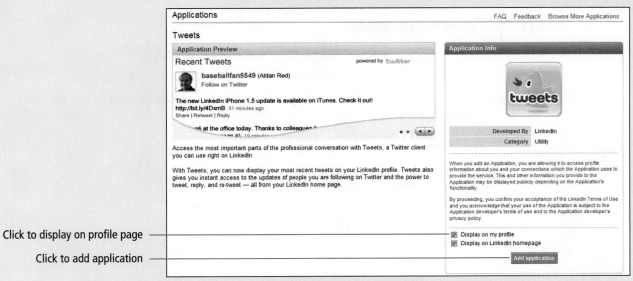

Click to display on profile page

Click to add application

Figure 5.27 Hands-On Exercise 1, Steps 9d and 9e.

Objective 3

Find New Connections

Who are your LinkedIn connections?

LinkedIn's equivalent of Facebook friends is called *connections*. These are business or professional contacts whom you know and trust. Anyone on the LinkedIn site can become a connection; you can also invite people who are not yet LinkedIn members to join your connections list.

How do you find new connections?

You can search for LinkedIn members in your email contacts list, or in your Palm, ACT!, or Mac Address contacts. In addition, LinkedIn can search for members who've gone to the same schools or worked at the same employers that you have. You can also invite non-LinkedIn members to be new connections.

Hands-On Exercises

2 | Finding New Connections

Steps: 1. Search Web Mail Contacts; **2.** Import Other Address Books; **3.** Find Present and Former Colleagues; **4.** Find Present and Former Classmates; **5.** Invite New Connections.

Use Figures 5.28 through 5.37 as a guide in the exercise.

Step 1 Search Web Mail Contacts

Refer to Figures 5.28 through 5.29 as you complete Step 1.

a. From the LinkedIn menu bar, select **Contacts > Add Connections**.

b. When the next page appears, make sure the **Add Connections** tab is selected.

c. Enter the email address for your web mail account into the *Email* box.

d. When prompted to enter your password, do so.

Some web mail services will display a *Password* box on the Add Connections page. Others will display a separate window for signing in.

e. Click the **Continue** or **Sign In** button.

> **Note** **Web Mail**
>
> Web mail refers to Windows Live Hotmail, Yahoo! Mail, Google Gmail, and most other email services you connect to using your web browser.

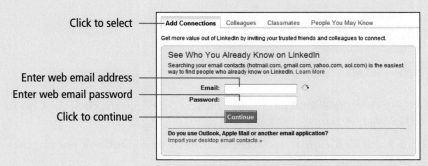

Click to select
Enter web email address
Enter web email password
Click to continue

Figure 5.28 Hands-On Exercise 2, Steps 1b through 1e.

LinkedIn will display all the people in your email contact list who are also LinkedIn members.

f. Check the names of those people you'd like to add to your LinkedIn connections list.

g. Click the **Send Invitations** button.

Check to select

Click to send invitations

Figure 5.29 Hands-On Exercise 2, Steps 1f and 1g.

The people you've invited to become connections will receive a message to that effect. If they accept your invitation, you will be added to each other's connections list.

Step 2 Import Other Address Books

Refer to Figures 5.30 through 5.31 as you complete Step 2.

LinkedIn can also import address books from desktop email applications, such as Microsoft Outlook. You can import files in the *.csv*, *.txt*, or *.vcf* formats.

a. From the LinkedIn menu bar, select **Contacts > Add Connections**.

b. When the next page appears, make sure the **Add Connections** tab is selected.

c. Click the **Import your desktop email contacts** link.

Click to select ———

Click to import address books ———

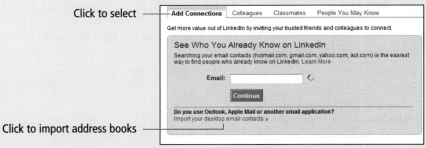

Figure 5.30 Hands-On Exercise 2, Steps 2b and 2c.

d. When the Import Your Desktop Email Contacts page appears, click the **Choose File** or **Browse** button.

If you use Outlook for email, you'll see an **Import from Outlook** button; click this button instead.

e. When the *Open* or *Choose File to Upload* window appears, navigate to and select your address book file; then click the **Open** button.

f. Click the **Upload File** button.

Click to choose address book file ———

Click to upload file ———

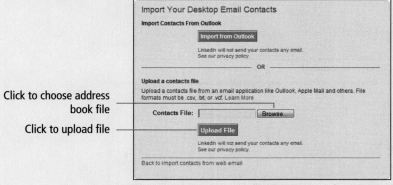

Figure 5.31 Hands-On Exercise 2, Steps 2d and 2f.

LinkedIn will display all the people in your address book who are also LinkedIn members.

g. Check the names of those people you'd like to add to your LinkedIn connections list.

h. Click the **Send Invitations** button.

Step 3 Find Present and Former Colleagues

Refer to Figures 5.32 through 5.33 as you complete Step 3.

The companies for whom you have worked represent another good source of connections. LinkedIn helps you find other people who've had the same employers and add them to your connections list.

a. From the LinkedIn menu bar, select **Contacts > Add Connections**.

b. When the next page appears, click the **Colleagues** tab.

   All the past and present employers you've added to your profile are now listed.

c. Scroll to a specific employer and click the **View All** button.

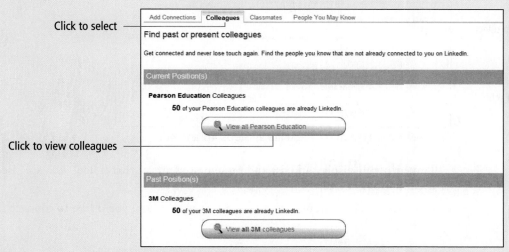

Figure 5.32 Hands-On Exercise 2, Steps 3b and 3c.

LinkedIn will display all past and present employees of that company who are also members of LinkedIn.

d. Check the names of those people you'd like to add to your LinkedIn connections list.

e. Click the **Send Invitations** button.

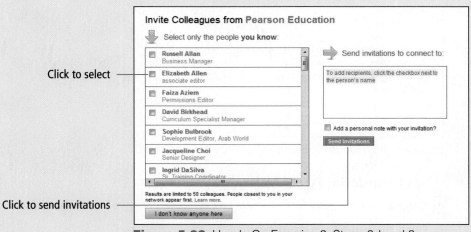

Figure 5.33 Hands-On Exercise 2, Steps 3d and 3e.

Step **4** Find Present and Former Classmates

Refer to Figures 5.34 through 5.36 as you complete Step 4.

People who attend your school are also good candidates for new connections. You can add both present and former classmates to your connections list.

a. From the LinkedIn menu bar, select **Contacts > Add Connections**.

b. When the next page appears, click the **Classmates** tab.

All the past and present schools you've added to your profile will appear.

c. Click the link for a specific school.

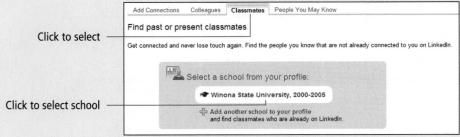

Click to select

Click to select school

Figure 5.34 Hands-On Exercise 2, Steps 4b and 4c.

LinkedIn will display all past and present students at that school who are also members of LinkedIn.

d. Click the **Invite** link next to each student with whom you'd like to connect.

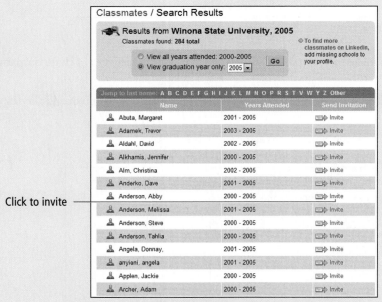

Click to invite

Figure 5.35 Hands-On Exercise 2, Steps 4d.

The Create Invitation page will appear.

e. Enter a personal note into the text box.

f. Click the **Send Invitation** button.

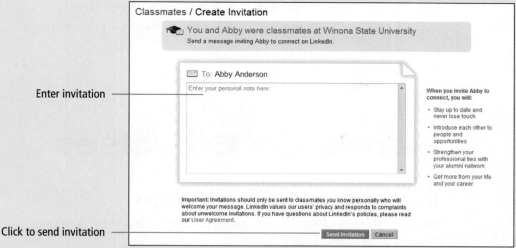

Enter invitation

Click to send invitation

Figure 5.36 Hands-On Exercise 2, Steps 4e and 4f.

Step 5 — Invite New Connections

Refer to Figure 5.37 as you complete Step 5.

You don't have to limit your connections to current LinkedIn members. You can also invite people who are not yet LinkedIn members to join your connections list.

a. From the LinkedIn menu bar, select **Contacts > Add Connections**.

b. When the next page appears, make sure the **Add Connections** tab is selected.

c. Enter the email addresses of the people you'd like to add into the *Enter Email Addresses* box.

Separate multiple addresses with commas.

d. Click the **Send Invitations** button.

LinkedIn will send invitations via email to the people you entered. If they respond positively, they will be added to your connections list.

Click to select

Enter email addresses

Click to send invitations

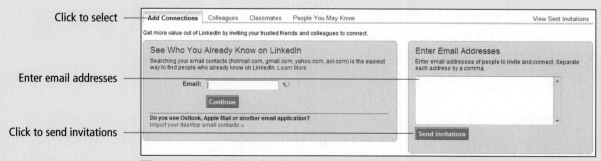

Figure 5.37 Hands-On Exercise 2, Step 5.

Objective 4

Send and Receive Messages

How can you contact other LinkedIn members?

LinkedIn offers its own internal email system. This system enables you to send messages to and receive messages from people on your connections list, as well as anyone else who is a member of the LinkedIn site.

Can you attach photos and other files to your LinkedIn messages?
In a word, no. LinkedIn lets you send only text messages to other members.

Hands-On Exercises

3 | Sending and Receiving Messages

Steps: 1. Read and Reply to Messages; **2.** Compose a New Message.

Use Figures 5.38 through 5.42 as a guide in the exercise.

Step 1 Read and Reply to Messages

Refer to Figures 5.38 through 5.40 as you complete Step 1.

a. From the LinkedIn menu bar, select **Inbox > View Received Messages**.

 Inbox Messages

If you have unread messages in your inbox, the Inbox item on the menu bar will show a number beside the Inbox text, indicating the number of unread messages waiting.

The LinkedIn inbox displays all messages you've received. The newest messages are listed first; unread messages are in bold.

b. To read a message, click the message header.

Figure 5.38 Hands-On Exercise 3, Steps 1a and 1b.

The full text of the message will be displayed.

c. To delete this message, click the **Delete** button.

d. To reply to this message, click the **Reply** button.

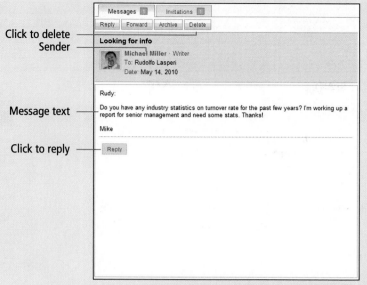

Click to delete

Sender

Message text

Click to reply

Figure 5.39 Hands-On Exercise 3, Steps 1c and 1d.

The reply form appears.

e. Type your reply into the text box.

f. Click the **Send Message** button.

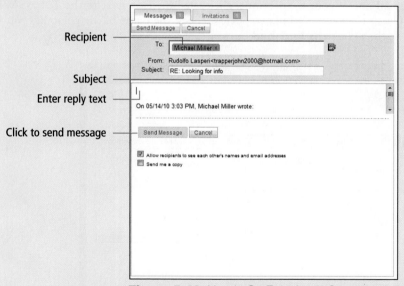

Recipient

Subject

Enter reply text

Click to send message

Figure 5.40 Hands-On Exercise 3, Steps 1e and 1f.

Step 2 Compose a New Message

Refer to Figures 5.41 through 5.42 as you complete Step 2.

a. From the LinkedIn menu bar, select **Inbox > Compose Message**.

The Compose Message page will appear.

b. Enter the recipient's name or email address into the *To* box.

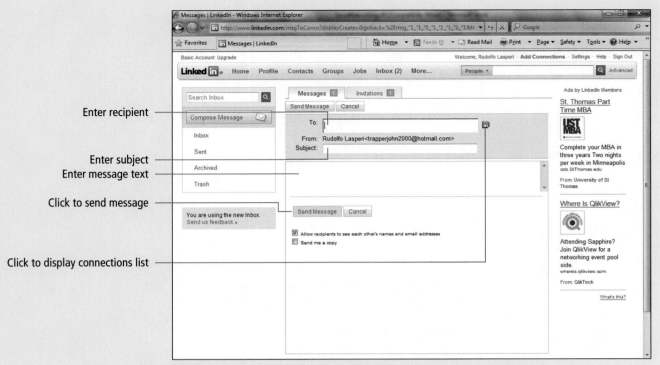

Enter recipient

Enter subject
Enter message text

Click to send message

Click to display connections list

Figure 5.41 Hands-On Exercise 3, Steps 2a, 2b, 2d, 2e, and 2f.

c. To email one of your connections, click the blue icon next to the *To* box. When the *Choose Connections* window appears, check the name of the person(s) you wish to email; then click the **Finished** button.

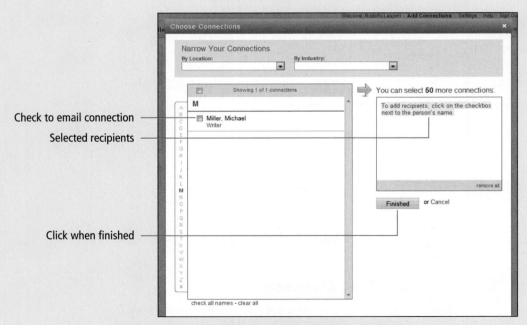

Check to email connection
Selected recipients

Click when finished

Figure 5.42 Hands-On Exercise 3, Step 2c.

d. Type the subject of the message into the *Subject* box.

e. Type your message into the large text box.

f. Click the **Send Message** button.

Objective 5

Join and Create Groups

What is a LinkedIn group?

On the LinkedIn site, a group is a means for professionals to connect with one another regarding a topic of mutual interest. You can join industry groups, professional groups (such as marketing or advertising groups), alumni groups, and more.

How do you join a group?

Most LinkedIn groups are public, which means that anyone can join. Some groups are private, which require the approval of group administrators before an application is accepted.

Can you create your own group?

Despite the large number of sometimes narrow groups available on the LinkedIn site, there may still be topics that have no group coverage. You can create your own group on any such topic by filling in a few forms on the site; any LinkedIn member can create a group in this fashion.

Hands-On Exercises

4 | Joining and Creating Groups

Steps: 1. Search for and Join a Group; **2.** Visit a Group; **3.** Create a New Group.

Use Figures 5.43 through 5.47 as a guide in the exercise.

Step 1 Search for and Join a Group

Refer to Figure 5.43 as you complete Step 1.

a. From the LinkedIn menu bar, select **Groups > Groups Directory**.

The LinkedIn Groups Directory page will appear, with featured groups displayed.

b. Go to the *Search Groups* panel in the sidebar and enter one or more descriptive keywords into the *Keywords* box.

c. Click the **Categories** arrow and select the type of group you're looking for: Alumni Group, Corporate Group, Conference Group, Networking Group, Non-Profit Group, Professional Group, All Categories, or Other.

d. Click the **Choose** arrow and select the desired language.

e. Click the **Search** button.

LinkedIn will display all the groups that match your query.

f. To view a group, click the group's name.

g. To join a group, click the **Join this group** link.

You will see the Join Group page, with information specific to each group.

h. Enter the information requested by the group and click the **Join Group** button.

Figures labeled at left:
Enter keywords
Select category
Select language
Click to search
Click to view group

Click to subscribe to group

Figure 5.43 Hands-On Exercise 4, Step 1.

Step 2 Visit a Group

Refer to Figures 5.44 and 5.45 as you complete Step 2.

Once you've joined a group, you can visit that group's page to interact with other group members.

a. From the LinkedIn menu bar, select **Groups > My Groups**.

The groups you belong to will be listed.

b. Click a group's title to visit that group's page.

Click to visit group page

Figure 5.44 Hands-On Exercise 4, Steps 2a and 2b.

A group page consists of several tabs, each related to a specific activity.

c. To read and comment on group discussions, click the **Discussions** tab.

d. To view group-related news, click the **News** tab.

e. To view job postings of interest to group members, click the **Jobs** tab.

Note that not all groups offer this option.

f. To view any subgroups within the group, click the **Subgroups** tab.

g. To view a list of group members, click the **More** tab and select **Members**.

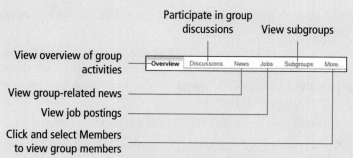

Figure 5.45 Hands-On Exercise 4, Steps 2c through 2g.

Step 3 · Create a New Group

Refer to Figures 5.46 and 5.47 as you complete Step 3.

a. From the LinkedIn menu bar, select **Groups** > **Create a Group**.

The Create a Group page will appear.

b. To display a group logo, click the **Browse** or **Choose File** button in the *Logo* section. When the *Choose File to Upload* window appears, navigate to and select the image file you want to use; then click the **Open** button. Make sure you check the "I acknowledge and agree ..." option on the Create a Group page.

c. Enter the name of the group into the *Group Name* box.

d. Click the **Group Type** arrow and select the type of group you're creating: Alumni Group, Corporate Group, Conference Group, Networking Group, Non-Profit Group, Professional Group, or Other.

e. Enter a brief description of the group into the *Summary* box.

This summary will appear in the Groups Directory.

f. Enter a longer description of the group into the *Description* box.

This description will appear on the group page.

g. If the group has an external website, enter the site's URL into the *Website* box.

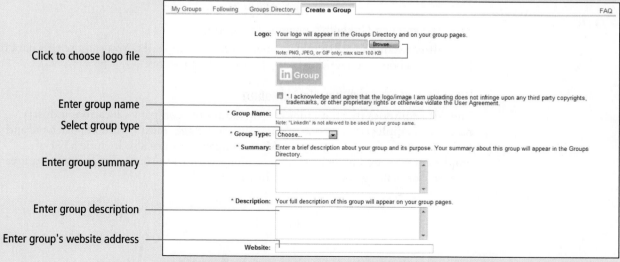

Figure 5.46 Hands-On Exercise 4, Steps 3a through 3g.

h. Enter your email address into the *Group Owner Email* box if it doesn't appear automatically.

i. Select whether this group has Open Access (anyone can join without approval) or needs a Request to Join. For either option, choose whether you want the group displayed in LinkedIn's Groups Directory and whether group members can display the group logo on their profiles.

j. Click the **Language** arrow and select the chosen language of the group.

k. If your group is location-based, check the *Location* option and enter the country and zip codes of the group.

l. Check the *Agreement* option to agree to the terms of service.

m. Click the **Create Group** button.

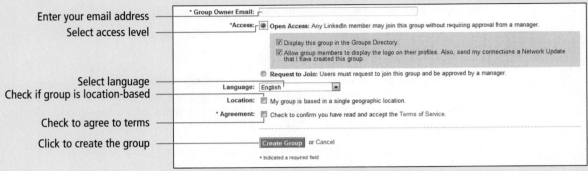

Enter your email address
Select access level
Select language
Check if group is location-based
Check to agree to terms
Click to create the group

Figure 5.47 Hands-On Exercise 4, Steps 3h through 3m.

LinkedIn will display the Send Invitations page. Use this page to invite new members to join your group.

Objective 6

Research Companies

How can you use LinkedIn's company research?

LinkedIn contains a wealth of data about specific companies. You can use this data to learn more about companies where you might like to work.

What type of research data is available?

LinkedIn compiles much useful data, including the company's location, industry, number of employees, revenue, median employee age, most common positions, and ratio of male to female employees. Most company profiles also include a list of employees who are LinkedIn members, along with their contact information, a great resource for making connections within a company.

Hands-On Exercises

5 | Researching Companies

Steps: 1. Finding a Company; **2.** Viewing Company Data.

Use Figures 5.48 through 5.54 as a guide in the exercise.

 Step 1 Finding a Company

Refer to Figures 5.48 through 5.50 as you complete Step 1.

a. From the LinkedIn menu bar, select **More > Companies**.

b. When the next page appears, if you know the name and location of the company, enter the name into the *Company Name or Keyword* box, click the **Location** arrow, and select the location. Then click the **Search Companies** button.

c. If you're not sure about the name or location of a company, or if you prefer to browse companies within a given industry, click the **Browse Industries** link.

Select location

Enter company name

Click to search for company

Click to browse companies by industry

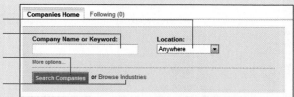

Figure 5.48 Hands-On Exercise 5, Steps 1b and 1c.

d. When the Browse All Industries page appears, click the name of a specific industry.

Click to view all companies in this industry

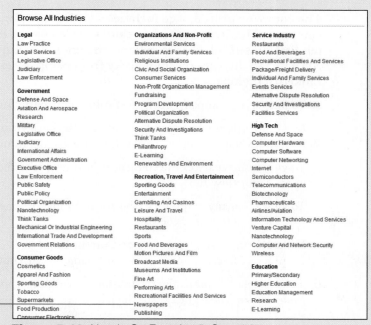

Figure 5.49 Hands-On Exercise 5, Step 1d.

e. When the next page appears, use the controls on the left side of the page to narrow the results.

For example, you can click the **Location** arrow to display only those companies in a given locale, or use the **Company Size** option to display only those companies with a set number of employees.

f. Click the name of a company to view the LinkedIn profile of that company.

Click to view company profile

Filter companies by industry

Filter companies by location

Filter companies by number of employees

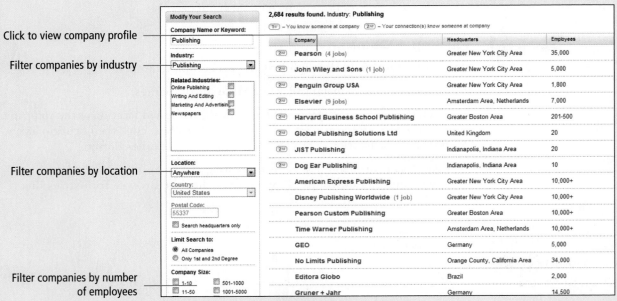

Figure 5.50 Hands-On Exercise 5, Steps 1e and 1f.

Step 2 Viewing Company Data

Refer to Figures 5.51 through 5.54 as you complete Step 2.

The company profile page includes a variety of information about the selected company. The Overview tab includes key company information; the Followers tab lists those LinkedIn members who are following this company; and the Activity tab displays recent activity from company employees who are LinkedIn members.

a. To follow the company, click the **Follow company** link.

LinkedIn will notify you of key company activities, including new job opportunities, and when employees join or leave the company, or are promoted.

b. To view a summary of the company's business, read the information at the top left of the **Overview** tab.

c. To view company employees who are also LinkedIn members, scroll through the lists on the left side of the page.

LinkedIn organizes employees by Current Employees, New Hires, Former Employees, Recent Promotions and Changes, and Popular Profiles.

d. To view related companies or divisions within this company, view the *Related Companies* box on the right side of the page.

Click to follow company

Company summary

Related companies

Employees

Figure 5.51 Hands-On Exercise 5, Steps 2a through 2d.

e. To view key information about the company, including location, industry, size, and the like, scroll to the *Key Statistics* box.

Key Statistics

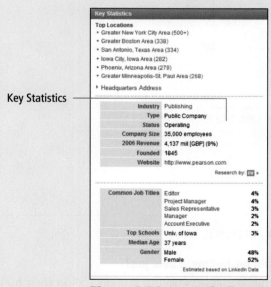

Figure 5.52 Hands-On Exercise 5, Step 2e.

f. To view recent activity by company employees, scroll to the *Recent Activity* box.

g. To view job openings at this company, scroll to the *Jobs* box.

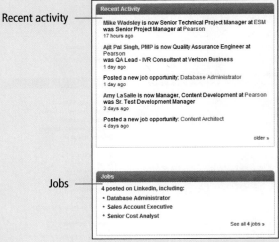

Recent activity

Jobs

Figure 5.53 Hands-On Exercise 5, Steps 2f and 2g.

h. If this is a public company, scroll to the *Stock Information* box to view recent stock performance.

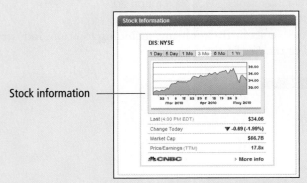

Stock information

Figure 5.54 Hands-On Exercise 5, Step 2h.

Objective 7

Look for Employment

How effective is LinkedIn for finding a new job?

Many job seekers today use social networking as a key tool in their hunt for employment. Employers, too, reference social networking sites when they have positions to fill, and when they're checking the qualifications of job applicants. While the full impact of social networking on hiring decisions is difficult to ascertain, CareerXroads' 9th Annual Source of Hire Study (2010) showed that, of hires directly attributed to social networks, 60 percent came from the LinkedIn site.

How do I find job openings on the LinkedIn site?

The most direct way to find potential employment on LinkedIn is to search the LinkedIn Jobs database. LinkedIn Jobs features thousands of job listings, organized by industry category; you can search the database by industry, company, title, experience level, date posted, and location.

You can access LinkedIn Jobs by clicking **Jobs > Find Jobs** on the LinkedIn menu bar. Enter the appropriate keywords into the search box; then click the **Search** button. You can also perform more targeted searches by clicking the **Advanced** link to use the Advanced Search page.

Search for specific job title
Enter keywords
Filter by location
Search for jobs at a given company
Filter results by function
Show jobs in specific industries
Filter results by experience level
Shows jobs posted within a specific date range
Sort results
Click to search

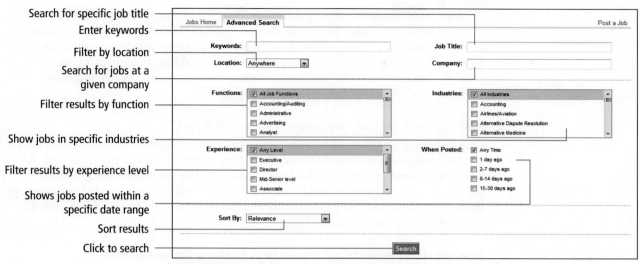

Figure 5.55 LinkedIn Jobs' Advanced Search page.

A LinkedIn job listing includes a brief summary of the job (type, experience desired, functions, industry, and date posted), along with a full job description, skill requirements, and company description. The *You're linked to* box lists those people in your network who work at this company; you can contact them directly to ask them questions or request assistance. Click the **Apply Now** or **Apply on Company Website** button to submit an application.

Click to apply
Position
Location
Company
Summary details
Network connections
Job description

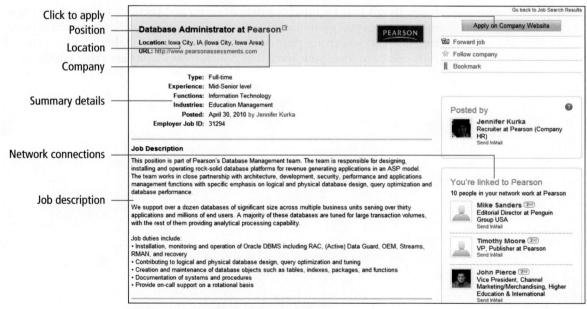

Figure 5.56 A typical job listing.

How can I edit my profile to maximize my employment potential?

Your LinkedIn profile functions as your online résumé to employers who post job openings on the LinkedIn site. As such, you need to treat your profile as you would a traditional résumé, and leverage the individual elements to present yourself in the best possible light.

You should start by making sure that all the elements in your profile are complete and up to date. Make sure that all relevant past employments are listed, as are any educational accomplishments of note. You should also focus on the summary section of the profile, highlighting your experience, skills, interests, and career aspirations. This section is the first one that most employers read and should reflect the most positive view of your prospects.

How can I use my LinkedIn connections to find a job?

One of the key features of LinkedIn, and a key benefit to job seekers, is the network of connections you establish. Given a large enough network, you may find that you have connections or connections of connections within the companies for which you'd like to work. You should leverage these connections at a potential employer to learn more about the company, its culture, and its people, and to establish "inside" contacts within the company.

How else can I enhance my prospects of finding a job on LinkedIn?

The more active you are on the LinkedIn site, the more visible you will be to future employers. To that end, you should take every opportunity to participate in the LinkedIn community, both to enhance your learning and make known your own interest and expertise.

One good way to demonstrate your expertise is to participate in LinkedIn Answers. This section of the site consists of questions posed and answered by members. Providing useful answers to these questions helps establish your credibility and value to potential employers.

Another useful part of the LinkedIn community is its groups feature. Find one or more groups that tie into your desired career and participate fully, learning from more experienced group members and contributing your own experience and expertise. You can even create your own groups of interest to others in your chosen field, thus demonstrating your initiative, which most employers value highly.

Summary

In this chapter you learned how to sign up for and navigate the LinkedIn site. You learned how to personalize your LinkedIn profile, find new connections, and send and receive messages. You also learned how to join and create groups, research companies of interest, and use LinkedIn to look for employment.

Key Terms

Multiple Choice Questions

1. Which of the following social networking sites is used most often for finding new employment?

    (a) Facebook

    (b) LinkedIn

    (c) MySpace

    (d) Twitter

2. Where does LinkedIn *not* look for potential connections?

    (a) Your Twitter followers

    (b) Your email contacts

    (c) Present and former work colleagues

    (d) Present and former classmates

3. Which of the following *cannot* be included in your LinkedIn profile?

    (a) Prior work experience

    (b) Link to your personal blog

    (c) Link to your Facebook page

    (d) Educational honors

4. Which of the following is displayed in a LinkedIn job listing?

    (a) Virtual tour of the facilities

    (b) Graph of expected salary increases, by year

    (c) Senior management bios

    (d) List of skill requirements

5. Which of the following contact information can you *not* include in your profile?

    (a) Phone number

    (b) Postal address

    (c) Instant messaging address

    (d) Digg button

6. Which of the following methods should you use to apply for a job via LinkedIn?

    (a) Send a message to the position's direct report via LinkedIn email.

    (b) Ask a mutual connection for a job application.

(c) Click the Apply Now or Apply on Company Website button on the job listing page.

(d) Fill in the form on the LinkedIn site.

7. Which of the following is *not* a category of LinkedIn group?

(a) Alumni Group

(b) School Group

(c) Corporate Group

(d) Non-Profit Group

8. Which of the following is *not* a tab in a LinkedIn group?

(a) Discussions

(b) News

(c) Photos

(d) Jobs

9. Which of the following can you attach to a LinkedIn message?

(a) Photos

(b) Videos

(c) Web links

(d) None of the above

10. Which of the following data is available via LinkedIn's company research?

(a) Number of employees

(b) Market share

(c) Average employee income

(d) All of the above

Fill in the Blank

Write the correct word in the space provided.

1. LinkedIn is used primarily by _____.

2. Your LinkedIn profile functions as an online _____ for job applicants.

3. If you're looking for employment, use the _____ database.

4. A friend on the LinkedIn site is called a(n) _____.

5. A group with _____ can be joined by any LinkedIn member without prior approval.

Practice Exercises

1. **Join LinkedIn and Create a Profile**

Before you can use LinkedIn, you must create an account and enter information for your profile.

(a) Create a new LinkedIn account.

(b) Fill in the appropriate information to complete your LinkedIn profile. Make sure you include educational experience and employment history.

(c) Email a copy of your LinkedIn résumé to your instructor, or print it out and hand it in.

2. **Find Connections**

One of the fascinating things about LinkedIn and other social networking sites is how closely most of us are connected to almost any given individual, through "friends of friends." This kind of "six degrees of separation" can help you locate connections within a given industry or company.

(a) Select a particular company where you might like to work.

(b) Identify all the LinkedIn connections you have within that company, or within the company's industry.

(c) Submit this list to your instructor.

3. **Send and Receive Messages**

LinkedIn's internal messaging system enables you to send private messages to and receive private messages from other LinkedIn users.

(a) Send a LinkedIn message to another member of your class and ask for a reply.

(b) When the other student replies, print that reply and hand it in to your instructor.

4. **Look for Employment**

LinkedIn is a powerful search tool for students seeking employment.

(a) Identify an industry in which you might like to work.

(b) Identify companies in that industry that are located within 100 miles of your school.

(c) From this list, identify all entry-level job listings posted on LinkedIn Jobs.

(d) Print out the first page of job listings and hand it into your instructor.

Critical Thinking

1. LinkedIn is an important resource for companies looking for new hires. Write a short paper discussing why this is the case, and why LinkedIn is more valuable to employers than other social networking sites.

2. LinkedIn is an important resource for job seekers, both graduating students and people who have been in the workplace for a number of years. Write a short paper discussing how an established employee can use LinkedIn to search for a new position with a different employer.

Team Projects

1. LinkedIn groups are typically targeted at a specific industry, profession, or skill set. As a team, identify a profession (teacher, doctor, accountant, etc.) and create a LinkedIn group for that profession. Find a way to make your group unique from similar existing groups. Make sure all team members are members of the group. Have all team members participate in at least one group discussion; then invite your instructor to join the group.

2. LinkedIn is a good resource for researching different companies within an industry. You can target an industry for employment, and then determine which companies within that industry you'd most like to work for. For this exercise, the team should identify a specific industry and then research the top companies within that industry; each team member should research a specific company. Write a short team paper comparing key data between the companies, and recommending one company as the best to work for.

Credits

LinkedIn screenshots. © LinkedIn. Used by permission.

CHAPTER 6

Using Twitter

Objectives

After you read this chapter, you will be able to:

1. Sign Up for and Configure Your Twitter Account

2. Personalize Your Profile

3. Tweet

4. Follow Others

5. Search for Hot Topics

6. Use Twitter Applications

The following Hands-On Exercises will help you accomplish the chapter objectives:

Hands-On Exercises

EXERCISES	SKILLS COVERED
1. Signing Up for and Configuring a Twitter Account	**Step 1:** Sign Up for a Twitter Account **Step 2:** Configure Twitter for Text Messaging
2. Personalizing Your Profile	**Step 1:** Edit Your Profile Information **Step 2:** Select a Profile Picture **Step 3:** Select a Profile Theme
3. Tweeting	**Step 1:** Post a Tweet **Step 2:** Mention Other Users **Step 3:** Use Hashtags **Step 4:** Tweet an Image with TwitPic **Step 5:** Send a Direct Message
4. Following Others	**Step 1:** Follow Users by Topic **Step 2:** Follow Email Friends **Step 3:** Follow Other People and Organizations **Step 4:** View Tweets **Step 5:** Reply to Tweets **Step 6:** Retweet a Message **Step 7:** Unfollow Others
5. Searching for Hot Topics	**Step 1:** Search for Tweets by Topic **Step 2:** Display Most Popular Topics

Sign Up for and Configure Your Twitter Account

What is Twitter?

Tweet A short, 140-character post on the Twitter social media network. Also used as a verb: to tweet.

Follower A Twitter user who subscribes to the tweets of another user.

Twitter is a microblogging service. Users post short text messages, called *tweets*, from their computers or mobile phones. Tweets are displayed to a user's *followers*, and are searchable via the Twitter site. Like most social media, Twitter is free for all members to use; it generates revenues by selling advertisements, via paid tweets.

How does Twitter work?

Twitter works much like a blogging service, but with restrictions on what can be posted. Tweets are like short text-only blog posts made to the Twitter site. People who subscribe to (follow) a given user see a feed of that user's tweets, much as a subscriber to a blog sees a feed of blog posts. This tweet feed can be viewed on a follower's computer or on most mobile phones.

How popular is Twitter?

Since its launch in 2006, Twitter has become one of the top three social media sites (after Facebook and MySpace) and one of the top 50 websites on the Internet. Twitter currently has more than 100 million users worldwide.

 Note **twttr**

Initially, Twitter's name was twttr. This may have been inspired by the Flickr photo-sharing site, or by the fact that short codes—special telephone numbers for SMS and MMS texting—are five characters in length.

Is Twitter a social network?

Unlike Facebook or LinkedIn, Twitter is not a full-featured social network. It offers only message posting and following; it does not offer any other community features, such as photo sharing, instant messaging, or groups.

Why do people tweet?

Some people use Twitter to inform friends and family of what they're doing and thinking. Others use Twitter as a kind of personal blog, posting random thoughts and comments for all to read. Businesses use Twitter to promote their brands and products, making announcements via their Twitter feeds. News organizations use Twitter to disseminate the latest news headlines. And celebrities and entertainers (arguably the most followed twitterers) use their Twitter feeds as a kind of public relations channel, feeding information of their comings and goings to their fans.

Hands-On Exercises

1 | Signing Up for and Configuring a Twitter Account

Steps: 1. Sign Up for a Twitter Account; **2.** Configure Twitter for Text Messaging.

Use Figures 6.1 through 6.5 as a guide in the exercise.

Step **Sign Up for a Twitter Account**

Refer to Figures 6.1 through 6.2 as you complete Step 1.

a. From your web browser, go to Twitter's main page, located at **www.twitter.com**.

b. Click the large yellow button, variously labeled **Sign Up, Let me in,** or **Join Today.**

   If you already have a Twitter account, click the **Sign in** button and enter your username or email address and password. Then click the **Sign in** button.

> **Note** **Comparing Your Screen with the Figures in This Book**
>
> Since Twitter is constantly updating its features and functionality, the pages you see on your own computer might not always match those displayed in this book.

Click to sign up —

Figure 6.1 Hands-On Exercise 1, Steps 1a and 1b.

c. When the Join the Conversation page appears, type your first and last name into the *Full name* box.

d. Enter your desired username into the *Username* box.

   Your username can be different from your real name or email address.

e. Enter your desired password into the *Password* box.

f. Enter your email address into the *Email* box.

g. If you want other Twitter users to find you via your email address, check the *Let others find me by my email address* option.

h. If you want to receive promotional emails from Twitter, check the *I want the inside scoop—please send me email updates* option. If not, uncheck this option.

i. Click the **Create my account** button.

   When prompted by the *Are you human?* dialog box, enter the captcha (security code text) as prompted and click the **Finish** button. You will receive an email message from Twitter; click the link in this message to confirm your registration. You will then be prompted to browse selected categories and find friends on the Twitter site. You can perform these actions right away, or at any time after you've signed up.

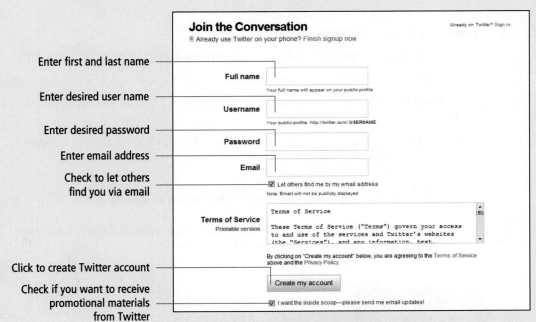

Enter first and last name

Enter desired user name

Enter desired password

Enter email address

Check to let others
find you via email

Click to create Twitter account

Check if you want to receive
promotional materials
from Twitter

Figure 6.2 Hands-On Exercise 1, Steps 1c through 1i.

Step 2 Configure Twitter for Text Messaging

Refer to Figures 6.3 through 6.5 as you complete Step 2.

To make tweets from your mobile phone, you first have to configure Twitter for your particular device. Once configured, you can then send tweets as text messages from your phone.

a. Click the **Settings** link at the top of any Twitter page.

b. When the Settings page appears, click the **Mobile** tab.

c. Select your country from the *Choose your country/region* list.

d. Enter your mobile phone number into the *Enter your mobile phone number* box.

e. Click the **Start** button.

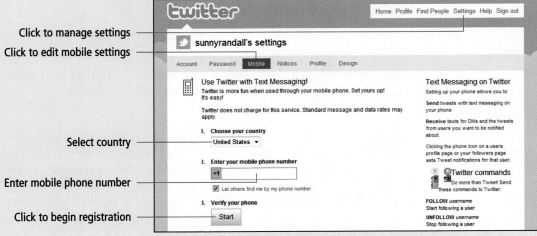

Click to manage settings
Click to edit mobile settings

Select country

Enter mobile phone number

Click to begin registration

Figure 6.3 Hands-On Exercise 1, Steps 2a through 2e.

f. When the Verify your phone page appears, follow the onscreen instructions to send a text message to the number displayed.

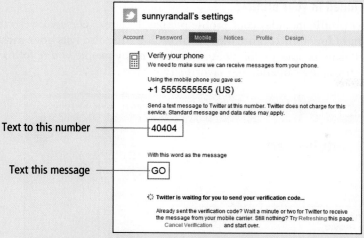

Figure 6.4 Hands-On Exercise 1, Step 2f.

When Twitter receives your message, it will display the Text messaging page. By default, new tweets from people you follow will be sent to your phone as text messages.

g. To stop receiving tweets on your phone, click the *Device updates* arrow and select *Off*.

h. To turn off updates between certain hours, such as when you're sleeping, check the *Turn off updates during these hours* option and enter the desired start and end times.

i. Click the **Save** button.

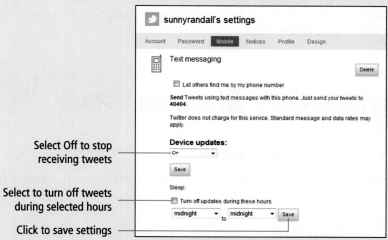

Figure 6.5 Hands-On Exercise 1, Steps 2g through 2i.

Objective 2

Personalize Your Profile

Who sees your Twitter profile?

Your Twitter profile page can be seen by anyone who clicks your username on the Twitter site. These could be existing followers, or anyone interested in possibly following you. An abbreviated version of your profile (your picture, real name, and location) also accompanies all your tweets on the site.

What is included in your profile?

Your Twitter profile includes your profile picture, location, personal website (if you have one), and biography (Figure 6.6). Your profile page also lists your most recent tweets, how many people are following you, how many people you're following, any *lists* in which you appear, and your favorite Twitterers.

List A grouping of tweets from selected Twitter users.

Real name
Username
Website
Bio
Number of users followed
Click to view favorites
Recent tweets
Number of followers
Location
Number of lists on which user appears
Total number of tweets made

Figure 6.6 A typical Twitter profile.

Can you personalize your profile?

You can personalize many aspects of your profile. In addition to personalizing the information itself (name, location, bio, and so forth), you can select the picture that accompanies your profile. You can also select a theme (background image and colors) to apply to your profile page.

Hands-On Exercises

2 | Personalizing Your Profile

Steps: 1. Edit Your Profile Information; **2.** Select a Profile Picture; **3.** Select a Profile Theme.

Use Figures 6.7 through 6.11 as a guide in the exercise.

Step 1 Edit Your Profile Information

Refer to Figure 6.7 as you complete Step 1.

a. Click **Settings** at the top of any Twitter page.

b. Click the **Profile** tab.

c. Type the full name you want displayed into the *Name* box.

d. Enter your location into the *Location* box.

e. If you have a website or blog, enter that URL into the *Web* box.

f. Type a short biography into the *Bio* box.

g. Click the **Save** button.

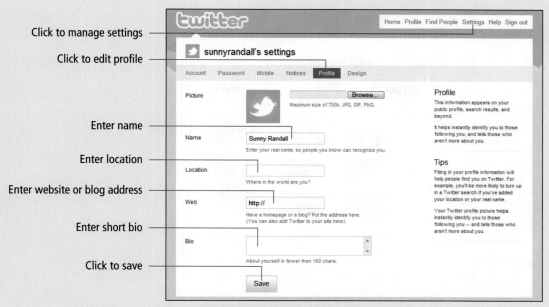

Click to manage settings

Click to edit profile

Enter name

Enter location

Enter website or blog address

Enter short bio

Click to save

Figure 6.7 Hands-On Exercise 2, Step 1.

Step 2 Select a Profile Picture

Refer to Figures 6.8 and 6.9 as you complete Step 2.

a. Click **Settings** at the top of any Twitter page.

b. Click the **Profile** tab.

c. In the *Picture* section, click the **Browse** or **Choose File** button.

 Note   **Picture Size**

You can upload photo files up to 700 MB in size, in.*jpg*, .*gif*, or .*png* formats.

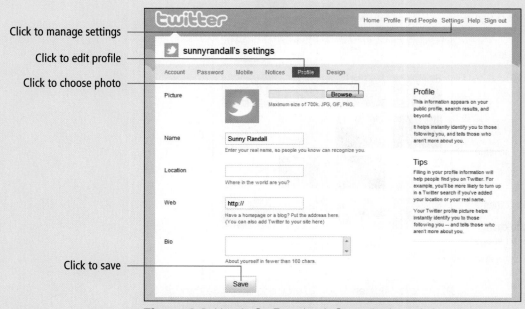

Click to manage settings

Click to edit profile

Click to choose photo

Click to save

Figure 6.8 Hands-On Exercise 2, Steps 2a through 2c.

d. When the *Choose File to Upload* or *Open* window appears, navigate to and select the desired photo, and click the **Open** button.

Select photo

Click to upload photo

Figure 6.9 Hands-On Exercise 2, Step 2d.

e. Click the **Save** button.

Step ③ Select a Profile Theme

Refer to Figures 6.10 through 6.11 as you complete Step 3.

a. Click **Settings** at the top of any Twitter page.

b. Click the **Design** tab.

c. To use a predesigned theme, click one of the themes displayed.

d. To use a different background picture, click the **Change background image** button. Click the **Browse** or **Choose File** button. When the *Open* or *Choose File to Upload* window appears, select a file and click the **Open** button.

Click to edit page design

Click to change color scheme

Click to select theme

Click to change background image

Click to save

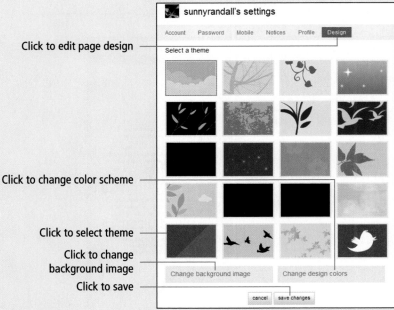

Figure 6.10 Hands-On Exercise 2, Steps 3a through 3d.

e. To use a different color scheme, click the **Change design colors** button. Click each of the page elements (background, text, links, sidebar, and sidebar border) in turn to display the color chooser. Click the color you want for that element; then click the **Done** button.

Click to edit page element

Select color

Click to save all changes

Click when done with item

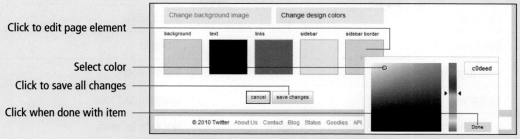

Figure 6.11 Hands-On Exercise 2, Step 3e.

f. Click the **save changes** button.

Objective 3

Tweet

What is a tweet?

A tweet is a text-based post to the Twitter service. Each tweet must be 140 characters or less in length. Tweets are displayed on the sender's profile page and are delivered to the sender's followers.

How does one tweet?

You can tweet from your computer, using your web browser to access the Twitter site. You can also tweet from your mobile phone, by sending a text message to the number provided by Twitter.

 Tweets Cannot Be Deleted

Once made, tweets cannot be edited or deleted. Because tweets are both permanent and public, be careful of what you post.

Is there a shorthand for posting on Twitter?

Because of the 140-character limitation, tweets do not have to conform to proper grammar, spelling, and sentence structure—and, in fact, seldom do. It is common to abbreviate longer words, use familiar acronyms, substitute single letters and numbers for whole words, and refrain from all punctuation.

For example, you might shorten the sentence "I'll see you on Friday" to read "C U Fri."

What are common acronyms?

Twitterers use many of the same acronyms that have been used for decades in Internet chat rooms, instant messaging, and text messaging. In addition, there are several Twitter-specific acronyms in widespread usage.

Table 6.1 details the most popular of these acronyms.

Table 6.1—Common Twitter Acronyms

Acronym	Description	Acronym	Description
AFAIK	As far as I know	IRL	In real life
b/c	Because	J/K	Just kidding
BFN	Bye for now	LI	LinkedIn
BR	Best regards	LMK	Let me know
BTW	By the way	LOL	Laughing out loud
DM	Direct message (a private tweet)	NSFW	Not safe for work
EM	Email	OH	Overheard
FB	Facebook	OMG	Oh my God
FTF	Face to face	PRT	Partial retweet
FTL	For the loss (bad)	RT	Retweet
FTW	For the win (good)	RTHX	Thanks for the retweet
FWIW	For what it's worth	TMB	Tweet me back
HTH	Hope that helps	YMMV	Your mileage may vary
IMHO	In my humble opinion	YW	You're welcome

What is a hashtag?

Hashtag A means of indicating an important word in a tweet; similar to identifying a keyword.

A *hashtag* is a word in a tweet that is preceded by the hash or pound character, like this: #hashtag. Hashtags function much like keywords, and help other users find relevant tweets when searching for a particular topic. A hashtag within a tweet is clickable; clicking a hashtag displays a list of the most recent tweets that include that word.

Can you include photos with your tweets?

By default, Twitter is a text-only service. However, certain third-party applications, such as TwitPic, enable you to include links to photos within your tweets.

Can you send private messages on Twitter?

Direct message A private tweet sent to another Twitter user.

While tweeting is by nature a public activity, Twitter does allow the sending of private tweets, in the form of *direct messages*, to anyone who follows your tweets. A direct message is essentially a tweet, with its inherent 140-character limit, sent directly and privately to another user.

Hands-On Exercises

3 | Tweeting

Steps: 1. Post a Tweet; **2.** Mention Other Users; **3.** Use Hashtags; **4.** Tweet an Image with TwitPic; **5.** Send a Direct Message.

Use Figures 6.12 through 6.18 as a guide in the exercise.

Step Post a Tweet

Refer to Figure 6.12 as you complete Step 1.

a. Go to the Twitter Homepage (**www.twitter.com**).

b. Type your message into the *What's happening?* box.

Remember that a tweet can be no more than 140 characters in length.

c. Click the **Tweet** button.

Number of characters left —
Enter message —
Click to post the tweet —

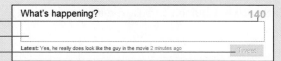

Figure 6.12 Hands-On Exercise 3, Step 1.

Tip ☆   **Add a Link**

To add a link to another website to your tweet, simply type the URL. You may wish to use a link-shortening service, such as bit.ly (**www.bit.ly**), to create shorter URLs to fit within Twitter's 140-character limit.

Tip ☆   **Tweet from a Mobile Phone**

You can also send tweets from your mobile phone. Simply send a text message, 140 characters or less, to the phone number Twitter provided when you configured your account for mobile service.

Step Mention Other Users

Refer to Figure 6.13 as you complete Step 2.

When you mention other Twitter users in your tweets, their names become clickable by anyone viewing the tweets. Clicking a referenced name displays that user's Twitter profile page.

a. Type your tweet into the *What's happening?* box.

b. Type an "at" sign (@) before the user's name, like this: @username.

c. Click the **Tweet** button to post the tweet.

Referenced username ———

Username with link in tweet ———

Figure 6.13 Hands-On Exercise 3, Step 2.

Step ❸ Use Hashtags

Refer to Figure 6.14 as you complete Step 3.

When you add a hash character before a specific word in a tweet, that word gets referenced by Twitter as a kind of keyword, and that word becomes clickable by anyone viewing the tweet. Clicking a hashtag in a tweet displays a list of the most recent tweets that include the same hashtag.

a. Type your tweet into the *What's happening?* box.

b. Type a hash or pound sign (#) before the word you want to reference, like this: #keyword.

c. Click the **Tweet** button to post the tweet.

Hashtag ———

Hashtag in tweet with link ———

Figure 6.14 Hands-On Exercise 3, Step 3.

Step ❹ Tweet an Image with TwitPic

Refer to Figure 6.15 as you complete Step 4.

You cannot, by default, include photos in your tweets. You can, however, use TwitPic to include links in your tweets to photos hosted on the TwitPic service.

Before you can include a photo link, you must sign up for a TwitPic account. A TwitPic account is free; sign up at www.twitpic.com with your Twitter ID.

a. Go to the TwitPic site (www.twitpic.com) and click the **Upload photo** link.

The first time you access the site you'll be prompted to sign into your Twitter account and then to allow TwitPic to access your account.

b. When the Upload and post a photo page appears, click the **Browse** or **Choose File** button.

c. When the *Open* or *Choose File to Upload* window appears, navigate to and select the desired photo. Then click the **Open** button.

d. Type the message for your tweet into the *Add a message* box.

e. Make sure the *Post to Twitter account* option is checked.

f. Click the **Upload** button.

TwitPic will post a tweet with a link to the photo you uploaded.

Click to select photo —

Enter tweet text —

Check to post to
Twitter account —

Click to tweet —

Figure 6.15 Hands-On Exercise 3, Step 4.

Step 5 Send a Direct Message

Refer to Figures 6.16 through 6.18 as you complete Step 5.

> **Note** **Direct Messages**
>
> You cannot send direct messages to people who are not following your tweets.

a. Click the **Profile** link at the top of any Twitter page.

b. Click the **Followers** link in the sidebar.

This displays a list of all Twitterers who are following your posts.

Click to display profile page —

Click to display followers —

Figure 6.16 Hands-On Exercise 3, Steps 5a and 5b.

c. Click the **tools** button and select *Direct message* [username].

The tools button will be visible only if you have followers.

Tools button

Click to send direct message

Figure 6.17 Hands-On Exercise 3, Step 5c.

d. When the Send [username] a message page appears, type your message into the text box.

As with all tweets, your direct message must be no longer than 140 characters.

e. Click the **Send** button.

Enter message

Click to send

Figure 6.18 Hands-On Exercise 3, Steps 5d and 5e.

Objective 4
Follow Others

How do you find people to follow on Twitter?

When you select other users to follow, you receive all their tweets on your Twitter Homepage. You can search for Twitterers by name or topic, or find people to follow in your email contacts lists.

Who can you follow on Twitter?

You can follow any Twitter user; your viewing another user's tweets doesn't require approval. The only exception to this is when a user blocks you as a follower; any user can block any other user, which helps to cut down on online stalking.

Can you reply to tweets?

You can reply to any tweet you read. All you have to do is click the **Reply** button next to the sender's username in the original tweet. Your reply will be sent as a tweet back to the original sender.

Can you resend tweets to other users?

Retweet A tweet forwarded to other Twitter users.

A *retweet* (RT) is a tweet that you resend, or "retweet," to people who are following you. This is an efficient way to obtain wide distribution for popular tweets.

Hands-On Exercises

4 | Following Others

Steps: 1. Follow Users by Topic; **2.** Follow Email Friends; **3.** Follow Other People and Organizations; **4.** View Tweets; **5.** Reply to Tweets; **6.** Retweet a Message; **7.** Unfollow Others.

Use Figures 6.19 through 6.28 as a guide in the exercise.

Step 1 Follow Users by Topic

Refer to Figures 6.19 and 6.20 as you complete Step 1.

There are several ways to find people to follow on Twitter. One approach is to browse Twitter for topics you like and to view a list of Twitterers who tweet on those topics.

a. Click the **Find People** link at the top of any Twitter page.

b. When the next page appears, click the **Browse Interests** tab.

c. Click the category in which you're interested.

Click to find people

Click to browse by category

Click to select category

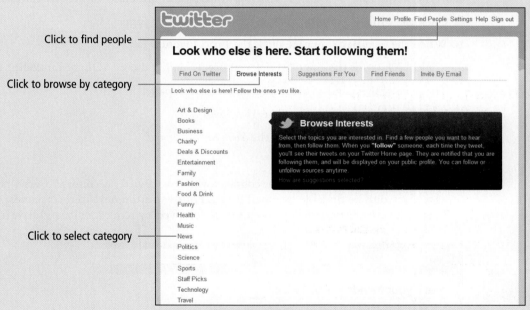

Figure 6.19 Hands-On Exercise 4, Steps 1a through 1c.

Twitter will display a list of users who post on that topic.

d. Click the **Follow** button for anyone you want to follow.

Figure 6.20 Hands-On Exercise 4, Step 1d.

Step 2 Follow Email Friends

Refer to Figure 6.21 as you complete Step 2.

You can also follow people who are in your email contacts lists. Twitter will search Gmail, Yahoo! Mail, America Online (AOL) Mail and LinkedIn contacts.

a. Click the **Find People** link at the top of any Twitter page.

b. When the next page appears, click the **Find Friends** tab.

c. Click the link for the email service you use: Gmail, Yahoo!, AOL, or LinkedIn.

   The page will expand to display an email sign in panel.

d. Enter your email address into the *Your email* box.

e. Enter your email password into the *Your password* box.

f. Click the **Find friends** button.

   Twitter will display a list of your contacts who have Twitter accounts. Users who have elected to be findable by email have a **Follow** button next to their names. Users who are not findable by email can be followed by request only, and have a

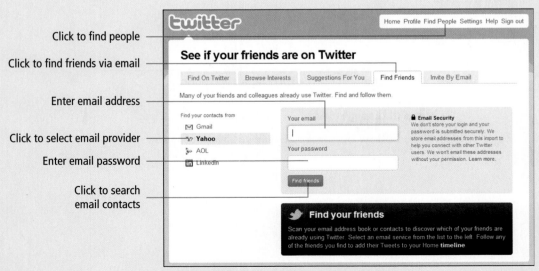

Figure 6.21 Hands-On Exercise 4, Step 2.

Send Request button next to their names. Click the appropriate button to follow or to send a request to that person.

Step 3 Follow Other People and Organizations

Refer to Figures 6.22 and 6.23 as you complete Step 3.

Twitter also lets you search for specific members and organizations to follow.

a. Click the **Find People** link at the top of any Twitter page.

b. When the next page appears, click the **Find On Twitter** tab.

c. Enter the name of the person or organization you want to follow into the *Who are you looking for?* box.

d. Click the **Search** button.

Twitter will display a list of members who match your search criteria.

Click to find people

Click to search for people or organizations

Enter name

Click to search

Figure 6.22 Hands-On Exercise 4, Steps 3a through 3d.

e. Click the **Follow** button for anyone you want to follow.

Click to follow

Figure 6.23 Hands-On Exercise 4, Step 3e.

Step 4 View Tweets

Refer to Figure 6.24 as you complete Step 4.

Once you sign into your Twitter account, tweets from members you're following will appear on the Twitter Homepage.

a. Click the **Home** link at the top of any Twitter page.

Tweets are listed in reverse chronological order, with the newest tweets at the top. How long ago the tweet was made is listed beneath each tweet.

b. To view older tweets, scroll to the bottom of the page and click **More**.

Click to display home page

Tweet

Person making the tweet

When the tweet was made

Figure 6.24 Hands-On Exercise 4, Step 4.

Step 5 Reply to Tweets

Refer to Figure 6.25 as you complete Step 5.

a. From the Twitter Homepage, point to the tweet to which you want to reply.

Twitter will display the **Reply** and **Retweet** links.

b. Click the **Reply** link.

The sender's name will appear in the *Reply to* box at the top of the page, preceded by the @ sign.

c. Enter your reply, as a tweet, into the *Reply to* box.

d. Click the **Tweet** button.

Original sender's address

Enter reply

Click to send reply

Point to tweet to display options

Click to reply

Figure 6.25 Hands-On Exercise 4, Step 5.

Step 6 Retweet a Message

Refer to Figure 6.26 as you complete Step 6.

You can forward, or retweet, any tweet to your followers.

a. From the Twitter Homepage, point to the tweet you want to forward.

Twitter will display the **Reply** and **Retweet** links.

b. Click the **Retweet** link.

The *Retweet to your followers?* pop-up will appear.

c. Click the **Yes** button.

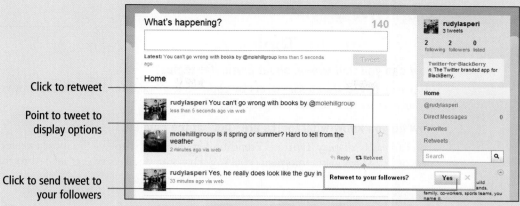

Click to retweet

Point to tweet to
display options

Click to send tweet to
your followers

Figure 6.26 Hands-On Exercise 4, Step 6.

Step ⑦ Unfollow Others

Refer to Figures 6.27 and 6.28 as you complete Step 7.

At any time, you can opt to no longer follow a particular Twitterer. This act is called *unfollowing*.

a. Click the **Home** link at the top of any Twitter page.

b. Click the **following** link in the sidebar.

Twitter will display a list of members you are following.

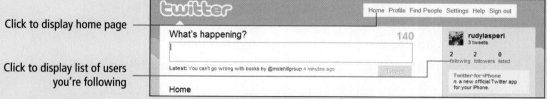

Click to display home page

Click to display list of users
you're following

Figure 6.27 Hands-On Exercise 4, Steps 7a and 7b.

Unfollow To no longer follow a given Twitterer.

c. Click the **tools** button to the right of the member you wish to unfollow. Then click **Unfollow** [username].

Click to unfollow

Figure 6.28 Hands-On Exercise 4, Step 7c.

Objective 5

Search for Hot Topics

How can you find tweets about particular topics?

Twitter lets you search for tweets by topic or keyword. In this way, you can view all recent tweets that match your criteria.

How do you know what topics are "hot" at the moment?

You can easily display Twitter's Trending list. This list displays the most tweeted hashtags or keywords at the moment; clicking a hashtag displays tweets related to that topic.

Hands-On Exercises

5 | Searching for Hot Topics

Steps: 1. Search for Tweets by Topic; **2.** Display Most Popular Topics

Use Figures 6.29 through 6.30 as a guide in the exercise.

Step 1 Search for Tweets by Topic

Refer to Figure 6.29 as you complete Step 1.

a. Click the **Home** link at the top of any Twitter page.

b. Type one or more keywords that describe the topic into the *Search* box.

c. Click the *Search* button (magnifying glass icon).

Twitter will display the most recent tweets that match your search query.

Click to display home page —

Click to search —

Enter search query —

Figure 6.29 Hands-On Exercise 5, Step 1.

Step 2 Display Most Popular Topics

Refer to Figure 6.30 as you complete Step 2.

The most popular topics on Twitter at any given moment are displayed in the Trending: Worldwide list.

a. Click the **Home** link at the top of any Twitter page.

b. Scroll to the *Trending: Worldwide* section in the sidebar.

The *Trending: Worldwide* section lists the most tweeted topics and hashtags.

c. Click a topic or hashtag to see all tweets related to that topic.

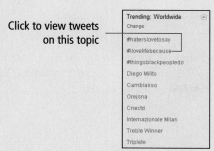

Click to view tweets
on this topic

Figure 6.30 Hands-On Exercise 5, Step 2.

Objective 6

Use Twitter Applications

What is a Twitter application?

Twitter applications are third-party software programs, web-based widgets, or mobile utilities that add functionality to the basic Twitter service. Some applications help automate the tweeting process; others consolidate tweets from people you follow; still others help you find tweets and Twitterers of interest.

What are the most popular Twitter applications?

There are literally thousands of Twitter applications available, many for free. Table 6.2 details some of the more popular of these applications.

Table 6.2—Popular Twitter Applications		
Application	**Website**	**Description**
bit.ly	www.bit.ly	URL-shortening service
Hello.txt	www.hellotxt.com	Lets you send a single post to multiple social media, including Twitter and Facebook; also consolidates posts from multiple sites
HootSuite	www.hootsuite.com	Manages multiple Twitter accounts; schedules future tweets
Ping.fm	www.ping.fm	Lets you send a single post to multiple social media, including Twitter and Facebook
Snaptweet	www.snaptweet.com	Creates a new tweet when you post a photo to Flickr
TweetDeck	www.tweetdeck.com	Manages multiple Twitter accounts; sends a single post to Twitter, Facebook, and other sites; schedules future tweets
Tweet-U-Later	www.tweet-u-later.com	Schedules future tweets
Twiddeo	www.twiddeo.com	Embeds links to videos in your tweets
TwitPic	www.twitpic.com	Embeds links to photos in your tweets
Twitterfall	www.twitterfall.com	Displays the latest tweets of upcoming trends and custom searches
Twitterfeed	www.twitterfeed.com	Feeds your blog posts to Twitter, Facebook, and other social networks
Twittershare	www.twittershare.com	Shares pictures, videos, music, and other files on Twitter
Twitxr	www.twitxr.com	Creates a new tweet when you snap a picture from your mobile phone

Summary

In this chapter you learned how to sign up for Twitter, configure your account, and personalize your profile. You learned how to tweet and follow other Twitterers. You also learned how to search for hot topics and find Twitter applications.

Key Terms

Multiple Choice Questions

1. Which of the following does Twitter let you include in a tweet?

   (a) Photos

   (b) Videos

   (c) Links to other websites

   (d) All of the above

2. A person who tweets is called a

   (a) Tweeter`

   (b) Twitterer

   (c) Tweetser

   (d) Twit

3. A person who subscribes to your tweets is called a

   (a) Follower

   (b) Subscriber

   (c) TwitFollower

   (d) Friend

4. To link to or mention other Twitter users in a tweet, type the following before the person's username:

   (a) !

   (b) *

   (c) #

   (d) @

5. Which of the following can you customize about your Twitter profile page?

   (a) Background image

   (b) Number of columns

   (c) Font family and size

   (d) Background music

6. Twitter is most like which of the following social media?

    (a) Facebook

    (b) MySpace

    (c) Blog

    (d) Media sharing site

7. Which of the following is *not* a way to find people to follow?

    (a) Email contacts

    (b) IM contacts

    (c) Search by name

    (d) Browse by topic

8. When you want someone to reply to your tweet, use this acronym:

    (a) b/c

    (b) TMB

    (c) RT

    (d) LMK

9. When you want to tweet a picture, which of the following applications would you use?

    (a) TwitPic

    (b) TweetDeck

    (c) Twitterfeed

    (d) bit.ly

10. You view tweets from users you follow on which of the following Twitter pages?

    (a) Profile

    (b) Follow

    (c) Feed

    (d) Home

Fill in the Blank

Write the correct word in the space provided.

1. A clickable keyword in a tweet is called a(n) _____.

2. A tweet can be no longer than _____ characters.

3. A private tweet is called a(n) _____.

4. A(n) _____ is a way to forward a tweet to other users.

5. When you _____ a user, you opt not to view his or her future tweets.

Practice Exercises

1. **Create a Twitter Account**

    The first step in tweeting is to create your own Twitter account and to personalize your profile accordingly.

    (a) Create a new Twitter account.

    (b) Personalize your profile with a picture and custom theme.

    (c) Print your profile page and hand it in to your instructor.

2. **Tweet**

   Any Twitter member can create tweets on any topic.

   (a) Provide your Twitter username to your instructor, so he or she can follow your tweets.

   (b) Post at least two tweets describing what you're doing in class today.

3. **Follow**

   You can follow the tweets of people and companies you know or like.

   (a) Obtain your instructor's Twitter username.

   (b) Become a follower of your instructor.

   (c) Print a copy of your Twitter Homepage that shows at least one tweet from your instructor.

4. **Find and Retweet**

   Twitter makes it easy to find tweets about any given subject.

   (a) Search for tweets about Ultimate Frisbee.

   (b) Retweet one of these tweets to your follower list.

Critical Thinking

1. Many entertainers and celebrities are heavy Twitter users. Write a short paper discussing the benefit an actor or musician might get from posting to Twitter on a regular basis. Also discuss the potential downsides of public figures using Twitter in this manner.

2. One of the challenges in using Twitter is fitting your message into the 140-character limit; it takes a bit of creativity to write in such a condensed fashion. Some have taken this creativity to the extreme, creating tweet-sized versions of classic literature.

   Now it's your turn to be creative. Write a Twitter version of the poem "The Road Not Taken," by Robert Frost. As an added challenge, try to do this in as few tweets as possible! (Hint: You can use slash marks to separate stanzas.)

   The Road Not Taken
   Robert Frost

   Two roads diverged in a yellow wood,
   And sorry I could not travel both
   And be one traveler, long I stood
   And looked down one as far as I could
   To where it bent in the undergrowth.

   Then took the other, as just as fair,
   And having perhaps the better claim,
   Because it was grassy and wanted wear;
   Though as for that the passing there
   Had worn them really about the same.

And both that morning equally lay
In leaves no step had trodden black.
Oh, I kept the first for another day!
Yet knowing how way leads on to way,
I doubted if I should ever come back.

I shall be telling this with a sigh
Somewhere ages and ages hence:
Two roads diverged in a wood, and I—
I took the one less traveled by,
And that has made all the difference.

Team Projects

1. Each member of your team should establish his or her own Twitter account and become a follower of the other members of the team. The first member of the team should post a tweet, which should then be retweeted by the second member, which should then be retweeted by the third member, and so forth.

2. Over the course of a 24-hour period, see which member of your team can get the most Twitter followers. Submit your lists to the instructor. (Printouts of your follower lists will be accepted.)

Credits

Twitter screenshots. © Twitter, www.twitter.com. Used by permission.

Poem: The Road Not Taken. Robert Frost, American Poet, (March 26, 1874–January 29, 1963)

CHAPTER 7

Using Virtual Worlds as Social Networks

Objectives

After you read this chapter you will be able to:

1. Understand Virtual Worlds
2. Sign Up for Second Life
3. Personalize and Control Your Avatar
4. Navigate the Virtual World
5. Network with Others in Second Life

The following Hands-On Exercises will help you accomplish the chapter objectives:

Hands-On Exercises

EXERCISES	SKILLS COVERED
1. Signing Up for Second Life	**Step 1:** Sign Up for Second Life **Step 2:** Get Started with Second Life **Step 3:** Log into Second Life
2. Personalizing and Controlling Your Avatar	**Step 1:** Personalize Your Avatar **Step 2:** Move Your Avatar with the Keyboard **Step 3:** Move Your Avatar with the Move Panel **Step 4:** Gesture
3. Navigating the Virtual World	**Step 1:** Teleport to Different Regions **Step 2:** Search for and Go to a Location **Step 3:** Create a Landmark **Step 4:** Return to a Landmark
4. Networking with Others	**Step 1:** Find Nearby People **Step 2:** Chat with Others **Step 3:** Add a Friend **Step 4:** Instant Message a Friend **Step 5:** Find and Join a Group **Step 6:** Visit Your Groups **Step 7:** Take and Email a Snapshot

Objective 1

Understand Virtual Worlds

What is a virtual world?

A virtual world is an online community that takes the form of an interactive simulated environment. Users inhabit this graphical 3D environment and interact with one another via cartoon-like avatars (onscreen alter egos), often participating in virtual activities and economies. Many virtual worlds let users expand on or create their own environments within the 3D world.

What is an avatar?

Each user is represented in the virtual world by an onscreen character called an avatar. Your avatar can be personalized to suit your personality, and you can use your computer's keys to move it around onscreen in the 3D virtual space. Your avatar can walk and talk (using your words, of course) and participate in various onscreen activities. Avatars can typically take any form the user chooses: human, animal, vegetable, mineral, or something more fantastical or abstract.

What are the characteristics of a virtual world?

A typical virtual world is part chat room, part multiplayer online game, all accessed via the user's onscreen alter ego. Most virtual worlds exhibit these six main characteristics:

- *Shared space,* where many users participate at the same time;
- *Graphical user interface,* which visually depicts the shared online space, typically in an immersive 3D environment;
- *Immediacy,* with all interaction taking place in real time;
- *Interactivity,* with users being able to create their own customized content;
- *Persistence,* so that the world continues to exist regardless of whether individual users are logged on;
- *Community,* in that the world encourages the formation of various types of social groups.

What is a virtual world like?

Some virtual worlds closely resemble the real world. Others present fantasy worlds, where your avatar might be a wizard or a knight or a superhero. This type of virtual world is descended from traditional role-playing games, although all virtual worlds incorporate role playing to some extent.

What can you do in a virtual world?

Most virtual worlds let you do virtually everything you can do in the physical world. You can talk to other users, play games with them, or shop for virtual merchandise; you can even participate in virtual political campaigns. A virtual world is simply a computerized version of the real world that you play on your computer, over the Internet.

How did virtual worlds develop?

MUD A multi-user domain or multi-user dungeon; an early text-based form of multiplayer gaming, with each user taking the role of a specific character.

Virtual worlds evolved as a form of online role playing. The first networked multi-user game was Maze War, which was played on Arpanet (the forerunner of today's Internet) as early as 1974. This type of Dungeons and Dragons–like game soon evolved into what was called a *MUD*, for multi-user domain or multi-user dungeon. A MUD is a multiplayer game where each player takes the role of a specific character in a text-based online environment.

MMPORG A massively multiplayer online role-playing game, where users play specific characters in a large online gaming environment.

MMORLG A massively multiplayer online real-life game, similar to an MMPORG, but one which imparts more control over the nature and features of their avatars to the users.

MUDs moved onto the Internet in the 1990s with larger and more complex environments. Today, users from around the world can engage in playing massively multiplayer online role-playing games, or *MMPORGs*, over the Internet. An MMPORG is a 3D online role-playing game where the user plays a specific character. Most MMPORGs are pure game-playing environments, lacking many of the social networking and customization features of today's more advanced virtual worlds.

MMPORGs have morphed into *MMORLGs*, or massively multiplayer online *real-life* games. An MMORLG is a virtual online environment where the user can more fully personalize his or her avatar, without a specific role within a game.

Is a virtual world a game?

Some virtual worlds are pure gaming environments. Others incorporate some form of game play within their worlds, but include other nongaming elements as well. That said, participating in some virtual worlds is a bit like playing a game; you manipulate your avatar to perform various tasks, just as you would a character in a video game.

How is a virtual world a social network?

Even game-oriented online environments have many social networking features, specifically the ability for users to interact via chat rooms, discussion forums, instant messaging, and the like. More sophisticated virtual worlds feature even more opportunities for social interaction by enabling entire communities to develop within their worlds. Users can interact with other users just as they would in the world, by "talking" directly to each other, forming groups and clubs, and even conducting e-commerce transactions with one another.

In many ways, a virtual world is a social network with avatars. That is, you engage in all the activities typical of a social network, but through your chosen onscreen graphical identity.

What are the most popular virtual worlds?

There are numerous online virtual worlds today. While many of these environments are within or in support of computer games, others more closely resemble nongame social networks. The most popular of these social virtual worlds include the following:

- ActiveWorlds (www.activeworlds.com)
- City of Heroes (www.cityofheroes.com)
- Cybertown (www.cybertown.com)
- Habbo (www.habbo.com)
- Kaneva (www.kaneva.com)
- Onverse (www.onverse.com)
- Poptropica (www.poptropica.com)
- Second Life (www.secondlife.com)
- SmallWorlds (www.smallworlds.com)

Some of these virtual worlds, such as Habbo and Poptropica, cater more to younger users. Others, such as City of Heroes, are more game oriented than community oriented. In any case, you need to spend some time getting a feel for any particular virtual world before you decide to dive in on a more serious basis.

Objective 2

Sign Up for Second Life

What is Second Life?

Second Life is one of the most popular virtual worlds today. It was developed by Linden Lab, launched in June of 2003. Second Life users, called *residents*, can explore the virtual world, meet and socialize with other residents, participate in individual and group activities, and trade virtual goods and services with one another.

What do you need to access Second Life?

Second Life can be played from any computer connected to the Internet. Users must download and install the Second Life Viewer, a client program that enables a connection to and interaction with the virtual world.

Who can use Second Life?

Second Life can be used by anyone aged 18 and over. Users aged 13 to 17 can access Teen Second Life, a similar but separate virtual world.

 Teen Second Life

When a teenager turns 18, he or she is automatically transferred from Teen Second Life to the main Second Life world.

Does it cost anything to use Second Life?

Linden Dollars The form of virtual currency in the Second Life virtual world, abbreviated L$.

Like most virtual worlds, Second Life is free to play, although subscriptions are available for more sophisticated game play. You can also purchase virtual dollars (called **Linden Dollars**, named after the game developer) to participate in the world's virtual economy—to buy, sell, rent, or trade virtual products, services, and land. Linden Dollars (abbreviated L$) can be purchased using U.S. dollars and other real-world currency on Second Life's LindeX exchange, or from other users or independent brokers.

 Premium Membership

Second Life's $9.95/month Premium Membership provides access to a higher level of technical support and pays a stipend of 300 Linden Dollars a week into the member's avatar account.

How do you start using Second Life?

To participate in Second Life, you first have to create an account (which is free). Once your account is confirmed (via email), you're prompted to download and install the Second Life Viewer program, which is necessary to access the virtual world.

Hands-On Exercises

1 | Signing Up for Second Life

Steps: 1. Sign Up for Second Life; **2.** Get Started with Second Life; **3.** Log into Second Life

Use Figures 7.1 through 7.6 as a guide in the exercise.

Step 1 | Sign Up for Second Life

Refer to Figures 7.1 through 7.4 as you complete Step 1.

> **Note** Comparing Your Screen with the Figures in This Book
>
> Since Second Life is constantly updating its feature set, the pages you see on your own computer might not always match those displayed in this book.

a. From your web browser, go to Second Life's main page, located at **www. secondlife.com.**

b. Click the **Join Now** button.

If you already have a Second Life account, click the **Login** link to sign in.

You will be prompted to create your onscreen personality. This personality does not need to include your actual name or attributes.

Click to log into an existing account

Click to create a new account

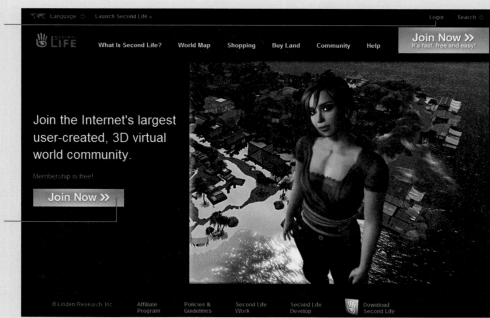

Figure 7.1 Hands-On Exercise 1, Steps 1a and 1b.

c. Enter the desired first name for your avatar into the *Create a First Name* box. Then click the **Find Last Names** button.

Second Life will display a list of available last names to match your chosen first name.

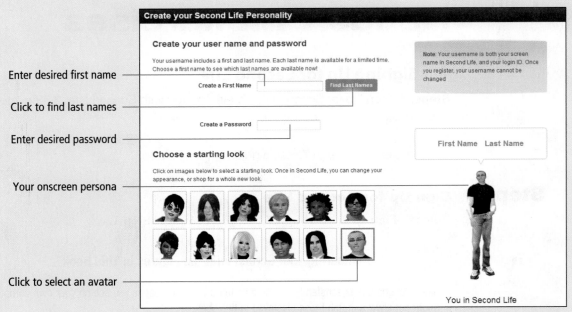

Enter desired first name —

Click to find last names —

Enter desired password —

Your onscreen persona —

Click to select an avatar —

Figure 7.2 Hands-On Exercise 1, Steps 1c through 1f.

d. Click the desired first/last name combination.

The screen will automatically return to the one shown in Figure 7.2.

Click to select first/last name —

Figure 7.3 Hands-On Exercise 1, Step 1d.

e. Enter your desired password into the *Create a Password* box.

f. Click the avatar you'd like to use.

Your selected name and avatar will be displayed on the right side of the screen.

 **Avatars**

Second Life presents only a small selection of avatars during the sign up process. Additional avatars are available after you sign up.

g. Scroll to the *Just a Few More Details …* section and type your email address into the *E-mail Address* box.

h. Use the *I was born* controls to select your date of birth.

i. Pull down the *Security Question* list and select a security question. Then type an answer to that question into the *Security Answer* box.

j. Enter the displayed captcha words into the *Security Check* box.

k. Click the **Create Account** button.

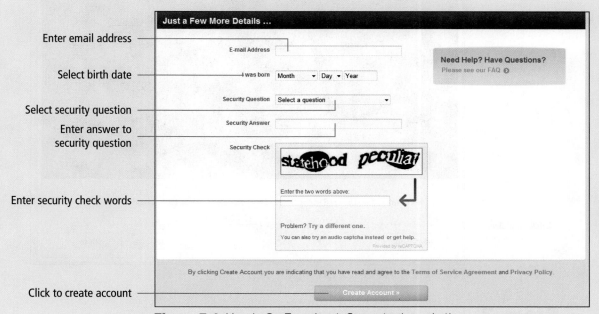

Enter email address

Select birth date

Select security question

Enter answer to security question

Enter security check words

Click to create account

Figure 7.4 Hands-On Exercise 1, Steps 1g through 1k.

Step 2 Get Started with Second Life

Refer to Figure 7.5 as you complete Step 2.

After you create your Second Life account, you should receive a confirmation email to the address you provided. When you click the link in this email to confirm your new account, Second Life will begin to automatically download and install the Second Life viewer. This software is necessary to display and access Second Life's 3D environment on your computer. If prompted to confirm the installation, click Yes.

a. When the *File Download* dialog box appears, click the **Run** button.

b. When the *Second Life Setup* dialog box appears, click the **Install** button.

The Second Life viewer is now downloaded and installed on your computer, and automatically launched.

Click to install ———

Figure 7.5 Hands-On Exercise 1, Step 2.

Step 3   Log into Second Life

Refer to Figure 7.6 as you complete Step 3.

Second Life does not run within your web browser. Instead, it uses a separate program, called the Second Life Viewer, which you downloaded and installed as part of the sign up process.

To access Second Life, your computer first needs to be connected to the Internet. You can then launch the Second Life Viewer program from the Windows *Start* menu or the Mac *Dock*. Once you've launched the Second Life Viewer and connected to the Second Life site, you will see the Second Life log in screen.

> **Alert**   **Terms of Service**
>
> When you log into Second Life the first time, you will be prompted to read and agree to the terms of service. Check the **I Agree to the Terms of Service and Privacy Policy** option. Then click the **Continue** button.

a. Enter your character's chosen name into the *Username* box.

b. Enter your password into the *Password* box.

By default, your avatar will return to its last location in the virtual world. On subsequent visits, you can launch your avatar into a different location by pulling down the *Start at* list and selecting another location you've recently visited.

c. Click the **Log In** button.

Figure 7.6 Hands-On Exercise 1, Step 3.

Click to change location
Click to log in
Enter password
Enter character's name

Objective 3

Personalize and Control Your Avatar

How do you access commands in Second Life?

There are many ways to access commands in the Second Life Viewer (Figure 7.7). There is a standard menu bar across the top of the screen, a series of avatar-specific

Menu bar

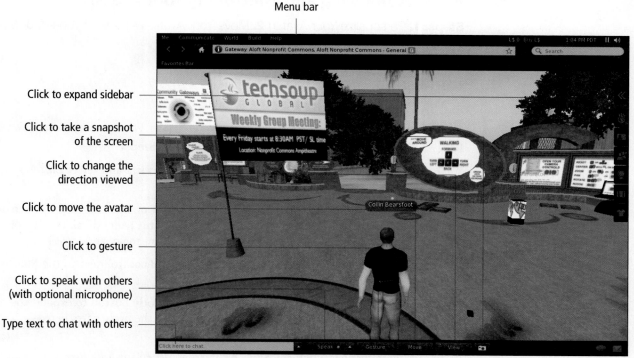

Click to expand sidebar
Click to take a snapshot of the screen
Click to change the direction viewed
Click to move the avatar
Click to gesture
Click to speak with others (with optional microphone)
Type text to chat with others

Figure 7.7 The Second Life Viewer screen.

buttons and controls along the bottom of the screen, and a sidebar on the right side of the screen. To expand the sidebar, click the left arrow pane; to hide the sidebar commands, click the right arrow pane.

Can you change the appearance of your avatar?

The initial avatar that you create when you sign up for Second Life is somewhat generic, and identical to avatars created by thousands of other new users. Fortunately, Second Life lets you customize all aspects of your avatar's appearance, from its gender and skin color to its facial features and clothing.

How do you control your avatar?

You can move your avatar throughout the virtual world using either your computer keyboard or your mouse.

Using the mouse is somewhat intuitive; click the avatar and drag your mouse in the direction you want it to face—left, right, up, or down. You then move the avatar by clicking the **Move** button at the bottom of the screen and selecting the desired direction and speed.

To use the keyboard, press the Left or Right Arrow keys to turn the avatar in those directions. Press the Up Arrow key to move the avatar forward; press the Down Arrow key to move the avatar backward.

How can your avatar express emotions?

Gesture In Second Life, a brief movement of the avatar to express some sort of emotion or feeling.

Your avatar can express emotions through the use of *gestures*. For example, you can instruct your avatar to clap its hands, stretch, shrug, laugh, or dance. Click the Gesture button at the bottom of the screen to select a gesture.

Hands-On Exercises

2 | Personalizing and Controlling Your Avatar

Steps: 1. Personalize Your Avatar; **2.** Move Your Avatar with the Keyboard; **3.** Move Your Avatar with the Move Panel **4.** Gesture

Use Figures 7.8 through 7.13 as a guide in the exercise.

Step 1 Personalize Your Avatar

Refer to Figures 7.8 through 7.10 as you complete Step 1.

a. To change your avatar's body type, right-click your avatar and select *Edit My Shape*.

The screen will change to display your current avatar on one side of the screen and the *My Appearance/Editing Shape* pane on the other. This panel displays a list of body parts—body, head, eyes, ears, nose, mouth, chin, torso, and legs.

b. To change the gender of your avatar, check the round control next to the Male or Female icons near the top of the pane.

c. To change the look of your avatar's body, click the **Body** button to expand the *Body* section of the pane. Make selections for each of the body parts listed— Height, Body Thickness, and Body Fat.

d. To save your changes, click the **Save As** button. When the *Save item to my inventory as* box appears, enter a name for your new shape; then click OK.

Click to change gender

Click to edit body parts

Avatar

Select body part to edit

Click to save changes

Figure 7.8 Hands-On Exercise 2, Steps 1b through 1d.

e. To change outfits, right-click your avatar and select **Change Outfit**.

The *My Appearance* pane will appear, with your current outfit displayed.

f. Select an outfit from the list; then click the **Save As** button. When the *Save what I'm wearing as a new Outfit* box appears, enter a name for your new outfit; then click **OK**.

Click to change outfit

Avatar

Click to save changes

Figure 7.9 Hands-On Exercise 2, Step 1f.

g. To edit the components of your outfit, right-click your avatar and select **Edit Outfit**.

The *My Appearance/Edit Outfit* pane will appear.

h. Click the tool button next to a given item of apparel and then select the desired attributes for that item.

i. To save your changes, click the **Save As** button. When the *Save item to my inventory as* box appears, enter a name for your new wardrobe; then click **OK**.

Avatar

Click to change fabric

Click to change color

Click to edit item of clothing

Click to edit clothing attribute

Click to save changes

Figure 7.10 Hands-On Exercise 2, Steps 1h through 1i.

Step 2 Move Your Avatar with the Keyboard

Refer to Figure 7.11 as you complete Step 2.

Your avatar appears at the bottom of the Second Life screen, always facing forward. You can use the arrow keys on your computer keyboard to turn and move the avatar.

a. Press the **right arrow key** to turn the avatar to the right.

b. Press the **left arrow key** to turn the avatar to the left.

c. Press and hold the **up arrow key** to move the avatar forward; release the key to stop moving.

d. Press and hold the **down arrow key** to move the avatar backward; release the key to stop moving.

Avatar facing forward

Figure 7.11 Hands-On Exercise 2, Step 2.

Step 3 Move Your Avatar with the Move Panel

Refer to Figure 7.12 as you complete Step 3.

A greater range of movement is possible by using your mouse to click the Move button at the bottom of the Second Life screen.

a. Click the **Move** button to display the move panel.

b. Click the **right** or **left arrows** to turn your avatar right or left.

c. Click and hold the **up arrow** to move your avatar forward; release the mouse button to stop moving.

d. Click and hold the **down arrow** to move your avatar backward; release the mouse button to stop moving.

By default, your avatar walks. You can also have your avatar run or fly.

e. Click the **running mode** button and then click the **up arrow** to run forward.

f. Click the **flying mode** button and then click the **up arrow** to fly forward.

 Note **Flying Mode**

Flying mode has different controls than walking or running mode. In addition to the normal forward, backward, left, and right arrows, there are Fly Up and Fly Down arrows to fly your avatar upwards or downwards.

g. Click the **walking mode** button to return to walking speed.

Move forward
Turn left
Click to walk
Click to run

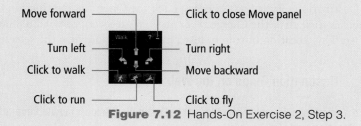

Click to close Move panel
Turn right
Move backward
Click to fly

Figure 7.12 Hands-On Exercise 2, Step 3.

Step 4 Gesture

Refer to Figure 7.13 as you complete Step 4.

Within Second Life, you can use gestures to have your avatar express emotions.

a. Click the **Gesture** button at the bottom of the screen. Then click **View All**.

The pop-up menu will display a short list of recently used gestures. A full list of gestures is available from the *GESTURES* panel.

b. When the *GESTURES* panel appears, double-click the gesture you want your avatar to make.

Click to close panel

Double-click to make the gesture

Click to open Gestures panel

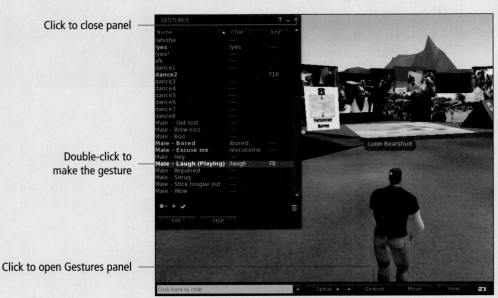

Figure 7.13 Hands-On Exercise 2, Step 4.

Objective 4

Navigate the Virtual World

What is the grid?

Grid The virtual world in Second Life.

The virtual world in Second Life is called the *grid*. The grid is divided into multiple regions. Some regions are public spaces, while others are private *islands* purchased by other users.

Island A private region in Second Life.

Where can you find out about the locations in Second Life?

Destination Guide A directory of the most popular locations in Second Life.

Second Life offers a *Destination Guide* that organizes its most popular locations into categories (Figure 7.14). From within Second Life, expand the sidebar and click the Home tab. When the Home panel opens, click the Destination Guide button. When the Destination Guide pane appears, click the Open the Destination Guide button. You can then click the Category list to view all locations within a category, or click the Visit This Location button to learn more about and view the selected location.

 Destination Guide on the Web

Second Life also offers a web-based version of the Destination Guide, at **www.secondlife.com/whatis/destinationguide/**.

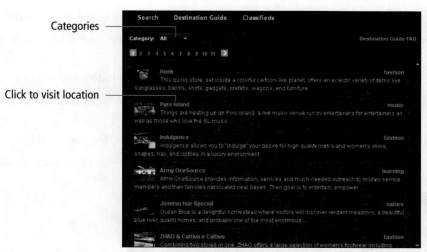

Categories

Click to visit location

Figure 7.14 The Second Life Destination Guide.

How do you move to another location?

The entire grid can be viewed from the overall Second Life map, which is accessible from the World menu; mini-maps can be displayed for smaller regions. Your avatar can *teleport* to any location by simply double-clicking that point on the map. You can also teleport directly to another location by searching for the location by name.

Teleport A means to rapidly move from one location to another in the Second Life world.

 Note | **Local Movement**

You can also walk, run, or fly to any location, but this is practical only for travel within a small region. Teleporting is the best way to travel long distances in Second Life.

Can you save locations you've visited?

Landmark A saved location in Second Life.

You can save any location you visit as a *landmark*. Your landmarks are listed in your My Landmarks list; double-click any listed landmark to return to that location.

Hands-On Exercises

3 | Navigating the Virtual World

Steps: 1. Teleport to Different Regions; **2.** Search for and Go to a Location; **3.** Create a Landmark; **4.** Return to a Landmark.

Use Figures 7.15 through 7.18 as a guide in the exercise.

 Step 1 **Teleport to Different Regions**

Refer to Figure 7.15 as you complete Step 1.

a. Click **World** on the menu bar and then click **World Map**.

Second Life will display a map of the entire virtual world, with a legend to map elements at the top right.

The *Zoom* slider at the bottom right allows you to zoom into or out of the map.

b. Move the *Zoom* slider to the left to zoom out; move the *Zoom* slider to the right to zoom in.

As you zoom into the map, you will see the names of individual regions.

c. To navigate to a specific region, enter the name of the location into the *Regions by Name* box and click the **Find** button.

d. To teleport to a specific location on the map, double-click that location.

Alternately, you can click the location and then click the **Teleport** button.

Double-click to
teleport to location

Regions by Name:
Enter the desired region

Click to locate region

Click to teleport

Move the slider to
zoom in or out

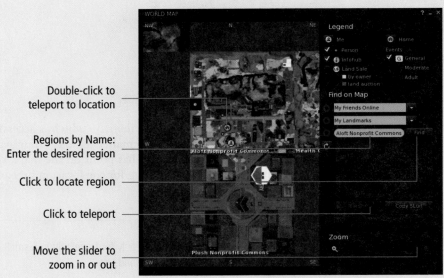

Figure 7.15 Hands-On Exercise 3, Step 1.

Step 2 Search for and Go to a Location

Refer to Figure 7.16 as you complete Step 2.

If you know the full or partial name of a location you want to visit, you may, for example, study the *Destination Guide* and search for and teleport directly to that location.

a. Type the name of the location into the search box in the upper right corner of the window and press Enter.

For example, to search for ISTE Island, enter "ISTE" into the search box. The location should appear in the search results (Find) panel. Note that some locations have more than one entry.

b. Click the name of the location to expand its entry.

c. Click the **Teleport** button to go directly to that location.

Enter name
of location

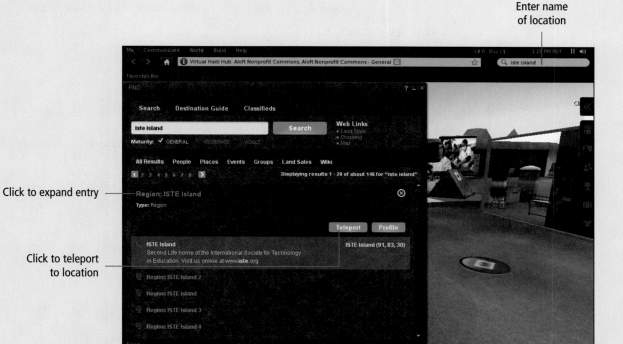

Click to expand entry

Click to teleport
to location

Figure 7.16 Hands-On Exercise 3, Step 2.

Step 3 **Create a Landmark**

Refer to Figure 7.17 as you complete Step 3.

You can create a landmark, like a bookmark, for any location you visit, and then return to that landmark at a future time.

a. Click **World** on the menu bar and then click **Landmark This Place**.

b. When the *Create Landmark* panel appears, accept the displayed name or enter a new name for this landmark into the *Title* box.

Enter landmark title

Enter description

Click to save

Figure 7.17 Hands-On Exercise 3, Step 3.

c. Enter an optional description of the landmark into the *My notes* box.

d. Click the **Save** button.

Step 4 — Return to a Landmark

Refer to Figure 7.18 as you complete Step 4.

a. Click **Places** on the sidebar.

   Second Life will display the *Places* panel. Your landmarks are listed here.

b. Click to expand the **MY LANDMARKS** item.

c. Double-click a landmark to teleport to that location.

Click to expand your landmarks

Click to display Places panel

Double-click to teleport to landmark

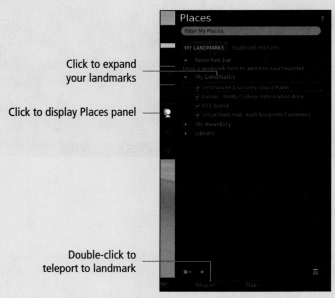

Figure 7.18 Hands-On Exercise 3, Step 4.

Objective 5

Networking with Others in Second Life

How can you communicate with other users?

Residents The other players in Second Life.

The people you meet within Second Life are called *residents*. You can socialize with other residents both publicly (through chats) or privately (through instant messaging).

What is the difference between a chat and an instant message?

In Second Life, a chat is a public conversation with any nearby resident or group of residents; anyone near you can take part in the chat. An instant message is a private message exchanged between two residents. Unlike with chats, residents do not have to be in proximity to each other in order to send and receive instant messages.

Does Second Life support voice chat?

If your computer is equipped with a microphone and speaker, you can speak your conversations instead of typing them, via voice chat. Voice chat is available for both chats and instant messages.

Does Second Life support friends lists?

As with most social networks, you can create lists of your friends in Second Life. You can then find and teleport directly to online friends, or communicate with them via instant message.

How can I share my Second Life activities with others?

Second Life lets you take a snapshot of any screen and email that snapshot to friends or colleagues. To save the current screen, click the snapshot button (looks like a camera) at the bottom of the screen. Then follow the onscreen directions to send the snapshot as an email.

What other social networking features does Second Life support?

One of the primary means of social networking in Second Life is via the groups feature. You can search for and join any number of topic-oriented groups, or create your own groups. Most groups are public and free to join, but Second Life also supports private and paid groups. Paid groups require Linden dollars to join.

 Creating a Group

It costs 100 Linden Dollars to create a new group. Groups with fewer than two members are deleted.

Hands-On Exercises

4 | Networking with Others

Steps: 1. Find Nearby People; **2.** Chat with Others; **3.** Add a Friend; **4.** Instant Message a Friend; **5.** Find and Join a Group; **6.** Visit Your Groups; **7.** Take and Email a Snapshot

Use Figures 7.19 through 7.31 as a guide in the exercise.

 Step 1 **Find Nearby People**

Refer to Figures 7.19 and 7.20 as you complete Step 1.

a. Click **Communicate** on the menu bar; then click **Nearby People**.

Second Life will display the *People* pane, which lists nearby residents. If there are no residents listed, move your avatar to a more populated area.

b. Point to a person's name and click the right arrow to display that person's profile pane.

Click to display profile

Figure 7.19 Hands-On Exercise 4, Steps 1a and 1b.

c. From the profile pane, click the **Add Friend** button to add this person to your friends list.

d. Click the **IM** button to send this person a private message.

e. To offer to teleport this person to your location, click the **Teleport** button.

Click to teleport this person to your location

Click to instant message

Click to add as friend

Figure 7.20 Hands-On Exercise 4, Steps 1c through 1e.

Step 2 Chat with Others

Refer to Figure 7.21 as you complete Step 1.

In the Second Life world, you can chat (through your avatar) with anyone close to you.

a. Type your text message into the chat box at the bottom of the screen.

b. Press Enter.

Your message will appear above the chat box, along with any replies from other users.

Ongoing chat ——

Enter text message ——

Figure 7.21 Hands-On Exercise 4, Step 2.

Step ③ Add a Friend

Refer to Figures 7.22 and 7.23 as you complete Step 3.

You can easily invite anyone near you to be your friend in Second Life.

a. Right-click a resident's avatar to display a pop-up menu.

b. Click **Add Friend**.

Click to add as friend ——

Right-click to
display pop-up menu ——

Figure 7.22 Hands-On Exercise 4, Steps 3a and 3b.

c. When the offer friendship dialog box appears, accept or edit the invitation message.

d. Click **OK** to send the invitation.

The other person must accept your invitation in order for you to be friends.

Edit invitation message ——

Click to send friend invitation ——

Figure 7.23 Hands-On Exercise 4, Steps 3c and 3d.

Step ④ Instant Message a Friend

Refer to Figures 7.24 and 7.25 as you complete Step 4.

a. Click **Communicate** on the menu bar; then click **My Friends**.

Second Life will display the *People* pane, with the **MY FRIENDS** tab selected.

b. Click the friend you want to talk to.

c. Click the **IM** button.

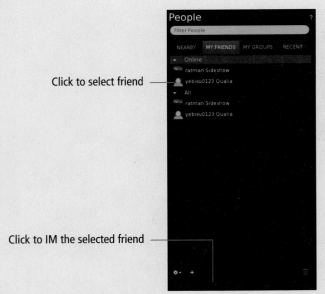

Click to select friend

Click to IM the selected friend

Figure 7.24 Hands-On Exercise 4, Steps 4a through 4c.

Second Life will display the chat panel for your friend.

d. Type your message into the text box; then press Enter.

Your ongoing conversation will appear in the chat panel.

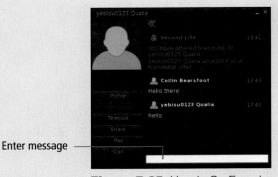

Enter message

Figure 7.25 Hands-On Exercise 4, Step 4d.

 Note **Offline Messages**

If you send an instant message to a resident who is not currently in the Second Life world, that message will be sent to that person via email instead.

Step 5 Find and Join a Group

Refer to Figures 7.26 through 7.27 as you complete Step 5.

a. Type a short description of the group or topic into the search box at the top right of the Second Life window. Then press Enter.

b. When the search results appear, click the **Groups** tab to display matching groups.

c. Click a group to expand its entry.

Enter search query

Click to display
matching groups

Click to select group

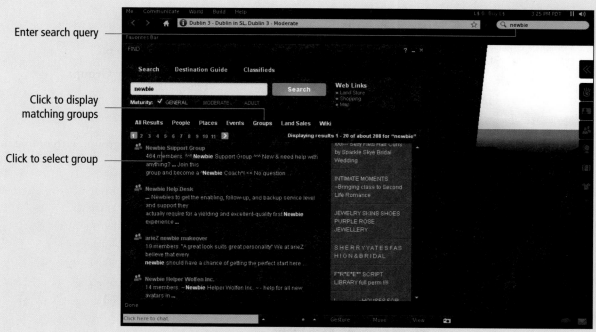

Figure 7.26 Hands-On Exercise 4, Steps 5a through 5c.

d. Click the **Profile** button to display more information about that group in the *People* panel.

e. Click the **Join Now!** button to join the group.

> **Note** **Public and Private Groups**
>
> Only groups that are open to the general public display the Join Now! button. Groups that don't have this option are private groups accessible via invitation only.

Click to join group

Click to display
more information

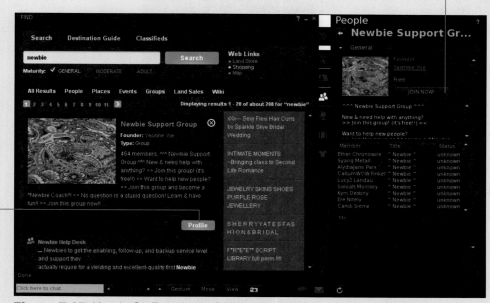

Figure 7.27 Hands-On Exercise 4, Steps 5d and 5e.

Step 6 Visit Your Groups

Refer to Figures 7.28 and 7.29 as you complete Step 6.

a. Click **Communicate** on the menu bar; then click **My Groups**.

Your groups will be displayed in the *People* panel.

b. Double-click the group you want to visit.

Second Life will display a chat panel for the selected group, with online members listed.

Double-click to visit group

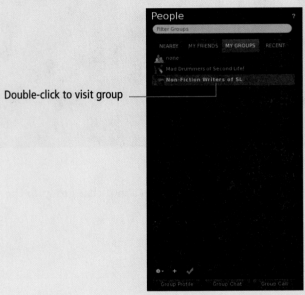

Figure 7.28 Hands-On Exercise 4, Steps 6a and 6b.

c. To chat with members of the group, enter your message into the text box and press Enter.

Online members

Enter message

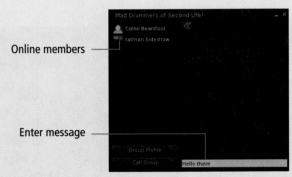

Figure 7.29 Hands-On Exercise 4, Step 6c.

Step 7 Take and Email a Snapshot

Refer to Figures 7.30 and 7.31 as you complete Step 7.

Second Life lets you take a snapshot of any screen and email that snapshot to friends or family.

a. Click the **Snapshot** button at the bottom of the current screen.

b. When the SNAPSHOT PREVIEW panel appears, check the **Email** option.

c. Click the **Send** button.

Snapshot Preview panel ——

Click to select email option ——

Click to send email ——

Click to take snapshot ——

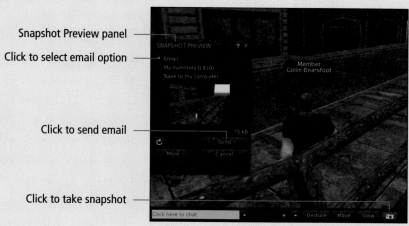

Figure 7.30 Hands-On Exercise 4, Steps 7a through 7c.

d. When the EMAIL SNAPSHOT panel appears, type the recipient's email address into the *Recipient's Email* box.

e. Confirm or retype your name into the *Your Name* box.

f. Type a subject for this email into the *Subject* box.

g. Type an accompanying message into the *Message* box.

h. Click the **Send** button.

Enter recipient's email address ——

Confirm or retype your name ——

Enter email subject ——

Enter accompanying message ——

Click to send ——

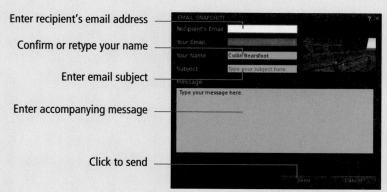

Figure 7.31 Hands-On Exercise 4, Steps 7d through 7h.

Summary

In this chapter you learned how virtual worlds work, and how to sign up for Second Life, one of the largest virtual worlds. You learned how to personalize and control your avatar, navigate the Second Life world, and network with others within Second Life.

Key Terms

Multiple Choice Questions

1. Which of the following is *not* a virtual world?

   (a) Facebook

   (b) Second Life

   (c) City of Heroes

   (d) Onverse

2. Which of the following is *not* a type of online game?

   (a) MUD

   (b) MADD

   (c) MMPORG

   (d) MMORLG

3. Many virtual worlds let you do the following:

   (a) Talk to other users

   (b) Play games

   (c) Shop for virtual merchandise

   (d) All of the above

4. Which of the following is *not* a necessary characteristic of an online world?

   (a) Graphical user interface

   (b) Community

   (c) Voice chat

   (d) Persistence

5. Which of the following features of your avatar can you customize?

   (a) Gender

   (b) Body type

   (c) Clothing

   (d) All of the above

6. Which of the following is *not* a way to move your avatar?

   (a) Run

   (b) Walk

(c) Crawl

(d) Fly

7. You use Second Life's virtual currency to purchase the following:

(a) Land

(b) Insurance

(c) Technical support

(d) All of the above

8. You access Second Life using:

(a) your web browser.

(b) your mobile phone.

(c) the Second Life Viewer.

(d) all of the above.

9. Users aged 13 to 17 can access a special version of Second Life called:

(a) Second Life for Kids.

(b) Teen Second Life.

(c) L'il Second Life

(d) Second Life Jr.

10. You can explore the most popular locations in Second Life by using the:

(a) Virtual Directory.

(b) Second Life Landowner's Handbook.

(c) 3D Atlas.

(d) Destination Guide.

Fill in the Blank

Write the correct word in the space provided.

1. A(n) _____ is a fellow user of Second Life.

2. Second Life's virtual world is called the _____.

3. The virtual currency in Second Life is called _____.

4. To rapidly move from one location to another in Second Life, you _____,

5. To express emotion, use a(n) _____.

Practice Exercises

1. **Join Second Life**

   Before you can explore Second Life, you have to create a new account.

   (a) Create a new Second Life account.

   (b) Give your avatar a unique name.

   (c) When you sign into Second Life at the end of the sign up process, take a snapshot of the screen and email it to your instructor.

2. **Personalize Your Avatar**

   You can customize just about everything about your avatar, from gender to hairstyle to clothing.

   (a) Right-click your avatar and make a selection to start the personalization process.

   (b) Take a snapshot of this initial avatar and email it to your instructor, with "Original Avatar" as your subject line.

(c) Work through the personalization process, changing your avatar's body and clothing.

(d) Take a snapshot of your final, personalized avatar and email it to your instructor, with "New Avatar" as your subject line.

3. **Explore Discovery Island**

Discovery Island is a popular location for learning about Second Life. It features a variety of interactive experiences that introduce you to the many features of the virtual world.

(a) Search for and teleport to Discovery Island.

(b) Walk through the world and watch the educational videos you find. (Videos are displayed on large screens throughout the island; click the Play arrow to view a video.)

(c) Take a snapshot of one of the videos playing and email it to your instructor.

4. **Find a Group.**

One of the best ways to interact with other users in Second Life is to join a group that revolves around a topic you find interesting.

(a) Search for and find a group related to a topic of interest.

(b) Email your instructor with the name of the group you just joined.

Critical Thinking

1. A virtual world such as Second Life offers many social networking features. Write a short paper comparing and contrasting the social networking features of Second Life with those of Facebook. Which of the two environments is best for which activities?

2. Hundreds of colleges and universities have established a presence on Second Life. Write a short paper discussing how the Second Life environment can be used for education. As research, find and visit one of these virtual schools, and discuss in the paper what you find. (And, if your school has a Second Life presence, present your comments on it.)

Team Projects

1. ISTE Island is the Second Life home of the International Society for Technology in Education. At a prearranged time, have all the members of your team congregate on ISTE Island. (Hint: You'll probably find yourself behind the main building; you'll have to walk around the building to get inside.) Go to the main building and find your way to the ISTE Island Teleport wall (just to the right of the Welcome Desk). Then double-click on the monitor for Discussion Skypark to teleport there. Start a chat with your team members, take a snapshot of all your avatars together, and email the snapshot to your instructor.

2. Make sure that all the members of your team are friends on Second Life. Now it's time for a game of "follow me." The first member should navigate to a location anywhere on the grid, landmark that location, and then teleport the second member of the team to that location. The second member should then navigate to a new location, landmark that location, and teleport the third member of the team to that location. This should continue until the final member of the team has been teleported to a location; the final member should then teleport the first member to this final location. The team should then write down the locations visited, in order, and submit this list to the instructor.

Credits

CHAPTER 8

Using Other Social Media

Objectives

After you read this chapter you will be able to:

1. Use Social Bookmarking Services
2. Share Photos with Flickr
3. Share Videos with YouTube
4. Microblog with Google Buzz
5. Create Your Own Social Network with Ning
6. Explore Other Social Media

The following Hands-On Exercises will help you accomplish the chapter objectives:

Hands-On Exercises

EXERCISES	SKILLS COVERED
1. Social Bookmarking with Digg	**Step 1:** Submit a New Web Page **Step 2:** Browse for Top-Rated Bookmarks **Step 3:** Search for Pages or Stories
2. Uploading and Sharing Photos with Flickr	**Step 1:** Upload a Digital Photo **Step 2:** Share a Digital Photo **Step 3:** Search for Photos **Step 4:** Join a Group
3. Uploading and Sharing Videos with YouTube	**Step 1:** Upload a Video File **Step 2:** Upload a Webcam Video **Step 3:** Find and View a YouTube Video **Step 4:** Share a YouTube Video
4. Using Google Buzz	**Step 1:** Find People to Follow **Step 2:** View Friends' Posts **Step 3:** Make a Post

Objective 1

Use Social Bookmarking Services

What is social bookmarking?

Social bookmarking is a method for sharing favorite web pages, websites, online articles, videos, and the like with friends and colleagues through dedicated social networking services. Instead of sharing an entire item, a user bookmarks the page on which the item appears and then sends that bookmark to interested parties. Bookmarks from all users are typically organized on the main site of the social bookmarking service, where other people can use those bookmarks to find items of interest.

How are bookmarks tagged?

Most social bookmarking services let users add descriptions to their bookmarks. These bookmarks often include tags or keywords, specific words that describe the content of the bookmarked page. Other users can then search the social bookmarking site by keyword to find bookmarks of interest.

 Social news

Social bookmarking sites are sometimes called social news sites, as news articles tend to be among the most bookmarked and shared items.

How did social bookmarking develop?

Today's social bookmarking services build on the concept of shared online bookmarks, which was first introduced in 1996. The itList website enabled users to create a web-based version of traditional web browser bookmarks, and thus access bookmarked sites from any web browser running on any computer. Over the next several years other online bookmarking services were launched, including Backflip, Blink, and HotLinks.

While these early bookmarking services failed to survive the so-called dot-com implosion of 2000/2001, newer, more fully featured online bookmarking services soon followed. StumbleUpon was launched in 2001 as the first true social bookmarking service, enabling users to share their bookmarks and "stumble upon" interesting web content. Delicious (then known as del.icio.us), launched in 2003, introduced the concept of tagged bookmarks, making it easier for others to find specific content. Other social bookmarking services soon followed, including CiteULike and Digg in 2004, reddit and ShareThis in 2005, and AddThis in 2006.

How does social bookmarking work?

With most social bookmarking services, a user clicks a button for that service on a given web page or on a toolbar installed in the user's web browser. Clicking the button saves a bookmark or reference to that page on the social bookmarking site. Bookmarks are typically saved in a user's personal folder on the bookmarking site, but are also made public for other users to reference from the site.

How does one find bookmarks on a social bookmarking site?

Bookmarks are typically tagged with descriptive keywords. Users can search the social bookmarking site by keyword; the site then displays all bookmarks that match the keyword *query*.

In addition, some social bookmarking sites organize their bookmarks by category, such as technology or entertainment, enabling users to browse bookmarks in this fashion. These sites often offer web feeds for their lists of bookmarks, which enable users to subscribe to particular lists and be automatically notified of new bookmarks as they're added.

What are the most popular social bookmarking services?

While there are dozens of active social bookmarking services, including those from Google (Google Bookmarks) and Yahoo! (Yahoo! Buzz), the following are the most popular among U.S. users:

- Digg (www.digg.com). Digg is, by most accounts, the largest and most popular social bookmarking site (Figure 8.1). In addition to bookmarking, tagging, and sharing functions, Digg lets users vote on the popularity of bookmarked items by "digging" (voting up) or "burying" (voting down) an item. The most popular (most "dugg") items appear on the home page of the Digg website. Digg share buttons appear on many news sites, making it easier to bookmark stories on Digg.

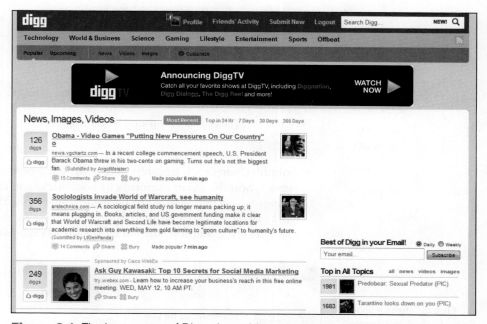

Figure 8.1 The home page of Digg, the web's most popular social bookmarking service.

> **Note**   **Comparing Your Screen with the Figures in This Book**
>
> Since social media sites are constantly updating their feature sets, the pages you see on your own computer might not always match those displayed in this book.

- reddit (www.reddit.com). Like Digg, reddit includes "up" and "down" voting on bookmarks, as well as discussion areas where users can discuss shared items. Sections of the site known as "reddits" focus on specific topics (Figure 8.2).

Figure 8.2 The reddit home page.

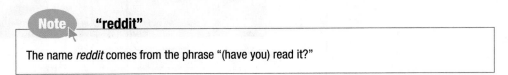

> **Note** **"reddit"**
>
> The name *reddit* comes from the phrase "(have you) read it?"

- StumbleUpon (www.stumbleupon.com). The first true social bookmarking service, StumbleUpon augments its bookmarks and thumbs-up, thumbs-down ratings with a personalized recommendation engine that suggests web pages to visit based on a user's ratings of previous pages. To view a list of suggested pages, users click the Stumble! button on the site's home page or toolbar (Figure 8.3).

Click to "stumble upon" new content

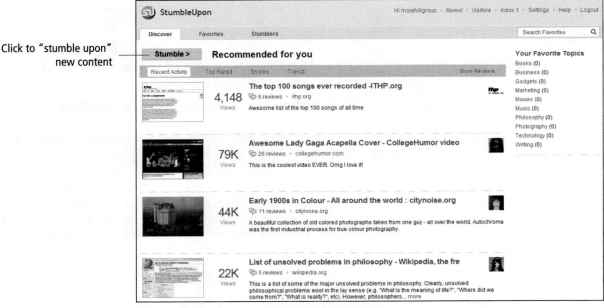

Figure 8.3 The StumbleUpon home page.

- Delicious (www.delicious.com). Unlike some other social networking services, Delicious makes all its bookmarks public by default. Delicious features a hotlist of the most popular bookmarked pages and articles on its home page, and offers RSS feeds of bookmarks by tag (Figure 8.4).

Figure 8.4 The Delicious home page.

 RSS Feeds

Most blogs, news-oriented websites, and some social bookmarking services offer feeds of their newest content, which are then fed to newsreader applications and websites. These feeds, in either RSS or Atom formats (they are similar), help interested users keep up to date with the latest postings.

 Social Bookmark Ownership

Digg is a private company. Reddit is owned by Conde Nast Digital, the company behind *Conde Nast* and *Wired* magazines. StumbleUpon, originally a private company, was acquired by eBay in 2007 but was then reacquired by a group of its original investors in 2009. Delicious, also originally a private company, was acquired by Yahoo! in 2005.

Hands-On Exercises

1 | Social Bookmarking with Digg

Steps: 1. Submit a New Web Page; **2.** Browse for Top-Rated Bookmarks; **3.** Search for Pages or Stories.

Use Figures 8.5 through 8.11 as a guide in the exercise.

Step 1 Submit a New Web Page

Refer to Figures 8.5 through 8.8 as you complete Step 1.

Digg is the most popular social bookmarking service; it works in much the same fashion as other similar sites. When you find a web page or article you'd like to share, you can submit the page to the Digg site with a few clicks of your mouse.

Before you use Digg, you must sign up for an account, which is free. You do so by navigating to www.digg.com, clicking Join Digg at the top of the page, and then creating a username and password. You can then return to the Digg home page and click Login to sign into your account.

> **Note** **Digging**
>
> When you submit or approve of a page or article, you are said to "digg" that page. The more people who approve of that page, the more it is "dugg," that is, the higher the Digg rating.

a. Use your web browser to navigate to a web page or an article you want to share.

b. If the page includes a **Digg** button, click that button.

You may need to click a **Share** link or button on the page in order to display the Digg button. If prompted to choose a topic, do so.

Click to Digg ————

Figure 8.5 Hands-On Exercise 1, Steps 1a and 1b.

> **Note** **Finding Digg**
>
> While not all websites have Digg functionality, most news-oriented websites should offer this feature.

If the page does not display a Digg button, proceed to Step d.

c. When the Submit to Digg page appears, select a category from the *Choose a topic* list and then click the **Digg it** button.

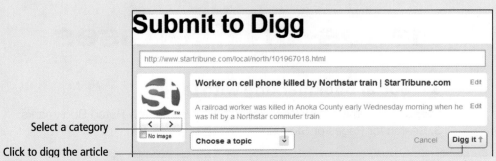

Figure 8.6 Hands-On Exercise 1, Step 1c.

d. If the page does not include a **Digg** button, click the **View on Digg** button in your browser's Favorites or Bookmarks bar.

Click to Digg →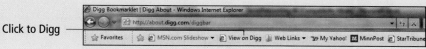

Figure 8.7 Hands-On Exercise 1, Step 1d.

If the page has not yet been submitted to Digg, you will see the Submit a New Link page. (If you clicked the **View as Digg** button in your browser, you may first see a Whoa! We couldn't find that URL on Digg page. Click the **Submit this URL now** link to display the Submit a New Link page.)

e. When the Submit a New Link page appears, accept or edit the Title of the page or article.

f. Accept or edit the Description of the page or article.

g. If the page displays a *Choose Thumbnail* section, select a thumbnail image to accompany your bookmark, or click **No Thumbnail** to include the bookmark without an image.

h. In the *Choose a Topic* section, click a category that best describes the bookmarked page or article.

i. In the *Are You Human?* section, enter the captcha text.

j. Click the **Submit Story** button.

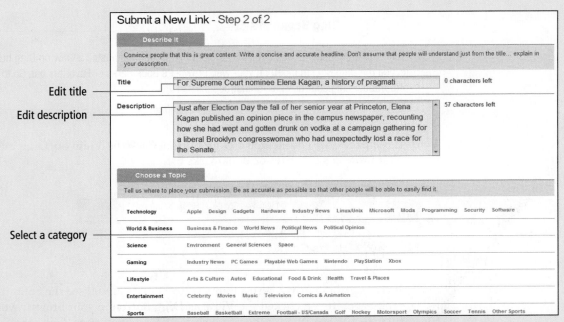

Figure 8.8 Hands-On Exercise 1, Steps 1e through 1h.

Step 2   Browse the Top-Rated Bookmarks

Refer to Figure 8.9 as you complete Step 2.

By default, the Digg home page displays the most recently "dugg" web pages and articles. You can also display the top-rated bookmarks.

a. Use your web browser to navigate to www.digg.com and log into your account.

b. Click the **Top News** tab.

c. To display the top-rated bookmarks for the past 24 hours, click **Top in 24 Hours** link above the story list.

> **Tip** ⭐ **Time Periods and Categories**
>
> To display the top-rated stories for the past 7 days or 30 days, click the appropriate links above the story list. You can also browse by topic by clicking the topic links along the left side of the Digg home page.

d. Click the title of a story to go to that web page.

Click to display top stories
in the past 24 hours

Click to view web page

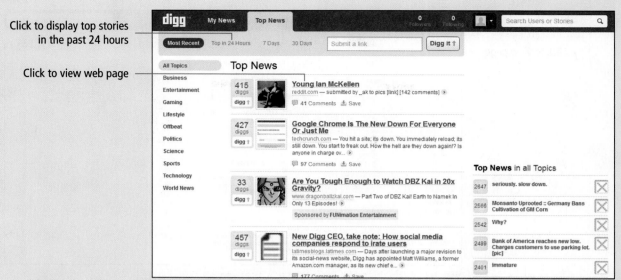

Figure 8.9 Hands-On Exercise 1, Step 2.

Step ③ Search for Pages or Stories

Refer to Figures 8.10 through 8.11 as you complete Step 3.

In addition to browsing by popularity or category, you can also search Digg for pages and stories about a particular topic.

a. Use your web browser to navigate to www.digg.com.

b. Enter one or more keywords into the *Search Users or Stories* box that describe the web page or article you're looking for. Then click the magnifying glass icon (the search button) or press your keyboard's Enter key.

Enter query

Click to search

Figure 8.10 Hands-On Exercise 1, Steps 3a and 3b.

c. When the search results page appears, click the title of a story to go to that web page.

 Tip **Comments and Sharing**

To view comments on a story by other Digg users, click the **Comments** link beneath the story summary. To share a story with a friend, click the right arrow icon to display the full story page. Then click the Email icon.

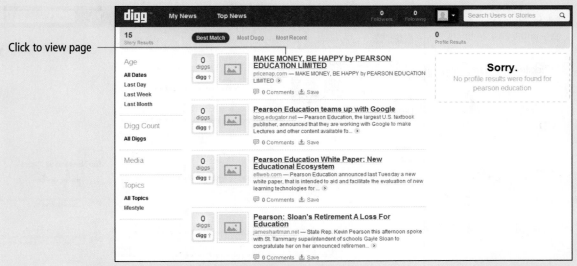

Click to view page

Figure 8.11 Hands-On Exercise 1, Step 3c.

Objective 2

Share Photos with Flickr

What is online photo-sharing?

Online photo-sharing enables you to upload your digital photos and let friends and family view those photos in their own web browsers. Most photo-sharing websites are free to use, thus providing both free file hosting and viewing. Photos are typically organized into virtual photo albums; you can usually specify who can view specific albums.

What other services are offered by photo-sharing sites?

Since most photo-sharing sites do not charge for file hosting, they make money by selling other photo-related services. Many of these sites, such as Shutterfly and Snapfish, are actually photo processing companies in disguise, and make their money by selling photo prints, photo calendars, photo greeting cards, and the like. Other photo-sharing sites, such as Flickr, offer fewer print services and instead generate income from selling subscriptions for advanced services.

In what ways is photo-sharing social networking?

Photo-sharing sites enable social networking via the sharing of uploaded digital photos. Communities are built not just around a particular user's photos, but also around specific topics or types of photos. For example, Flickr offers user-created groups for sharing and discussing photos of a specific type, such as still lifes or portraits, as well as user-selected *galleries* of photos from other users.

Gallery On Flickr, a collection of photographs of a given type or topic.

What are the top photo-sharing sites?

In addition to commercial sites such as Shutterfly and Snapfish, there are many free photo-sharing sites that present true social communities. The most popular of these sites include:

- Flickr (www.flickr.com). Owned by Yahoo!, Flickr is the largest photo-sharing community on the web, with more than 40 million users. Because of its large user base, Flickr offers the most opportunities for social networking. Basic membership is free, although paid memberships are available that let users store and

Photostream On Flickr, a feed of photos from a given user.

share a larger number of photos online. Flickr displays a user's *photostream* on its main page; you can then search for photos by keyword, or browse the most recent uploads.

- Fotki (www.fotki.com). Like Flickr, Fotki is a free photo-sharing community. You can easily search Fotki for photos by keyword, or for photos from a specific member.

- Photobucket (www.photobucket.com). Similar to Fotki and Flickr, Photobucket is a free photo-sharing community that lets you search for photos by keyword.

- Picasa Web Albums (picasaweb.google.com). Owned by Google, Picasa Web Albums is a less fully featured photo-sharing site. You can upload your photos into albums and specify who can view your albums. You can also perform simple keyword searches for photos from other users.

Before you can upload and share photos on any of these sites, you first have to establish a free membership.

Hands-On Exercises

2 | Uploading and Sharing Photos with Flickr

Steps: 1. Upload a Digital Photo; **2.** Share a Digital Photo; **3.** Search for Photos; **4.** Join a Group.

Use Figures 8.12 through 8.22 as a guide in the exercise.

Step 1 | Upload a Digital Photo

Refer to Figures 8.12 through 8.17 as you complete Step 1.

Flickr is the most popular and fully featured photo-sharing site, although it works in much the same fashion as other similar sites. As with all photo-sharing sites, you must first create an account, which is free, before you can upload and share photos.

a. Use your web browser to navigate to **www.flickr.com** and either create a new account or sign into your existing account.

b. Click the **Upload Photos & Video** link.

Figure 8.12 Hands-On Exercise 2, Steps 1a and 1b.

c. When the Upload to Flickr page appears, click the **Choose photos and videos** link.

Figure 8.13 Hands-On Exercise 2, Step 1c.

d. When the *Select file(s) to upload* window appears, navigate to and select the files you wish to upload; to upload multiple files, hold down the Ctrl key while selecting. Then click the **Open** button.

The Upload to Flickr page will list the photo(s) you've selected.

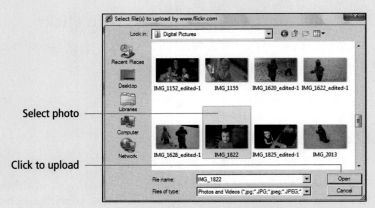

Figure 8.14 Hands-On Exercise 2, Step 1d.

e. To let all Flickr users see your photos, go to the Set privacy section and check *Public*. To hide your photos from public view, check the *Private* option. To show your photos only to friends, check the *Visible to Friends* option; to show your photos only to family members, check the *Visible to Family* option.

f. Click the **Upload Photos and Videos** button.

When the photos are uploaded, Flickr will ask if you want to add a description.

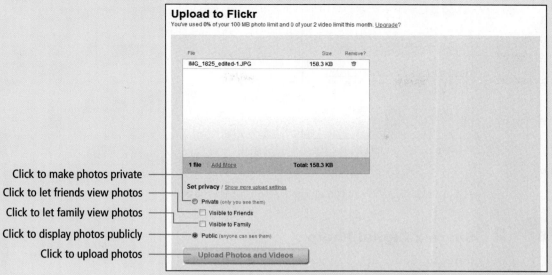

Upload to Flickr

You've used 0% of your 100 MB photo limit and 0 of your 2 video limit this month. Upgrade?

File	Size	Remove?
IMG_1825_edited-1.JPG	158.3 KB	🗑

1 file   Add More   Total: 158.3 KB

Set privacy / Show more upload settings

Click to make photos private ⟶ ⦿ Private (only you see them)
Click to let friends view photos ⟶ ☐ Visible to Friends
Click to let family view photos ⟶ ☐ Visible to Family
Click to display photos publicly ⟶ ⦿ Public (anyone can see them)
Click to upload photos ⟶ [Upload Photos and Videos]

Figure 8.15 Hands-On Exercise 2, Steps 1e and 1f.

g. Click the **add a description** link.

h. When the Describe this upload page appears, scroll to the Titles, descriptions, tags section for the first photo you uploaded. Enter a title for this photo into the *Title* box.

i. Enter a brief description of this photo into the *Description* box.

j. Enter one or more tags (keywords) that describe this photo into the *Tags* box.

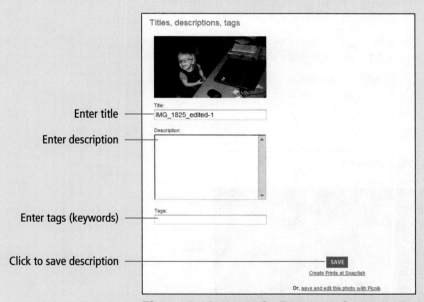

Titles, descriptions, tags

Title:
Enter title ⟶ IMG_1825_edited-1

Description:
Enter description ⟶

Tags:
Enter tags (keywords) ⟶

Click to save description ⟶ SAVE
Create Prints at Snapfish

Or, save and edit this photo with Picnik.

Figure 8.16 Hands-On Exercise 2, Steps 1h, 1i, 1j, and 1l.

Set Flickr's name for a digital photo album.

Flickr lets you organize your photos into *Sets,* which is its equivalent of photo albums.

k. Go to the *Add to a Set* panel on the page. If you want to add this photo to an existing Set, click the **Choose a Set** arrow and select the set. To create a new Set for this photo, click the **Create a new Set** link. When the panel expands, enter a name and description for the Set. Then click the **Create Set** button.

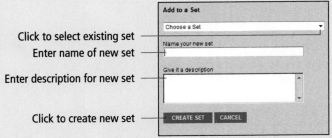

Click to select existing set
Enter name of new set
Enter description for new set

Click to create new set

Figure 8.17 Hands-On Exercise 2, Step 1k.

1. Click the **SAVE** button at the bottom of the page.

Step 2 Share a Digital Photo

Refer to Figure 8.18 as you complete Step 2.

Flickr lets you share any public photo with other Flickr users or non-Flickr users, via email.

a. Navigate to the photo you want to share.

b. Click the **Share This** link to the right of the photo.

The *Share this photo* panel will appear.

c. To share with another Flickr member, enter that member's screen name into the name box.

d. To share with a non-Flickr user, enter that person's email address into the name box.

e. To add a message to the photo, click the **Add a message?** link. When the panel expands, type your message into the *Message* box.

f. Click the **SEND** button.

Click to share photo

Enter email addresses or screen names

Click to add a message

Click to send

Figure 8.18 Hands-On Exercise 2, Step 2.

Step 3 Search for Photos

Refer to Figures 8.19 through 8.20 as you complete Step 3.

The easiest way to find photos of a particular type or of a specific subject is by using the *Search* box that appears at the top of every Flickr page.

a. Enter one or more keywords to describe what you're searching for into the *Search* box at the top of the page. Then press your keyboard's Enter key.

Flickr will display the most relevant photos to your query.

Enter search query ⟶

Figure 8.19 Hands-On Exercise 2, Step 3a.

b. To display the most recent photos, click the **Recent** link. To display what Flickr says are the most interesting photos, click the **Interesting** link.

c. To view a specific photo, click the thumbnail for that photo.

Click to display most
interesting photos

Click to display most
recent photos

Click thumbnail to view photo ⟶

Figure 8.20 Hands-On Exercise 2, Steps 3b and 3c.

Step 4 Join a Group

Refer to Figures 8.21 through 8.22 as you complete Step 4.

Flickr offers a variety of groups, each dedicated to a specific topic or type of photograph. Flickr Groups display photos by group members and offer online discussion forums.

a. To find a specific group, click the Groups arrow at the top of any Flickr page and select **Search for a Group**.

Click to search for group ⟶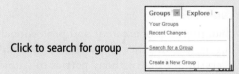

Figure 8.21 Hands-On Exercise 2, Step 4a.

b. When the Search page appears, enter one or more keywords describing that group into the search box. Then click the **SEARCH** button.

Groups that match your query will be displayed on the search page.

c. To view a particular group, click the group's name.

d. To join a group, click that group's **Join?** link.

Click to search

Enter search query

Click to view group

Click to join group

Figure 8.22 Hands-On Exercise 2, Steps 4b through 4d.

Objective 3

Share Videos with YouTube

What is YouTube?

YouTube is, in its own words, "the world's most popular online video community." It is a site that enables users to upload their own digital videos and share those videos with other users. It is also a site where viewers can find millions of short videos for viewing on their computers and other devices.

> **Note** **YouTube Community**
>
> YouTube claims more than 300 million users worldwide, with more than 120 million videos available for viewing. It would take more than 600 years to view all the videos currently available and there are 200,000 new videos uploaded every day.

What types of videos can be found on YouTube?

YouTube offers an interesting and ever-changing mix of amateur and professionally produced videos. Many videos on YouTube are the Internet equivalent of *America's Funniest Home Videos*, amateur videos of everything from birthday parties to stupid human tricks. Also popular are video blogs, or *vlogs*, video versions of traditional text-based blogs; these are personal journals, typically captured via webcam and posted to YouTube on a regular basis.

Vlog A video blog, or a personal journal in video form.

YouTube is also host to a variety of educational and informational videos, which makes the site ideal for finding "how to" information on a variety of topics. In addition, many businesses post both informational and promotional videos to the YouTube site.

Finally, YouTube is a repository for "historical" items, such as old television commercials, music videos, clips from classic television shows, and the like. It's also host for a large number of music videos from both past and present, as well as a growing number of current television programs, documentaries, and feature films.

What are the specifications for uploading a video to YouTube?

You can transfer videos to YouTube "live" from a computer webcam or upload digital videos shot on a video camcorder and edited with a computer video editing program. YouTube accepts videos that meet the following specifications:

- Length: No longer than 10 minutes

- File size: No larger than 2 GB

- File formats: 3GP (cell phone video), *.avi, .flv, .mk4 (h.264) .mp4, .mpeg, .mov, .wmv.*

- Resolution: Up to 1080p (1920 × 1080 pixels), in either standard or widescreen aspect ratio

Videos you upload cannot contain any copyrighted content, including any commercial music that may be playing in the background. This rule also means that you cannot record and upload television programming. In addition, videos may not contain offensive or adult content.

 Viewing YouTube Videos

YouTube stores and serves its videos in Flash movie (FLV) format. YouTube offers a dedicated application for viewing its videos on Apple's iPhone, since the iPhone is not compatible with Flash videos.

How is YouTube a social network?

YouTube is a video sharing community. It's the community aspect that makes YouTube a social network. You can comment on other users' videos, share videos with other users or non-YouTube members, subscribe to other users' videos, and post YouTube videos on your blog or Facebook page. The key is to participate; while you can be a passive viewer, social networking comes from fully participating in the YouTube community.

Hands-On Exercises

3 | Uploading and Sharing Videos with YouTube

Steps: 1. Upload a Video File; **2.** Upload a Webcam Video; **3.** Find and View a YouTube Video; **4.** Share a YouTube Video.

Use Figures 8.23 through 8.40 as a guide in the exercise.

 Upload a Video File

Refer to Figures 8.23 through 8.26 as you complete Step 1.

Before you upload a video to YouTube, you must register for a free account at www.youtube.com. Most YouTube videos are recorded on a video camcorder, transferred to a computer for editing, and then uploaded to the YouTube site.

a. Click the **Upload** link at the top of any YouTube page.

Click to upload video ———

Figure 8.23 Hands-On Exercise 3, Step 1a.

b. When the Video File Upload page appears, click the **Upload video** button.

Click to upload video ———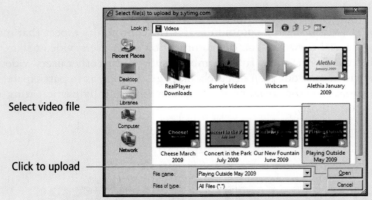

Figure 8.24 Hands-On Exercise 3, Step 1b.

c. When the *Select file(s) to upload* window appears, navigate to and select the desired video file. Then click the **Open** button.

As your file uploads, YouTube will display the Video File Upload page. The progress of your upload will be displayed at the top of this page; uploading a video can take several minutes more for longer videos, or if you have a slow Internet connection.

Select video file ———

Click to upload ———

Figure 8.25 Hands-On Exercise 3, Step 1c.

d. Click the thumbnail you'd like displayed for the video.

Thumbnails may not be displayed until the video is almost finished uploading.

e. Enter a title for the video into the *Title* box.

f. Enter a short description for the video into the *Description* box.

g. Enter one or more keywords that describe the video into the *Tags* box.

h. Click the *Category* list and select the appropriate category for the video.

i. If you want all YouTube viewers to see your video, check the *Share your video with the world* option in the Privacy setting. (This is the default.) If you want to share your video only with viewers you select, check the *Private* option.

j. Click the **Save changes** button.

When your video is done uploading, YouTube displays a link to the video. Click this link to view the video.

Select thumbnail image

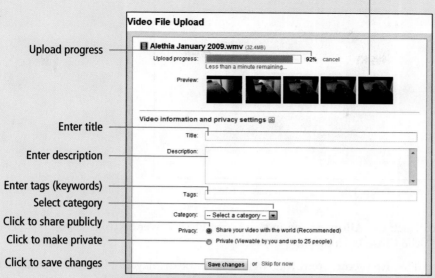

Upload progress

Enter title

Enter description

Enter tags (keywords)
Select category
Click to share publicly
Click to make private

Click to save changes

Figure 8.26 Hands-On Exercise 3, Steps 1d through 1j.

Step 2   Upload a Webcam Video

Refer to Figures 8.27 through 8.31 as you complete Step 2.

YouTube also enables you to record video from a computer webcam directly to the YouTube site. Before you proceed, make sure your webcam is enabled and functional.

a. Click the **Upload** link at the top of any YouTube page.

b. When the Video File Upload page appears, click the **Record from webcam** link.

YouTube will display the Record Video from Webcam page, along with the Adobe Flash Player Settings dialog box.

Click to record from webcam

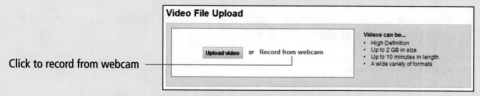

Figure 8.27 Hands-On Exercise 3, Step 2b.

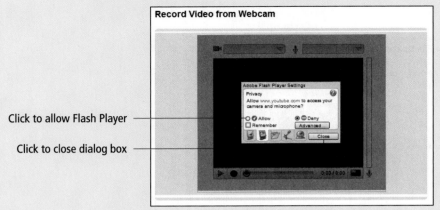

Click to allow Flash Player

Click to close dialog box

Figure 8.28 Hands-On Exercise 3, Step 2c.

c. Click the **Allow** option in the Adobe Flash Player Settings dialog box. Then click the **Close** button.

The live picture from your webcam will be displayed. Make sure you have the proper webcam and microphone selected from the dropdown lists above the picture.

 Tip | **Audio Level**

The audio level is displayed in a vertical meter to the right of the picture on the Record Video from Webcam page. As you talk, watch the audio level meter rise and fall. Try to keep the audio level in the green range; if the meter goes higher into the red, you're talking too loud and the sound on your recording could be distorted.

d. Click the record button to begin recording.

The record button will change to a red stop button.

e. Click the stop button when you're done recording.

When you stop recording, YouTube will give you the options to Preview your recording, Re-record the video, or Publish the video.

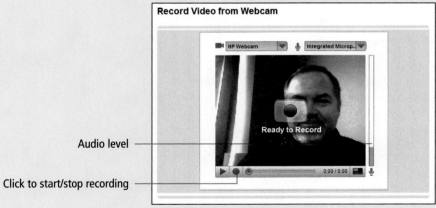

Audio level

Click to start/stop recording

Figure 8.29 Hands-On Exercise 3, Steps 2d and 2e.

Click to re-record video

Click to publish video

Click to preview video

Figure 8.30 Hands-On Exercise 3, Step 2f.

f. Click **Publish** to publish the video to the YouTube site.

   YouTube will display the Video Information page for this video.

g. Edit the title information in the *Title* box.

h. Enter a short description of this video into the *Description* box.

i. Enter one or more keywords to describe the video into the *Tags* box.

j. Click the *Category* list to select a category for this video.

k. Click the thumbnail image you want to display for this video.

> **Note** **Thumbnail Images**
>
> Thumbnail images are displayed only after YouTube is done processing the video.

l. In the *Privacy* section, check the *Share your video with the world* option to share your video with all YouTube users. If you want to share your video only with viewers you select, check the *Private* option.

m. Make any other changes to the *Broadcasting and Sharing Options* section that you wish.

n. Click the **Save Changes** button.

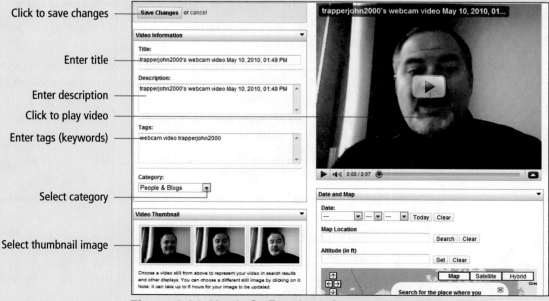

Click to save changes

Enter title

Enter description

Click to play video

Enter tags (keywords)

Select category

Select thumbnail image

Figure 8.31 Hands-On Exercise 3, Steps 2g through 2n.

Step 3 ▸ Find and View a YouTube Video

Refer to Figures 8.32 through 8.34 as you complete Step 3.

You can browse YouTube videos by category or search for specific videos you want to watch.

a. Enter one or more keywords that describe what you want into the search box at the top of any YouTube page. Then click the **Search** button.

Enter query ——
Click to search ——
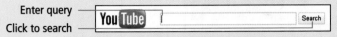

Figure 8.32 Hands-On Exercise 3, Step 3a.

YouTube will display videos that match your query on the resulting search results page.

b. To view a video, click either the video title or the thumbnail.

Click to select video ———

Figure 8.33 Hands-On Exercise 3, Step 3b.

YouTube will display the video page for the video you selected. The video will be displayed in its own playback window, and playback starts automatically.

c. To pause playback, click the pause icon, which then changes into a play icon. To resume playback, click the play icon.

d. To mute the audio, click the audio icon. To adjust the volume, place your cursor over the audio icon to display the volume slider; use your mouse to adjust the slider left (softer) or right (louder).

e. To display the video at a higher resolution (if available), place your cursor over the resolution icon and click a different resolution.

f. To display the video in a larger playback window across the width of your web browser, click the expand icon.

g. To display the video full screen, click the full screen icon. To exit full screen mode, press Esc.

h. To view more details about the video, click the down arrow next to the description beneath the video.

i. To vote for the video, click either the thumb up icon (I like this) or the thumb down icon (I dislike this).

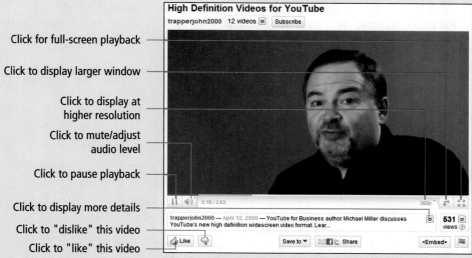

High Definition Videos for YouTube
trapperjohn2000   12 videos ⌄   Subscribe

Click for full-screen playback

Click to display larger window

Click to display at higher resolution

Click to mute/adjust audio level

Click to pause playback

Click to display more details

Click to "dislike" this video

Click to "like" this video

0:18 / 2:53   360p

trapperjohn2000 — April 12, 2009 — YouTube for Business author Michael Miller discusses YouTube's new high definition widescreen video format. Lear...   531 views

Like   Save to ▼   ✉ f ⌐ Share   <Embed>

Figure 8.34 Hands-On Exercise 3, Steps 3c through 3j.

Step 4   Share a YouTube Video

Refer to Figures 8.35 through 8.40 as you complete Step 4.

YouTube offers several ways to share a video you like with your friends. You can share a link to the video via email, post the video to a Blogger-hosted blog, or post the video as a status update or tweet to Facebook, MySpace, Twitter, Google Buzz, StumbleUpon, and other social media.

a. Navigate to the YouTube video you want to share.

b. Click the **Share** button beneath the video.

The Share panel will be displayed.

Click to share

Click to post to Twitter

Click to email

Click to post to Facebook

Click to post to Google Buzz

Click to post to MySpace

Like   Save to ▼   ✉ f ⌐ Share   <Embed>

http://www.youtube.com/watch?v=yDStHquECKg

✉ Email   f Facebook   ⌐ Twitter   MySpace   ⊙ orkut   hi5   ⓑ Blogger

Live Spaces   ⓑ Bebo   Buzz   StumbleUpon

Want to share your favorites, ratings, or comments to **Facebook**, **Twitter**, and **Google Reader**? Connect your accounts! (You control when messages are posted.)

Connect Accounts   Not interested now

Figure 8.35 Hands-On Exercise 3, Steps 4a and 4b.

c. To share the video via email, click the **Email** button. When the email window appears, enter the recipient's email address into the *To* box, enter an accompanying message into the *Message* box, and click the **Send** button.

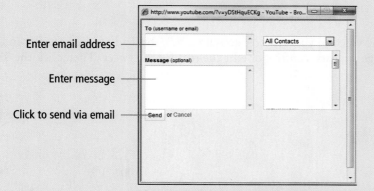

http://www.youtube.com/?v=yDStHquECKg - YouTube - Bro...

To (username or email)

All Contacts

Enter email address

Message (optional)

Enter message

Click to send via email

Send or Cancel

Figure 8.36 Hands-On Exercise 3, Step 4c.

d. To post this video as a status update to your Facebook account, click the **Facebook** button. When the Facebook window appears, enter a short message to accompany the video link, and click the **Share** button.

Enter message —

Click to post to Facebook —

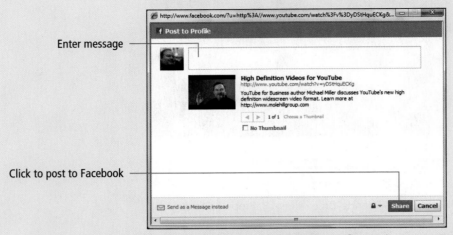

Figure 8.37 Hands-On Exercise 3, Step 4d.

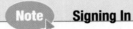

Note **Signing In**

The first time you try to share a video with your Facebook, MySpace, Twitter, or other account, you will be prompted to sign into your account. Follow the onscreen instructions to enter your user name and password and sign in.

e. To post this video as a status update to your MySpace account, click the **MySpace** button. When the *Share on MySpace* window appears, enter a short message to accompany the video link, and click the **Share** button.

Enter message —

Click to post to MySpace —

Figure 8.38 Hands-On Exercise 3, Step 4e.

f. To post this video to your Twitter account, click the **Twitter** button. When the Twitter page appears, confirm or edit the text for the tweet. Then click the **Tweet** button.

Edit text

Click to tweet

Figure 8.39 Hands-On Exercise 3, Step 4f.

g. To post this video to your Google Buzz account, click the **Buzz** button. When the *Google Buzz* window appears, enter a short message to accompany the video link. Then click the **Post** button.

Enter message

Click to post to Google Buzz

Figure 8.40 Hands-On Exercise 3, Step 4g.

Objective 4

Microblog with Google Buzz

What is Google Buzz?

Google Buzz is a social networking tool from Google that exists within Google's Gmail web-based email application. You do all your Buzzing from the Gmail home page, and all your status updates appear in your Gmail inbox. Buzz lets you post short status updates as you do with other social networking and microblogging services. However, it also integrates these updates with a variety of other social networking sites. When you post to Buzz, you also cross-post to these other sites and vice versa.

What social media can you consolidate with Google Buzz?

Google Buzz lets you cross-post text messages and other media with Twitter, Friend-Feed, Google Reader, Blogger, Picasa, Flickr, YouTube, and identi.ca. Other services are likely to be added in the future.

How does Google Buzz work?

To use Google Buzz, you have to create a list of people you wish to follow. These people should have a Google or Gmail account, or subscribe to one of the services that consolidate with Buzz. Posts from these people will then appear on your Gmail page.

Other users may opt to follow you, as well. Posts you make will appear on your followers' Gmail pages.

Hands-On Exercises

4 | Using Google Buzz

Steps: 1. Find People to Follow; **2.** View Friends' Posts; **3.** Make a Post.

Use Figures 8.41 through 8.47 as a guide in the exercise.

Step ① Find People to Follow

Refer to Figures 8.41 through 8.43 as you complete Step 1.

> **Note** **Gmail Account**
>
> To use Google Buzz, you must have a Gmail account. To sign up for a free account, go to **mail. google.com**.

a. Use your web browser to navigate to the Gmail home page at **mail.google.com**.

b. Click the **Buzz** link in the sidebar.

Click to display Google Buzz —

Figure 8.41 Hands-On Exercise 4, Steps 1a and 1b.

Google will display the main Google Buzz page.

> **Tip** **Follow Back**
>
> To follow someone who's following you, click the Follow Back button next to that person's name on the main Google Buzz page.

c. Click the **Find more people to follow** link.

Click to find people to follow —

Figure 8.42 Hands-On Exercise 4, Step 1c.

d. When the *Following* dialog box appears, enter the name or email address of the person you want to follow into the *Follow more people* box. Then click the **Search** button.

Google will display a list of people who match your query.

e. Click the **Follow** link next to the person you want to follow.

f. Click the **Done** button to close the follow window.

Enter name or email address —

Click to search —

Click to follow —

Click when done —

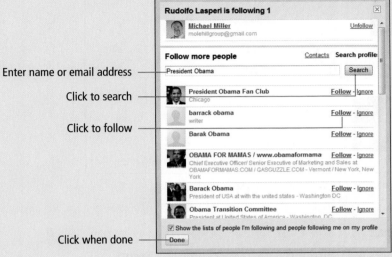

Figure 8.43 Hands-On Exercise 4, Steps 1d through 1f.

Step ➋ View Friends' Posts

Refer to Figure 8.44 as you complete Step 2.

a. Navigate to the Gmail home page (**mail.google.com**).

b. Click the **Buzz** link in the sidebar.

c. Scroll down the page to the Buzz section.

The most recent posts from the people you're following will be displayed.

d. To comment on a post, click the **Comment** link. When the post expands, enter your comment into the text box. Then click the **Post Comment** button.

e. To express approval of a post, click the **Like** link.

Click to "like" post
Click to comment on post
Posts

Figure 8.44 Hands-On Exercise 4, Steps 2c through 2e.

Step 3 Make a Post

Refer to Figures 8.45 through 8.47 as you complete Step 3.

a. Navigate to the Gmail home page (**mail.google.com**).

b. Click the **Buzz** link in the sidebar.

The first time you use Google Buzz you may be asked to set up a profile. If you are prompted to do so, follow the onscreen instructions.

c. Type the text of your message into the text box at the top of the page.

d. To attach a web page link to your post, click the **Link** link. When the posting area expands, enter the URL into the *Add a link to this post* box. Then click the **Add link** button.

e. To attach a photo to this post, click the **Photo** link. When the *Add photos to post* window appears, click the **Choose photos to upload** button. When the *Select file(s) to upload* dialog box appears, navigate to and select the photos you wish to attach. Then click the **Open** button. When you're returned to the *Add photos to post* window, click the **Add Photos to post** button.

f. To post your update, click the **Post** button.

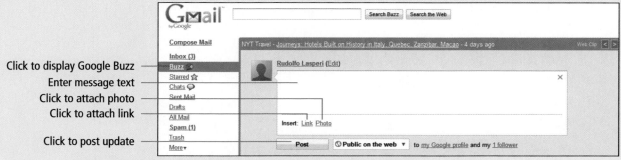

Click to display Google Buzz
Enter message text
Click to attach photo
Click to attach link
Click to post update

Figure 8.45 Hands-On Exercise 4, Step 3.

Objective 5

Create Your Own Social Network with Ning

What is Ning?

Ning is a platform for creating social networks. The company was launched in 2005; one of its cofounders, Marc Andreessen, also cofounded Netscape, a company that created one of the earliest Web browsers.

Who uses Ning?

Any individual or group can use Ning to create a Facebook-like social network of any size. Some users create Ning networks around specific topics or hobbies; others create Ning networks for causes or companies. For example, you could create a Ning network for your favorite club or nonprofit organization, or even for a class or local community.

What features does a Ning network offer?

A Ning network is like a mini-Facebook, with many of the same features: discussion forums, photo albums, videos, music, chat rooms, member pages and blogs, and the like. It's essentially a small, private social networking site that is open only to those you wish to invite.

Unlike a Facebook or MySpace group, a Ning network has its own identity; it has its own unique URL and its own distinct look and feel. The owner of each network determines who can join that particular network.

Figure 8.46 A typical Ning network.

How much does it cost to use Ning?

Initially, Ning offered both free and paid networks; free networks carried advertisements. As of July 2010, Ning phased out its free networks and now offers only paid networks, with subscriptions running from $2.95/month to $49.95/month. The higher priced plans allow more members per group, additional customization options, and additional features.

How do you create a Ning network?

Once you've signed up for a Ning account, creating a Ning network is a matter of filling in a few web-based forms. You have to specify a name for your new network, as well as your desired Ning address. You then determine whether it will be a private or public network (private networks are open only to specific invitees) and enter a description and keywords.

Ning then lets you choose the features you want for your network, and the layout for the network's home page. You can also select a theme for your network's appearance. Your network is now launched, and you can invite others to join.

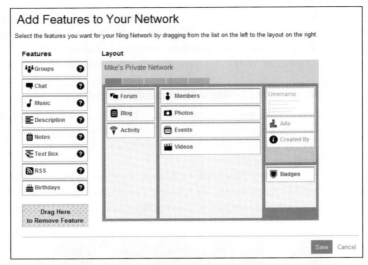

Figure 8.47 Selecting the features for a new Ning network.

Objective 6

Explore Other Social Media

What other social networks are popular today?

Due to space limitations, many popular social networks are not discussed in this book. Some of these networks are more popular outside of the United States, or among specific audiences.

These other social networks include the following:

- BlackPlanet (www.blackplanet.com), targeting the African-American community

- Buzznet (www.buzznet.com), focusing on music and pop culture

- Flixter (www.flixter.com), focusing on movies

- Friends Reunited (www.friendsreunited.com), based in the United Kingdom

- Friendster (www.friendster.com), popular in Asia

- Habbo (www.habbo.com), targeting teenagers worldwide

- hi5 (www.hi5.com), popular in India, Thailand, Central America, Latin America, and other countries

- identi.ca (www.identi.ca), a Canadian-based microblogging service

- Mixi (www.mixi.jp), based in Japan

- Netlog (www.netlog.com), popular with young people in Europe

- Orkut (www.orkut.com), popular in Brazil and India

- Qzone (qzone.qq.com), popular in China

- Skyrock (www.skyrock.com), popular in the French-speaking world

- Sonico (www.sonico.com), popular in Latin America

- VKontakte (www.vkontakte.ru), popular in the Russian-speaking world

What other websites offer social networking features?

Wiki A website that enables the easy creation and editing of interlinked articles, typically for the consolidation of user-supplied information.

Wikipedia An online user-created and edited encyclopedia.

Many websites offer the same sort of community features found on social networking sites. For example, *wiki* websites, such as *Wikipedia* (www.wikipedia.org), enable group collaboration and discussion on encyclopedia-like articles. Community question and answer sites, such as Yahoo! Answers, encourage the community to provide answers to questions posed by other users. And opinion websites, such as epinions.com, provide a community of product and service reviews.

In addition, many of the larger blogs offer thriving community discussions around popular blog posts, and numerous websites provide topic-oriented discussion boards and chat rooms for the community of users.

In reality, there are numerous opportunities to participate in social networking on the web. You're not limited to just Facebook or Twitter; look for communities of users focused on those topics that interest you. There no doubt will be many options open to you.

Summary

In this chapter you learned how to use social bookmarking services to share interesting articles and web pages. You also learned how to share photos with Flickr and videos with YouTube, and to use Google Buzz to microblog across a variety of social media. In addition, you learned how to create your own social network with Ning, and explore other types of social media.

Key Terms

Multiple Choice Questions

1. When you want to share an article you've found online, use this type of service:

    (a) Social networking site

    (b) Social bookmarking service

    (c) Microblog

    (d) Article sharing site

2. For-profit commercial photo-sharing sites generate revenue by doing the following:

    (a) Selling photo prints

    (b) Selling advertising

    (c) Charging member fees

    (d) All of the above

3. Which of the following is *not* a social bookmarking service?

    (a) Digg

    (b) StumbleUpon

    (c) Twitter

    (d) Delicious

4. What is the maximum resolution you can use when you upload a video to YouTube?

    (a) 320 × 240 pixels

    (b) 640 × 480 pixels

    (c) 1280 × 720 pixels

    (d) 1920 × 1080 pixels

5. Google Buzz is most like which of these websites?

    (a) Facebook

    (b) Twitter

    (c) MySpace

    (d) Digg

6. YouTube lets you share videos with the following sites:

    (a) Facebook

    (b) Twitter

    (c) MySpace

    (d) All of the above

7. When you want to create your own social network, use the following service:

    (a) Wikipedia

    (b) Ning

    (c) Google Buzz

    (d) None of the above

8. Which of the following social networking websites is more popular outside the United States?

    (a) Orkut

    (b) MySpace

    (c) Facebook

    (d) LinkedIn

9. Which of the following types of sites does *not* offer social networking features?

    (a) Wikis

    (b) Photo-sharing sites

    (c) Opinion websites

    (d) Search engines

10. Which of the following is *not* true about social bookmarking?

    (a) Most social bookmarking sites organize their bookmarks by category.

    (b) Social bookmarking services started as email links shared by friends.

    (c) Delicious introduced the concept of tagged bookmarks.

    (d) Many news sites include quick-click buttons for the major social bookmarking services.

Fill in the Blank

Write the correct word in the space provided.

1. Social bookmarks are typically _____ with descriptive keywords.

2. Use a(n) _____ sharing community to upload and share home movies.

3. When you vote down a bookmark on Digg, you _____ the item.

4. You access Google Buzz via the _____ web page.

5. To share a photo or video with all members of a site, make that item _____.

Practice Exercises

1. **Create and Populate a Flickr Set**

   On Flickr, photos are organized into sets. Once you've created a set, you can then upload photos to that set.

       (a) If you do not yet have a Flickr account, create one.
       (b) Create a set named "Favorite Photos."
       (c) Upload at least three photos into this new set.
       (d) Print a copy of the Flickr set page and hand it in to your instructor.

2. **Digg a Web Page**

Digg enables you to share with friends those web pages that you find most interesting.

(a) If you do not yet have a Digg account, create one.

(b) Use Google or another search engine to find a recent news article about social networking that has not yet been dugg.

(c) Digg this article.

(d) Print a copy of the Submit a New Link page and hand it in to your instructor.

3. **Share a YouTube Video via Email**

YouTube makes it easy to share your favorite videos. Any public video on the YouTube site can be shared via email or social media.

(a) Search the YouTube site for a video that demonstrates how to post videos on YouTube.

(b) Share this video via email with your instructor.

4. **Invite Followers on Google Buzz**

Google Buzz lets you post status updates to those who follow your posts. You can invite anyone to become a follower.

(a) If you do not yet have a Gmail account, create one.

(b) Invite your instructor to become a follower.

(c) Once your instructor is following your posts, make a new post announcing that you've completed this exercise.

Critical Thinking

1. Social bookmarking services, such as Digg and Delicious, help you share interesting articles and web pages with other users. They also help you find articles and pages of interest. Write a short paper discussing how you can use social bookmarking services to research papers for other classes.

2. Ning enables anyone to create his or her own social network around any topic. Some social networking sites, such as Facebook, enable users to create their own topic-oriented groups, using the site's established social networking tools. Write a short paper discussing the advantages and disadvantages of creating a social network with Ning versus creating a similar Facebook group.

Team Projects

1. Using either a camcorder or webcam, make a short video of the group discussing the benefits of social networking. Upload the video to the YouTube account of one of the group members, providing a brief description and appropriate tags for the video. Once the video is uploaded, share the video with your classmates via Facebook and Twitter, and via email with the instructor.

2. In this chapter we discussed several social bookmarking services, including Digg, Delicious, reddit, and StumbleUpon. Assign one social bookmarking service to each member of the group, trying not to duplicate services unless necessary. (Feel free to use one of the social bookmarking services not discussed in depth in this chapter.) The group should then decide on a topic and each member should search for and bookmark at least one article on that topic. After the bookmarks have been posted, the group should write a short collaborative paper comparing and contrasting the bookmarking experience of each social bookmarking service.

Credits

Figure 8.1, Digg.com. Reprinted by permission of Digg.com.

Figure 8.2, Reddit.com. Conde Nast Publications, Inc.

Figure 8.3, Stumbleupon.com. © StumbleUpon, Inc. Used by Permission.

Figures 8.4, 8.12–8.22, Delicious.com. Reproduced with permission of Yahoo! Inc. © 2010 Yahoo! Inc. DELICIOUS, the DELICIOUS logo, FLICKR and the FLICKR logo are registered trademarks of Yahoo! Inc.

Figures 8.6–8.11, Digg.com. Reprinted by permission of Digg.com.

Figures 8.23–8.24, 8.26–8.36, YouTube.com. Reprinted by permission of Google Inc.

Figure 8.25, FullShot 9.5 Professional (screenshot). Used by permission of Fullshot. © Informer Technologies.

Figure 8.37, Facebook.com. © Facebook. Used by Permission.

Figure 8.38, MySpace.com. © MySpace, www.myspace.com. Used by Permission.

Figure 8.39, Twitter.com. © Twitter, www.twitter.com. Used by permission.

Figure 8.40, Google.com. Reused by Permission of Google, Inc.

Figures 8.41–8.45, Gmail.com. Reused by Permission of Google, Inc.

Figures 8.46–8.47, Ning.com. Reused by Permission of Ning, Inc.

Appendix

Comparing Social Networks

SOCIAL MEDIUM	WEBSITE	TYPE	DESCRIPTION
ActiveWorlds	www.activeworlds.com	Virtual world	3D virtual community similar to Second Life
BlackPlanet	www.blackplanet.com	Social network	Targets the African American community
Buzznet	www.buzznet.com	Social network	Focuses on music and pop culture
City of Heroes	www.cityofheroes.com	Virtual world	Massively multiplayer online role-playing game
Cybertown	www.cybertown.com	Virtual world	Family-friendly 3D virtual community
Delicious	www.delicious.com	Social bookmarking service	Popular worldwide
Digg	www.digg.com	Social bookmarking service	Largest social bookmarking service, more than 23 million users
Facebook	www.facebook.com	Social network	Largest general social network on the web, more than 400 million users
Flickr	www.flickr.com	Photo sharing	Largest free photo sharing community, more than 40 million users
Flixter	www.flixter.com	Social network	Focuses on movies
Fotki	www.fotki.com	Photo sharing	Free photo sharing community
Friends Reunited	www.friendsreunited.com	Social network	Based in the United Kingdom
Friendster	www.friendster.com	Social network	One of the first social networks, popular in Asia
Google Buzz	www.google.com/buzz	Microblogging service	Built into Google's Gmail service
Habbo	www.habbo.com	Virtual world	3D virtual community, popular with teenagers
hi5	www.hi5.com	Social network	Popular in India, Thailand, Central America, Latin America, and other countries
identi.ca	www.identi.ca	Microblogging	Based in Canada
Kaneva	www.kaneva.com	Virtual world	3D virtual community
LinkedIn	www.linkedin.com	Social network	Popular with business professionals
Mixi	www.mixi.jp	Social network	Based in Japan
MySpace	www.myspace.com	Social network	Popular with musicians and entertainers worldwide
Netlog	www.netlog.com	Social network	Popular among European young people
Ning	www.ning.com	Social network	Service for building custom social networks

(Continued)

SOCIAL MEDIUM	WEBSITE	TYPE	DESCRIPTION
Onverse	www.onverse.com	Virtual world	3D virtual community and gaming platform
Orkut	www.orkut.com	Social network	Owned by Google, popular in Brazil and India
Photobucket	www.photobucket.com	Photo sharing	Free photo sharing community
Picasa Web Albums	picasaweb.google.com	Photo sharing	Google's free photo sharing community
Poptropica	www.poptropica.com	Virtual world	3D virtual community targeting children ages 6 to 15
Qzone	www.qzone.com	Social network	Popular in China
reddit	www.reddit.com	Social bookmarking service	Popular worldwide
Second Life	www.secondlife.com	Virtual world	Most popular virtual community, more than 16 million users
Skyrock	www.skyrock.com	Social network	Popular in the French-speaking world
SmallWorlds	www.smallworlds.com	Virtual world	Game-oriented 3D virtual community
Sonico	www.sonico.com	Social network	Popular in Latin America
StumbleUpon	www.stumbleupon.com	Social bookmarking service	First true social bookmarking service, enables users to "stumble upon" new topics
Tumblr	www.tumblr.com	Microblogging service	Up and coming Twitter-like service, approximately 3 million users
Twitter	www.twitter.com	Microblogging service	Largest microblogging service, more than 100 million users
VKontakte	www.vkontakte.ru	Social network	Popular in the Russian-speaking world
YouTube	www.youtube.com	Video sharing	Largest video sharing community, more than 300 million users

Glossary

Admin Short for group administrator, the person responsible for managing and posting content to a group.

Application On Facebook, a utility or game that runs on the Facebook site.

Avatar A graphical representation of a computer user, typically in the form of a cartoon character.

Blog Short for *web log*, a shared online journal consisting of entries from the site's owner or creator.

Bookmark A means of identifying a web page for future viewing or sharing with other users.

Bulletin board system (BBS) A private online discussion forum, typically hosted on a single computer and accessed by other computers via a dial-up telephone connection. BBSs were popular before the advent of the Internet.

Captcha A type of challenge-response test to ensure that the user is a human being, rather than a computer program. Captchas typically consist of warped or otherwise distorted text that cannot be machine read; by requiring input of the captcha text, a web page cuts down on the amount of computer-generated spam.

Chat Facebook's proprietary instant messaging system, which facilitates one-to-one real-time communication between two friends.

Chat room A web page that hosts real-time text communication between multiple users.

Comment A short message left on a MySpace user's Profile page.

Computer virus A malicious software program capable of reproducing itself across multiple computers and causing damage to an infected computer.

Connection On LinkedIn, a professional contact or "friend."

Contextual Relating to or determined by the context of the item. Contextual advertising places ads on pages that share similar content.

CSS Short for cascading style sheets; a technology used within HTML to define and format specific elements on a web page.

Delicious Formerly known as del.icio.us, a popular social bookmarking service that enables users to tag bookmarked pages with their own index terms. Delicious (www.delicious.com) was launched in 2003 and acquired by Yahoo! in 2005.

Destination Guide A directory of the most popular locations in Second Life.

Dial-up computer network A commercial online service that connects multiple computers via a dial-up telephone connection and offers various community-based features, such as email and message forums. These early online networks, such as CompuServe, Prodigy, and America

Online, typically charged some combination of monthly fee and hourly access fee.

Digg A social bookmarking service that enables users to submit web pages and other content and then rate that content. Digg (www.digg.com) was launched in 2004.

Direct message A private tweet sent to another Twitter user.

Discussion forum An online space where users can read and post messages on a given topic. Many commercial online services and websites offer discussion forums; Usenet is that part of the Internet devoted solely to such discussion forums.

Email Short for *electronic mail*, a means of sending messages over the Internet or a closed computer network.

Emoticon Also known as a *smiley*, a graphic representation of the user's mood. For example, a happy mood might be indicated by an emoticon of a smiling face.

Event On the Facebook site, a scheduled activity, much like an item on a personal schedule.

Facebook The largest social networking site on the web. Facebook (www.facebook.com) was launched in 2004 and currently has more than 500 million users.

Facebook toolbar A strip of buttons or commands located at the top of every Facebook page. Use the Facebook toolbar to navigate to key pages on the Facebook site.

Flame war A heated or hostile interaction between two or more people in an online forum.

Follower A Twitter user who subscribes to the tweets of another user.

Foursquare A location-based social networking service for mobile phones. Users check into a particular location, and nearby friends are notified of their presence.

Friend On a social network, another user with whom you communicate. Most social networks enable you to create lists of friends, who are authorized to view your posts, photos, and other information.

Friending The act of adding someone to a social network friends list.

Friendster One of the earliest social networking websites. Launched in March 2003, Friendster (www.friendster. com) enjoyed a brief period of success. Ironically this success brought about a series of technical problems that drove users to competing sites. Friendster was purchased by News Corporation in 2005, and is today one of the largest social networking sites in Asia.

Gallery On Flickr, a collection of photographs of a given type or topic.

Gesture In Second Life, a brief movement of the avatar to express some sort of emotion or feeling.

Google Buzz A social networking tool that integrates data from a variety of social media, including Twitter, Blogger, and FriendFeed. Google Buzz (**www.google.com/buzz/**) was launched in 2010, and integrates with Gmail, Google's web-based email service.

GPS Short for *global positioning system*, a technology that uses satellites to provide positioning and navigation services.

Grid The virtual world in Second Life.

Group On Facebook, a topic- or activity-oriented community page.

Hashtag A means of indicating an important word in a tweet; similar to identifying a keyword.

Homepage The main page for Facebook members, located at **www.facebook.com**. The Facebook Homepage consists of a news feed of status updates from a member's friends.

HTML Short for hypertext markup language; the markup language used to create web pages.

Identity theft A form of fraud in which one person pretends to be someone else, typically by stealing personal information, such as a bank account number, credit card number, or Social Security number. The intent of identity theft is often to steal money or obtain other benefits.

Inbound link A link from another website to a given website.

Instant messaging A means of conducting a one-to-one text communication in real time over the Internet or a closed computer network.

Island A private region in Second Life.

Keyword A word or phrase used to construct a search.

Landmark A saved location in Second Life.

Linden Dollars The form of virtual currency in the Second Life virtual world, abbreviated L$.

LinkedIn A social network for business professionals, launched in 2003. LinkedIn (**www.linkedin.com**) currently has more than 60 million users.

Linkworthy Content that is useful or interesting enough to warrant linking to.

List On Facebook: A collection of specified Facebook friends; a subset of the member's overall collection of Facebook friends. On Twitter: A grouping of tweets from selected Twitter users.

Malware Short for malicious software. Any computer program designed to infiltrate or damage an infected computer. Computer viruses and spyware are the two most common types of malware.

Media sharing The act of uploading, storing, and sharing various types of media files (photos, videos, and music) with other users over the web.

Menu bar A horizontal strip that contains clickable or pull-down menus to access specific items or actions.

Microblog A web-based service, such as Twitter, that enables users to post short text messages to interested followers.

MMORLG A massively multiplayer online real-life game, similar to an MMPORG, but one which imparts more control over the nature and features of their avatars to the users.

MMPORG A massively multiplayer online role-playing game, where users play specific characters in a large online gaming environment.

Mood On the MySpace site, a graphic indication of the user's emotional condition, as represented by the appropriate emoticon.

MUD A multi-user domain or multi-user dungeon; an early text-based form of multiplayer gaming, with each user taking the role of a specific character.

Multiplayer online game A computer game that can be played by multiple users over the Internet.

MySpace A social networking site that is popular among musicians and other entertainers. MySpace (**www.myspace.com**) was launched in 2003 and currently has more than 125 million users.

Network On Facebook, a group devoted to a particular school or company; only students and teachers of a school, and employees of a company, can join that school or company's network.

News feed On a social network, a collection of posts or status updates from a person's friends.

Officer An honorary title for a high-level member of a Facebook group. Officers have no privileges beyond that of normal members.

Open Graph Formerly known as Facebook Connect. Facebook's technology platform for connecting other sites and content to the Facebook social network.

Page Sometimes called a fan page, a group for fans of an entertainer, celebrity, company, or product.

Photo album On Facebook, a collection of digital photos organized by some underlying theme or topic.

Photo-sharing site A website where users can upload, store, and share digital photos with other users.

Photostream On Flickr, a feed of photos from a given user.

Playlist A collection of songs.

Profile A collection of personal information, including photos, contact information, likes and dislikes, and recent posts for a member of a social networking site. The Profile page serves as a member's home page on a social networking site.

Profile page The personal page for each Facebook member. All a member's personal information and status updates are displayed on his or her Profile page.

Publisher box The box at the top of your Profile and Homepages; used to post status updates. There is also a Publisher box at the top of friends' Homepages; use this Publisher box to post a message to that friend's Profile page.

Residents The other players in Second Life.

Retweet A tweet forwarded to other Twitter users.

RSVP A response to an invitation to a Facebook event; an indication as to whether you are attending an event or not. (The acronym *RSVP* comes from the French phrase *répondez s'il vous plaît*, or "please reply.")

SAP The self-named enterprise planning software distributed by the German SAP software company.

Set Flickr's name for a digital photo album.

Smartphone A mobile phone with advanced computer-like capability, typically including Internet access.

Social bookmarking service A web-based service, such as Digg and Delicious, that helps users bookmark and share popular websites, web pages, and articles.

Social media Websites, services, and platforms that people use to share experiences and opinions with each other. The most common social media include social networks, social bookmarking services, blogs, and microblogs.

Social network A website, such as Facebook or MySpace, where users can form communities with like-minded people and share details of their lives with friends, family, fellow students, and coworkers.

Spam Unsolicited commercial email, or junk email.

Spyware A malicious software program that obtains information from a user's computer without the user's knowledge or consent.

Status A short text message that indicates what a Facebook user is doing or thinking at the moment. Status updates are displayed in the News Feed of friends' Homepages.

Status update A short text post from a member of a social networking site, conveying the user's current thoughts, actions, and such.

Stream On MySpace, a constantly updated feed of status updates and other posts from friends.

Tag A label used to describe a specific item.

Tagging The act of formally identifying a Facebook member in a photo uploaded to the Facebook site.

Teleport A means to rapidly move from one location to another in the Second Life world.

Theme On the MySpace site, a preset combination of layout, colors, and graphical elements applied to a Profile page.

Tweet A short, 140-character post on the Twitter social media network. Also used as a verb: to tweet.

Twitter A popular microblogging service where users post short text messages (tweets) of no more than 140 characters, which other users can then follow. Twitter (**www. twitter.com**) was launched in 2006, and currently has more than 100 million users.

Unfollow To no longer follow a given Twitterer.

Usenet A subset of the Internet that hosts and distributes topic-based discussion forums, called *newsgroups*. Usenet was created in 1980 and continues to this day.

vCard A specific file format for electronic or virtual business cards.

Viral Achieving immense popularity via word of mouth on the Internet.

Virtual world An online community that takes the form of a computer-based simulated environment.

Vlog A video blog, or a personal journal in video form.

Wall The primary section of a Facebook member's Profile page, which displays the member's status updates as well as messages from other users.

Wall-to-wall Direct communication between two Facebook members, accomplished via consecutive posts on each member's Wall.

Website community A website designed to promote a community around a specific topic. Most website communities feature topic-specific articles and other content, along with discussion boards, chat rooms, and the like.

Widget A small single-purpose application installed on a web page.

Wiki A website that enables the easy creation and editing of interlinked articles, typically for the consolidation of user-supplied information.

Wikipedia An online user-created and edited encyclopedia.

YouTube The Internet's largest video sharing community, located at www.youtube.com, where members upload and view millions of video files each day.

Index

A

Acronyms for Twitter, 157, 158t
Admin, 61
Advertising on social networks, 11–12. *See also* Professional networking
Alexa, 2
Anderson, Tom, 80
AOL Instant Messenger (AIM), 26
Applications
    Facebook, 18, 41–42, 70
    LinkedIn, 125–126
    Twitter, 158, 169
Associations on LinkedIn Profile page, 123
Avatars, 13, 175, 176, 180, 184–188. *See also* Virtual worlds
Awards, 123

B

Bands. *See* Music
BBSs (bulletin board systems), 2
Birthdays. *See* Events
BlackPlanet, 232
Block Lists, 74–75
Blogs and bloggers. *See also* Microblogging
    defined, 1
    described, 95
    of entertainers or musicians, 106
    managing blogs on MySpace, 95–96
    vlogs, 218
Bookmarking sites. *See* Social bookmarking services
Bulletin board systems (BBSs), 2
Business. *See* Professional networking
Business cards, 113
Buzznet, 232

C

Captcha, 20
CareerXroads' 9th Annual Source of Hire Study, 142
Celebrities and entertainers, 105–106, 150
Cell phones. *See* Mobile phones
Chats
    chat rooms, described, 3
    Facebook, 38–39, 40–41
    Second Life, 192, 194–195
Children, 13
Classmates, 26–27, 63, 130–131
Collaborative websites, 233
Colleagues. *See* Professional networking
College students, 13
Comments

on MySpace Profile pages, 86, 93–94
on Profile pages of musicians or entertainers, 106
on status updates, 30–32
Communicating with friends on Facebook, 38–41
Community Pages, 66
Community question and answer sites, 233
Computer viruses, 6
Connections, described, 126. *See also* LinkedIn
Consumer reviews, 233
Contact information, disclosing, 8–9, 70
Contact lists, 26, 126–128, 164
CSS, 86, 88–89
Custom Privacy window, 37

D

Deleting photos, 24, 51
Deleting tweets, 157
Deleting updates, 37
Delicious, 3–4, 204, 207. *See also* Social bookmarking services
Destination guides, 188, 190
Dial-up computer networks, 2
Digg, 3–4, 4f, 205, 207–212. *See also* Social bookmarking services
Direct messages (DM), 158, 161–162
Discretion, 10
Discussion forums, 2, 233
DM (direct messages), 158, 161–162

E

Early history of social networks, 2
Education information, 121–122
Electronic business cards, 113
Email
    described, 3
    finding friends via email contact lists, 26, 126–128, 163
    sending messages on Facebook, 17, 38–41, 39–40
    sending messages on LinkedIn, 131–134
    sending messages on MySpace, 94–95
    sharing YouTube videos via, 225
    spam, 7, 20, 70
    Web mail, 127–128
Emotions
    emoticons, 82
    gestures, 178
Entertainers, 105–106, 150
epinions.com, 233
eUniverse, 80
Events
    attaching Facebook events to status updates, 35–36
    creating, 59–60

described, 56
managing events on Facebook, 47, 56–60
RSVP, 56, 58–59

F

Facebook, 3f, 17–78
    Block Lists, 74–75
    communicating with friends, 17, 38–41
    described, 2, 18
    early history of, 2
    Facebook applications, 18, 41–42, 70
    Facebook plug-in, 50
    Facebook toolbar, 18–19, 19f
    fan pages, 47, 60–62, 63–64, 66–67
    finding friends, 17, 21, 24–30
    Friends of Friends, 71, 72
    getting started, 17, 18–22
    groups, 47, 60–63, 64–66
    hands-on exercises, 17, 19–22, 25–33, 34–41, 47–56, 57–60, 62–67, 70–75
    hiding information and posts, 69, 73
    for job hunters, 68
    Login, 19, 55
    managing events, 47, 56–60
    managing privacy settings, 47, 69–75
    managing the homepage, 17, 30–33
    mixing personal and professional lives on Facebook, 69
    networks, 37, 47, 60, 63
    Open Graph, 13
    personalizing the Profile page, 17, 23–24
    popularity of, 2
    professional networking, 68–69
    reliability of Facebook's privacy settings, 70
    safety concerns, 69
    sharing photos and videos, 47, 48–56, 225–226
    status updates, 17, 33–37
    user statistics, 18
Facebook Connect, 13
Face-to-face communication vs. social networking, 7
Fake names, 7
Fan pages, 47, 60–62, 63–64, 66–67
Flame wars, 10
Flickr
    described, 212–213
    groups, 217–218
    photostream, 213
    searching for photos, 216–217
    sets, 215–216
    uploading and sharing photos, 213–216
Flixter, 232
Fotki, 213